SOUNDSCAPES OF UYGHUR ISLAM

FRAMING THE GLOBAL
Hilary E. Kahn and Deborah Piston-Hatlen, *series editors*

SOUNDSCAPES OF UYGHUR ISLAM

Rachel Harris

INDIANA UNIVERSITY PRESS

This book is a publication of

Indiana University Press
Office of Scholarly Publishing
Herman B Wells Library 350
1320 East 10th Street
Bloomington, Indiana 47405 USA

iupress.org

© 2020 by Rachel Harris

All rights reserved

No part of this book may be reproduced or utilized in any form or by any means, electronic or mechanical, including photocopying and recording, or by any information storage and retrieval system, without permission in writing from the publisher. The paper used in this publication meets the minimum requirements of the American National Standard for Information Sciences—Permanence of Paper for Printed Library Materials, ANSI Z39.48-1992.

Manufactured in the United States of America

Library of Congress Cataloging-in-Publication Data

Names: Harris, Rachel (Rachel A.), author.
Title: Soundscapes of Uyghur Islam / Rachel Harris.
Description: Bloomington, Indiana : Indiana University Press, 2020. | Series: Framing the global | Includes bibliographical references and index.
Identifiers: LCCN 2020006281 (print) | LCCN 2020006282 (ebook) | ISBN 9780253050182 (hardback) | ISBN 9780253050205 (paperback) | ISBN 9780253050199 (ebook)
Subjects: LCSH: Muslims China—Xinjiang Uygur Zizhiqu—Social conditions. | Muslim women—China—Xinjiang Uygur Zizhiqu—Social conditions. | Uighur (Turkic people)—China—Xinjiang Uygur Zizhiqu—Social life and customs. | Uighur (Turkic people)—China—Xinjiang Uygur Zizhiqu—Music. | Xinjiang Uygur Zizhiqu (China)—Ethnic relations. | China—Ethnic relations.
Classification: LCC BP63.C52 X554 2020 (print) | LCC BP63.C52 (ebook) | DDC 297.082/09516—dc23
LC record available at https://lccn.loc.gov/2020006281
LC ebook record available at https://lccn.loc.gov/2020006282

1 2 3 4 5   25 24 23 22 21 20

*This book is dedicated to Rahile Dawut:
inspirational scholar, teacher, and friend.*

CONTENTS

Acknowledgments ix

1 Sound, Place, and Religious Revival *1*

   Interlude 1 Rabiya Acha's Story

2 Affective Rituals in a Uyghur Village *40*

3 Text and Performance in the Hikmät of Khoja Ahmad Yasawi *70*

4 Style and Meaning in the Recited Qur'an *101*

   Interlude 2 *Tutiwalidu* (They'll Arrest You)

5 Mobile Islam: Mediation and Circulation *134*

6 Song and Dance and the Sonic Territorialization of Xinjiang *168*

7 Erasure and Trauma *203*

References 223

Index 237

ACKNOWLEDGMENTS

As this book goes to press, there is still no sign of relief from the radical policies of social reengineering in the Xinjiang Uyghur Autonomous Region in northwest China, which have seen more than a million Uyghurs and other Muslim minorities incarcerated in massive detention camps and subjected to coercive regimes of reeducation and forced labor. The religious rituals described in this book have been labeled violent extremism, everyday expressions of faith have been outlawed, and places of worship have been destroyed. All this has taken place under a thick veil of secrecy. Uyghurs in Xinjiang live under extreme forms of high-tech surveillance, and contact with the outside world is strictly controlled. For several years now, I have had no news of the well-being or whereabouts of the Uyghur village women who welcomed me into their homes and taught me about their faith.

The projects of reengineering and deracination currently underway in Xinjiang have targeted the landscape and the soundscape, its inhabitants' minds and bodies, the living and the dead. Cities and villages are being razed and rebuilt in ways that facilitate surveillance and control and promote assimilation. Far from being a reasonable and necessary response to violent extremism as the Chinese government claims, these measures add up to a comprehensive policy of cultural erasure that has targeted Uyghur language and culture, uprooted communities, separated children from parents, and incarcerated leading Uyghur artists and intellectuals.

Among them is my long-term collaborator, Professor Rahile Dawut of Xinjiang University, who has been detained without charge since November 2017. I have shared many productive and inspiring conversations with Rahile over the years. She has been a constant model for me, for her extraordinary generosity as a colleague, her evident passion for her research, and her tireless work as fieldworker and academic mentor. The injustice of her ongoing detention is a constant personal reminder of the need to speak out about the destruction of the culture she loved, and the cruel and dehumanizing treatment of the people with whom we both worked.

Another key figure in this project is my husband, Aziz Isa, without whom this book would not have been written. He has been my constant collaborator for the past decade: travel companion, fixer, interpreter, interlocutor, and frequent coauthor. Like so many Uyghurs in the diaspora, he lives with terrible uncertainty for the safety of his relatives, and he has responded with courage and resolve. I owe my thanks also to our daughters, who have grown up with this project. We've been through some scary moments together, but they seem to have survived intact and even developed a taste for travel, and I think that now they understand what it's all about.

A huge thank-you to my magnificent colleagues who have contributed in various ways to this book. To my fellow ethnographers of Uyghur culture for their excellent and engaged scholarship: Ildikó Bellér-Hann, Darren Byler, Joanne Smith Finley, Rune Steenberg, Rian Thum, and many more. To photographer Lisa Ross for her extraordinary images and commitment to the cause. To my fellow ethnomusicologists for their support and motivation over the years: Stephen Jones, Ted Levin, Laudan Nooshin, Anne Rasmussen, Martin Stokes, Abigail Wood, Owen Wright, Xiao Mei, and Zhou Ji, to name just a few. To my old (but young) friend and coconspirator Rowan Pease, who heroically read the whole manuscript; to Angela Impey, Richard Widdess, and Darren Byler (again), for their helpful comments on individual chapters. To Jennika Baines at Indiana for her careful curation, and to my anonymous readers whose feedback helped enormously to strengthen and shape the final manuscript.

Thanks also to the young Uyghur scholars who are a constant source of strength and hope, especially Mukaddas Mijit and Aynur Kadir; to all my collaborators on the *Sounding Islam in China* project, which helped frame this book, especially Maria Jaschok, Ha Guangtian, Mu Qian, and Ruard Absaroka: it's been a massive pleasure working with you. My thanks are also due to the UK Arts and Humanities Research Council and the Leverhulme Trust for their generous support of this project. Audio and video recordings relating to this book and much more can be found on the *Sounding Islam in China* project website, http://www.soundislamchina.org.

Some of the material that appears in this book has been published elsewhere, but all of it has been substantially reworked and revised. Parts of the introduction and chapter 5 appear in *Performing Islam* and *Central Asian Survey*; parts of chapter 2 appear in *Ethnomusicology Forum*; and parts of chapter 6 appear in *World of Music*.

Finally, my enduring gratitude and love to all our Uyghur friends, hosts, and interlocutors, whose names I do not record here for obvious reasons. They taught me so much about different ways of being in this world. Although they are not named, their voices appear throughout this book, and I hope I have respected their intentions and beliefs in the way I have shaped my narrative around the stories they so generously shared with me. *Allagha Amanät!*

SOUNDSCAPES OF UYGHUR ISLAM

1

SOUND, PLACE, AND RELIGIOUS REVIVAL

Snapshots in Sound from Xinjiang

The massive development of recent decades in the Xinjiang Uyghur Autonomous Region in northwest China has brought rapid advances in infrastructure, the wholesale extraction of natural resources, and large-scale Han Chinese immigration into a region until recently dominated by Turkic Muslim peoples, the most numerous of whom are the Uyghurs. This development has wrought huge changes, not only in the landscape but also in the soundscape. By 2012, coal mines and oil refineries had come to dominate the desert landscape, and heavy trucks thundered up and down the new highways transporting minerals and building materials. In Xinjiang's provincial cities, bulldozers rumbled over demolition sites and mud-brick shacks crashed to the ground, fracturing precarious communities of Uyghur rural migrants. The thudding of pile drivers echoed around the high-rise residential developments that were shooting up in their place. In the manicured town squares, the evening soundscape became carnivalesque. Groups of Han Chinese women performed American line dancing or Chinese *yang'ge* dancing to techno soundtracks that competed with tinny music from children's fairground rides. In the Muslim graveyard in Ürümchi, there was an audible hum from the electricity pylons and the mass of wires that passed overhead; relatives complained that the noise was disturbing the sleep of the dead. In the Uyghur villages of the rural south, the roar of motorbikes had all but replaced the groan of the donkeys, and the nights throbbed to the sound of water pumps as farmers took advantage of cheap electricity to pump water to their cotton fields. The village loudspeaker, that supreme sonic marker of the Chinese Cultural Revolution, was once again filling the village streets with a mixture of popular songs and news of the latest political campaigns.

What can attention to sound contribute to our understanding of the patterns of social and religious change, and the extreme political upheavals that have affected Uyghur communities in Xinjiang and in the Central Asian states? How do social and ideological transformations entwine with the soundscape? The sonic snapshots just sketched give fleeting impressions of the diverse ways in which local people in Xinjiang experienced development, Han migration, and state propaganda in 2012. The sounds of development are ubiquitous, but they signify different things to different listeners. They might be a welcome marker of private achievements: a new home or a good cotton crop. Equally, the sounds might index the destruction of a family home and loss of a way of life or the bulldozing of ancestral graves to make way for a new tourist destination. The heat and noise of the public squares marked not only the increasing number of Han Chinese migrants but also their increasing confidence to claim and dominate public space in this border region.

Equally important for an understanding of the soundscape are the sounds that are not heard, sounds that do not circulate in the public sphere. In this majority-Muslim region, no call to prayer resounded from the village mosque, and the women's religious gatherings that lie at the heart of this book were conducted behind closed doors and windows to muffle the sound of recitation and protect the participants from unwanted attention by the local police. By 2018, the government campaign to "cleanse" Uyghurs of the "virus" of Islam was in full swing. Western journalists who traveled to the region commented repeatedly on the silence of local people in response to their questions. This silence, born of the fear of incriminating oneself through a careless word, had permeated every aspect of daily life. The very use of the Uyghur language in public was labeled an unpatriotic act, one that might lead to the speaker's detention in the new network of internment camps or "reeducation centers," as the authorities termed them. Meanwhile, the public soundscape was dominated by organized demonstrations of Uyghurs' love for the Chinese motherland and the Chinese language and culture: mass performances of revolutionary songs, song-and-dance shows, and street parades celebrating the Chinese New Year.

Researching Religious Revival in China and Central Asia

Over the past three decades, Islamic revival movements and revivalist trends have had a profound impact across the former Soviet Central

Asian states and China. Within Uyghur society, this religious revival is best understood as rooted at the local level. In part, these trends can be read as a response to the relaxing of the tight controls on religious life under Soviet rule and during China's "revolutionary period" of the 1950s–70s. At this level, they represented a revitalization of family and community religious traditions, but they also responded to the increased mobilities and contacts and access to global flows of knowledge that became possible in the 1980s. Thus, they must also be understood as part of the transnational spread of Islamic revival movements with their emphasis on a return to "orthodox" practice and the scripturalist Islamic tradition and on forms of ethical self-cultivation. It is this broad and diffuse revival movement that the Chinese government has depicted wholesale as "religious extremism" and sought to crush through the intense securitization of the Xinjiang region and the mass internment of Uyghurs and other Turkic Muslims.

My research on this topic is based on fieldwork across borders, working with Uyghur communities in the Xinjiang Uyghur Autonomous Region of China (also known by Uyghurs as East Turkistan) and in the Central Asian states of Kazakhstan and Kyrgyzstan. Between 2006 and 2012, I was able to spend several extended periods living in a village in southern Xinjiang, working together with my Uyghur husband, Aziz Isa, to whom I am indebted for his many contributions to this study. Where I write "we" in this book, it refers to our family fieldwork team. During this period, we took part in religious and family rituals and we recorded the oral histories of women who lived in the village. The women had their own individual reasons for engaging with my research. They requested copies of my videos so that they could watch and assess the power of their rituals. They had little experience of tailoring their life stories for the consumption of outsiders, and I found that their oral histories were always recounted with particular audiences, such as their families or friends, in mind. Rabiya Acha, whose story follows this introduction, asked us to pass on the recording we made to her children after her death. She wanted to impress on them the suffering that their mother had endured over a lifetime in the village.

Because of the increased tensions in Xinjiang after 2012, we were unable to continue work there and began to spend time with Uyghur communities across the border in eastern Kazakhstan and Kyrgyzstan. For at least a hundred years, Uyghurs have been migrating westward out of the homeland (*wätän*), following the trade routes across the Heaven Mountains (Tängri Tagh or Tian Shan) and settling in the region now encompassed by the nation-states of Kazakhstan and Kyrgyzstan. Uyghurs arrived here in larger numbers in the 1950s, fleeing from the first wave of communization under the People's Republic of China (PRC) and arriving in what was then a relatively settled Soviet system (Clarke and Kamalov 2004; Harris 2012). In the period that we conducted fieldwork in the Central Asian states, between 2014 and 2015, the relationship between Islam and the state was less oppositional than it was in Xinjiang, and it was easier to attend religious gatherings and schools and conduct interviews that revealed a spectrum of views and often sharp debates within the Uyghur community over the influx of new religious practices and ideologies.

In Xinjiang, the situation throughout my research period has been marked by escalating violence and an anti-religious-extremism campaign that has included mass arrests, sweeping securitization of the region, new forms of discrimination against Uyghurs, and intensified restrictions on religious life. As access to the field became increasingly difficult and potentially dangerous for my local associates, I turned to other forms of data gathering, mainly via the internet and social media platforms, and I listened in on a rich array of mediated expressions of piety and discussions on the nature of faith. I am keenly aware of the ethical challenges posed by this method of research (Fiesler and Proferes 2018) and the potential harms to profiled users, given the sensitivity of much of this material. Under the increasingly severe sanctions on religious expression, foreign connections, and social-media use, it has been impossible to gain individual permission to use these sources, but I have taken every care to anonymize this material and protect my sources from harm.

As state sanctions against religion grew more punitive, my research was inevitably drawn toward a consideration of the relationship between religious revival and the state. A key question addressed in this book, following developments in the anthropology of the state (Sharma and Gupta 2006; Reeves, Rasanayagam and Beyer 2013), is how the Chinese state is discursively reproduced and materially constituted through everyday social practice among Uyghur communities in Xinjiang. In this region, the state is generally understood as a powerful and monolithic entity, an ever-present force that is deeply implicated in the minute texture of everyday life (Gupta 2006). The state is experienced through the constant admonitions of propaganda campaigns; through direct intrusions into daily life in the form of security checkpoints and police visits; as a constant check on private discourse in the form of an imagined listening ear; in everyday bureaucratic practices such as the issuing of "convenience cards," without which people may not travel outside their home towns; and in ritual and symbolic performances such as mass performances of revolutionary songs and organized celebrations of the Chinese New Year on the streets of Khotan.

In China and in Central Asia, notions of tradition and cultural authenticity are used as tools of governance, and there is little middle ground within the opposition that is drawn between idealized national traditions and foreign religious extremism. Muslims in China have striven to align themselves with government initiatives in heritage, development, and tourism. In some cases they have represented their revivalist moves to the outside world as a tourist-friendly cultural renaissance (Hillman 2004), in other cases as examples of "spiritual civilization," but gaining acceptance of such efforts is not always easy. Uyghurs, as marginalized cultural others, have been less able to position themselves advantageously in these shifting fields than have the Hui Chinese Muslims. Religious practice in China occupies an uneasy ground between tolerance and criminalization and is subject to constant shifts in policy. One important effect of state-imposed constraints on debate and restrictions on the flow of information is that lived experience is privileged over debate as a site for religious revival, and thus sounded practice and other sensory media assume particular prominence.

The book arises from the interdisciplinary research project "Sounding Islam in China."[1] The project drew on ethnographic research with special attention to sound in order to cut through the polarized nature of the contemporary political debates, to provide insights into the lived experience of Islam in China, and to enhance our understanding of how transnational trends in Islam are locally reproduced, negotiated, and reconfigured. This book pursues a set of related questions: How does a distinctively Uyghur Islamic soundscape reflect the rise of new forms of Islam? How do these new religious modalities circulate within Uyghur society, and how do people listen to them? Thus, I am interested not only in how these sounds reflect new realities but also how they help to construct new ways of being Muslim and being Uyghur. In the later chapters of this book, responding to the fast-changing events in the region, I turn my focus to the ways in which state campaigns seek to remodel the soundscape and to discipline the embodied practices of its citizens: unmaking Muslims.

As Jonathan Lipman (2014) has argued, Muslims in China reverse the normative Chinese geographies of inside and outside (*nei/wai*). The geography of the "Middle Kingdom" (*zhongguo*) places imperial rule at its civilized heart and relegates the barbarians (including the Uyghurs) to the outer regions beyond the Great Wall. Chinese Muslims, on the other hand, both historically and today, regard the Middle East as their heartland, the source of correct practice and authentic religious sound, and thus they situate themselves on a different periphery. Uyghurs are outsiders from both perspectives. Living in China's northwestern borderlands, they are accustomed to the mainstream Chinese notion that they reside "outside" or "beyond the pass," while China proper is situated "within the mouth" (*kouli*) of the Gansu corridor, "inside" the Great Wall. As Muslims, they regard themselves as far from the Muslim heartlands, distant from the birthplace of Islam, the source of "true Islam" and models for living a proper Muslim lifestyle.

Lives lived in political borderlands are typically marked by tensions between outside and inside, between center and margin, and the Uyghur Islamic soundscape is inscribed in conditions of tension and conflict. Uyghurs, positioned on the borderlands of both Chinese culture and Islamic culture, must constantly engage in the cultural work of absorbing new ideologies and practices, synthesizing and recreating them in the light of local social and political realities and cultural norms. Thus, the notion of the Uyghur Islamic soundscape entails a series of interlocking themes related to the transnational flows of Islamic ideologies and practice and notions of geographical inside and outside, national borders, and gendered divisions of sacred space.

Uyghur Islam in the Twentieth Century

In order to understand the rapid and sometimes violent changes that are the subject of this book, it is important to grasp the nature of religious belief and practice in the region prior to the major political and social upheavals of the mid-twentieth century and to understand the way that the relationship between Uyghur Muslims and the Chinese state has been forged over the decades of Chinese Communist Party (CCP) rule. Several authors have helped to piece together a picture of Islamic faith and practice in the region before the People's Republic was founded in 1949. Ildikó Bellér-Hann's (2008) historical ethnography of Uyghur society in the late nineteenth and early twentieth centuries draws on local textual sources and the accounts of Russian and European travelers in the region. It builds a detailed picture of Islamic practice embedded in local custom, calendric and life-cycle rituals, and relationships of mutual obligation within Uyghur communities. Community life was also dominated by Islamic structures: religious schools (*mädräsä*), sharia courts, and the mosque community (*jäma'ät*).

Studies of local pilgrimage practices build up a picture of a distinctively local form of Islam, inflected by Sufi traditions and regional historiography. Rian Thum (2014) draws primarily on local textual sources in Turkic and Persian languages in his study of Uyghur Islam before the twentieth century. Thum considers the role of a range of texts in daily life, including manuals used for teaching basic knowledge of Islam in the region's religious schools and the prayer manuals carried by individuals both as handbooks and as talismans, often compiled specifically for members of particular crafts and guilds. Central to Thum's account are the hagiographies (*tazkira*) that were written to be recited by pilgrims at the tombs of the saints. Uyghur pilgrims traveled considerable distances across the region to ask favors of the saints or to reaffirm their faith and also to understand more of their history and identity, performing local circuits of pilgrimage around the shrines that dotted the Taklamakan desert in a period when the hajj was an unimaginable dream for the vast majority.

None of the foregoing should be taken as an indication of a monolithic "traditional" Uyghur Islam as a backdrop against which contemporary reformist trends can be measured (Rasanayagam 2006). The history of Islam in this region is one of contestation and change, from the bitter legacy of power struggles between branches of the Naqshbandi Sufi order throughout the eighteenth century (Thum 2014; Brophy 2018) to the early twentieth century revival movement of the Uyghur Jadidists who, influenced by movements in Ottoman Turkey and in Russian Central Asia, first sought to modernize a national form of Uyghur Islam by introducing new styles of education (Brophy 2016).

Under CCP rule, religious practice in Xinjiang came under a tightly organized system of state controls and carefully defined rights. The Islamic Association of China was formed in 1953 to coordinate relations between the party, the Muslim masses, and overseas Muslims and to represent the rights of China's Muslims, who were divided into distinct ethnic categories (Hui Chinese-speaking Muslims, Uyghurs, and other smaller groups: e.g., Salar, Kazakh, Kyrgyz, Uzbek, Tajik, Tatar). A 1953 meeting laid out the aims of the Islamic Association: to interpret Islamic law in accordance with Party policy, to develop regulations to implement Party policy on Islam, and to train and oversee officially sanctioned religious clerics. It was also responsible for producing and ratifying religious scholarship and developing the educational curriculum for China's ten officially approved Islamic institutes, including one in Xinjiang.

The PRC constitution guarantees freedom of religion, but CCP policy—which takes precedence over state law—specifies that only "normal" religious activities receive state protection. This stipulation allows government officials to decide which practices qualify as "normal," and therefore legal, and which are "deviant," and thus illegal (Erie 2016, 12). In practice, this policy has brought about a situation where constant negotiations are required, at all levels of government from the neighborhood to the national, to decide whether a particular practice should be regarded as normal or illegal. This situation has disadvantaged Uyghur Muslims, whose marginal position within Chinese culture has made their religious practice especially prone to be viewed as deviant.

During the first few years of CCP rule in Xinjiang, the Party adopted a relatively cautious and tolerant approach toward Islam. Sharia courts and the office of *qazi* (religious judge) were abolished in 1950, but the rights of Muslims to mosque land were protected. A state Islamic institute was established in Ürümchi, the regional capital of Xinjiang, to teach a curriculum that included study of the Qur'an, hadith, law, the Arabic language, and communist ideology. Only its graduates could serve as official imams in the region's mosques (Fuller and Lipman 2004). This system effectively collapsed under the growing political radicalism of the late 1950s and 1960s. Islam was classified as part of the "four olds": customs, cultures, habits, and ideas fostered by the exploiting classes to poison the minds of the people. Religious books were publicly burned, and religious authority figures were humiliated in public meetings organized by the Red Guards in Xinjiang. Ordinary people, however, as many of my interviews confirmed, continued to practice and transmit their faith privately. As was also the case in Central Asia under Soviet rule, this period saw the domestication of religion, with the household becoming the primary locus for religious activities (Waite 2007).

When the Cultural Revolution ended, a period of relative calm and carefully circumscribed tolerance for religious practice prevailed. Officially approved mosques reopened, and births, marriages, and deaths could once more be celebrated with religious rituals. The Islamic Association of China was reconvened in 1980 after a break of seventeen years, the Islamic Institute in Ürümchi resumed teaching, officially approved religious literature returned to state bookshops, and the Islamic Association began to organize an official annual hajj for a select group of well-connected pilgrims. Officially appointed imams generally came to command the respect of local communities, and they played a key role in providing religious guidance for their local communities and negotiating the space between government directives and community practice. In many ways, however, state policies remained hostile to religious practice and transmission. State employees and students, for example, could not be seen to follow any religion and were not permitted to fast or wear the veil.

In the same period, as controls on travel and cross-border contact were relaxed, Uyghurs began to establish new trading links with Central Asia and the Middle East. Religious families sent their elders on the hajj and sent their children to study in Egypt, Turkey, or Saudi Arabia, and they began to encounter the reformist trends then sweeping the Islamic world. Islamic reformist ideas were soon being disseminated within Uyghur society. As Paula Schrode (2008) argues, these trends represented a new fusion of social prestige, economic power, staged piety, and religious knowledge. Wealthy local merchants acquired social prestige by completing the hajj. They cemented their status by sponsoring the building of new community mosques, and these soon became a prominent feature of the landscape across Xinjiang. Traders and religious students who returned from the Middle East began to compare local religious practice with the kinds promoted in Saudi Arabia and elsewhere, and they often found local practices inadequate and unorthodox. Gradually the number of voices demanding the purification of traditional Islam began to grow. Uyghurs returning from the Middle East were viewed within their communities as religiously cosmopolitan and knowledgeable, and they gained further prestige from their reformist stance. Some began to preach, serving local communities as unofficial imams. Others joined the *dawah* missionary movement and traveled around rural communities in the south, spreading their own messages of piety. The dawah movement in Xinjiang was loosely connected to the Tablighi Jama'at, a global organization with historical roots in the Deobandi movement in India and a strong institutional base in Pakistan. Its followers were active in many parts of the world at this time, including Central Asia (Mostowlansky 2017) and China (Stewart 2016). Many of the Uyghur dawah preachers who were active in southern Xinjiang had little formal education and had acquired their religious knowledge in piecemeal fashion, but people responded strongly to their call to cleanse local practice and return to orthodox forms of Islam.

Through these various routes, new forms of piety began to permeate Uyghur society. The rise in pious practice should not be understood as a coherent trend in Uyghur society, still less as an organized movement. Many styles and interpretations of "correct" Islam circulated in Uyghur society. This circulation was largely unofficial and often semi-underground because of the uncertain and often punitive state policies toward religious practice and the restrictions on religious literature and teaching. In this situation, people with an uncertain grasp of basic religious education sampled and enthusiastically debated the merits of decontextualized styles of religious teaching in often random ways (Waite 2006). These trends in Uyghur society played out in ways very similar to the ways revival movements developed across the border in Kyrgyzstan and Uzbekistan (Rasanayagam 2011; Montgomery 2016) and further east in Hui Muslim Chinese communities in Qinghai and Yunnan (Hillman 2004; Stewart 2016). Sometimes, as in the case of the mid-1990s *mäshräp* movement in the Ili valley in northern Xinjiang (Dautcher 2009), local revivalist groups sought to counter social issues such as alcoholism or drug abuse, and they were frequently engaged in organized charity.

By the mid-1990s, the Xinjiang authorities were viewing these developments with deep suspicion, and they began to move against reformist preachers or organized local groups, especially when their message seemed to be attracting a large audience, thus posing a potential challenge to government control (Dautcher 2009; Waite 2006). The government implemented a series of "strike hard" campaigns, targeting a wide range of religious practices that lay outside the sphere of the officially controlled mosques. Numerous ordinary aspects of Muslim observance, such as abstinence from pork, daily prayers and fasting, veiling or growing beards, were criticized as antisocial. Activities that involved groups of people gathering together—including shrine pilgrimage, religious instruction of children, and home-based healing rituals—were designated as "illegal religious activities." Illegal religious activities were in turn conflated with Uyghur "separatism" (i.e., ethnic nationalist projects to split the Chinese motherland).

Soon after the US announcement of a Global War on Terror in the aftermath of the September 11, 2001, attacks on New York and the Pentagon, China began to adopt the rhetoric of religious extremism and terrorism to explain and justify its internal security policies (Roberts 2018). Since then, designated illegal religious activities in Xinjiang have in turn been conflated with religious extremism in official discourse, and practitioners have been subject to fines, imprisonment, and even torture and execution (Becquelin 2004; Uyghur Human Rights Project 2013). State media began to designate local incidences of violence as terrorist incidents, although the specific reasons underlying local violence were more often to do with local power struggles, official corruption, and police brutality.

Who's a Wahhabi?[2]

Many encounters during our fieldwork serve to illustrate the complexities of the new religious identities that developed in this period. Räyhan, a retired doctor living in the Kyrgyz capital Bishkek, offered us an even-handed assessment: "Now we are more religious than before. It's good. People don't follow bad ways. Our young people don't drink or smoke. On the other hand, there are Wahhabis. They preach sharia in a different way. They say that after a death you shouldn't give the [ritual for the] seven days, you shouldn't give the forty days. They say, this isn't right, that isn't right. They want to get rid of everything" (Räyhan, Bishkek, August 2016). In fact, reformist Muslims in Central Asia were more likely to refer to themselves as *sunnatchi* (followers of the sunna),[3] and their affiliation with any particular group was usually far from clear. In the Central Asian states and in Xinjiang, however, religious revivalists were commonly labeled as Wahhabis, both in state media and by ordinary people who resisted their reforms. Violent incidents in the region were routinely attributed to the Wahhabis, and a reformist stance was regularly conflated with antistate activity (Gladney 2004a; McBrien 2006; Mostowlansky 2017; Roberts 2018).

In 2012, in the regional capital Ürümchi, we attended a *näzir*[4] (death ritual) held by a pious family from southern Xinjiang who had set up a successful information technology business in the regional capital. An elderly official imam from their hometown also attended. During the meal, the brothers of the family criticized the imam aggressively: "Why do you preach about unity of the nationalities in your mosque? Why do you allow the Chinese flag to hang on your mosque? Why don't you preach about how to be a good Muslim? Tell them, don't drink, don't smoke, work hard! We will all die. You should preach true Islam before you die." They also clashed over the details of ritual procedure. When the imam tried to pray for the soul of their father, who had died several years previously, they stopped him short. "Let our father rest in peace; why do you pray for him now when he has been dead for years?" The imam was upset and afterward privately accused them of being Wahhabis, yet the näzir that they were hosting was itself a practice heavily criticized by reformists in Xinjiang.

A government worker in the south of the region complained that religion had overtaken nationality as a marker of identity. "The other day a family came to ask me for help, and they said, please help us because we are all Muslims. I asked, why don't you say, because we are all Uyghurs?" There is no such thing as Wahhabism, he told us. Uyghur young women were adopting the "Arab style" of full-face veiling not because of any serious religious belief but because it annoyed the Chinese. But his wife was fasting during Ramadan, which was possible for her even though she was a teacher in a state school because in that year it coincided with the school holidays. His son had been drinking heavily a few years before, but lately he had started to perform his daily prayers (*bäsh waqit namaz*) and given up alcohol. A Uyghur colleague, commenting on the diversity of views of Islam prevalent in Ürümchi in 2012, said, "If you sit five people down and ask them about Islam they will argue about five different interpretations."

Recent studies of Muslim societies have paid close attention to forms of negotiation, contestation, and control over sacred authority and correct practice (Asad 1986; Marsden and Retsikas 2013; Soares and Osella 2009). Saba Mahmood (2005) calls for scholars to interrogate the practical and conceptual conditions under which different forms of faith and ideology emerge: "the terms that people use to organize their lives are not simply a gloss for universally shared assumptions about the world and one's place in it, but are actually constructive of different forms of personhood, knowledge, and experience" (16).

These studies propose an approach to Islam that takes into account the complexity of interactions between everyday religious experience, interpersonal relationships, and global forms of religious transformation (Marsden 2005, 22–23). In order to understand exactly what constitutes correct religious practice in specific contexts, it is important to examine the genealogies of particular ideas and practices and the relationship between orthodoxy, power, and political authority. They also emphasize the diversity of individual experience and the need to examine the experiences through which different actors develop and cultivate their own understandings of what it means to be a Muslim and live a Muslim life (Henig 2012). In a context where the overwhelmingly dominant state narratives have established a collective image of Uyghur Muslims as violence-prone extremists, this call for attention to diversity and contestation takes on particular importance.

Why Sound?

These ongoing, often deeply polarizing, debates were the defining factor in the changes occurring in religious life in Uyghur communities in Xinjiang and in the diaspora in Kazakhstan and Kyrgyzstan. Rather than focusing on religious ideology, these debates were typically centered on ritual practice, and they very often concerned embodied and sounded practices. In the small border town of Karakol in eastern Kyrgyzstan, an elderly woman called Jännät Hajim, a retired doctor and leader of a women's prayer group, also complained bitterly about the Wahhabis:

> We used to have a respected mulla [religious scholar] called Päyzulla Hajim. They [the reformists] were always arguing with him. In the end, he gave up on this town and moved away . . . because of the Wahhabis. When Päyzulla's wife died, the imam wouldn't do the graveside prayers for his wife. He said, "This is not in sharia." So after they carried the body to the graveyard, and they'd all left, Päyzulla Hajim did the prayers for his wife himself, all on his own. And then he left. That imam was a Wahhabi. (Jännät Hajim, Karakol, July 2016)

This bitter description of Päyzulla Hajim, all alone beside his wife's grave mouthing a silent prayer, illustrates the intimate social aspect that the revival often took, and the way that these debates over "correct" forms of sounded and embodied practice could drive huge rifts through communities.

Attention to sound has become more mainstream in anthropology during the past decade, along with critiques of the dominance of the textual turn. Anthropologists have called instead for "an ethnography of the ear" (Erlmann 2004, 3), seeking approaches to ethnographic research that place listening at their core. Steven Feld has coined the term *acoustemology* to define "an exploration of sonic sensibilities, specifically of ways in which sound is central to making sense, to knowing, to experiential truth" (Feld 1996, 97). This approach, and especially Feld's emphasis on "listening to histories of listening" (Feld 2015), lays emphasis on the ways that communities attribute meaning to sonic environments, and the ways in which listening technologies emerge within particular cultural and historical contexts. It is an approach that takes particular account of agency and positionality: listening practices are social markers, indexes of knowledge, taste, and social distinction.

Developments in sound studies have complemented those in anthropology. Jonathan Sterne, for example, furnishes us with the notion of the sonic imagination exhorting us to "think across sounds," that is, to consider sounds in relation to each other rather than as things in themselves. We may think about the contexts in which sounds happen, and the practices, people, and institutions associated with them; and we can think about multiple competing conceptions of sound, each of which has its own politics, history, and cultural domain (Sterne 2012). The notion of sonic imagination explicitly offers emancipatory potential: the possibility of reworking culture through the development of new narratives, new histories, and new technologies.

In 2009, I began working with a group of Uyghur village women in southern Xinjiang. I attended their meetings, which involved reciting the Qur'an and the practice of *zikr* (Arabic *dhikr*): the rhythmic repetition of Arabic language religious formulas in order to achieve a closer relationship with God through emotional catharsis (Shannon 2004). Although highly musical, the practice was not defined as music and, as such—as nonmusic— it was the principal form of sounded expressive practice open to respectable women in this religiously conservative village (Harris 2013a). As I spent more time in the village, I came to understand the importance of thinking across the whole range of sounded and listening practices related to the expression and embodiment of faith. This perspective provided important insights into the changing nature of Uyghur Islamic faith and religious practice. Many of the debates and conflict about Uyghur Islam centered on the nexus of sound, bodily practices, and musicality: should you have music and dancing at weddings; should you pray at the grave of the recently deceased; should the recited Qur'an sound like singing? Often, the call to "return" to Islam took the sounded form of an inner voice, and listening to its call produced great spiritual relief. As Bäkhtiyar, a newly religious wealthy businessman in Karakol, explained, "One evening at dusk, an idea came into my head . . . it was like a mysterious voice spoke in my heart, and it said I should face *maghrib* [the sunset; the evening prayer]. I felt like someone was calling me to pray. I didn't tell anyone about this feeling, not even my family, but I went to pray. Then I felt deep happiness in my soul" (Bäkhtiyar, Karakol, July 2016). Bäkhtiyar listened to the exhortation and began to follow a pious lifestyle, performing the daily actions of prayer, undertaking the hajj, and funding the building of a new mosque in the town bazaar. This change in lifestyle, he said, brought him a profound sense of spiritual relief.

As a part of the wider field of sensory studies (Pink 2009), sonic imaginations work to displace the privileged visual and promote a democracy of

Fig. 1.1. A depiction of women's veiling practices in a 2014 peasant art propaganda competition, part of the anti-religious-extremism campaign in Xinjiang.

the senses. This work is important in the fraught sphere of the discourse about Islamic revivals in which dominant narratives privilege the visual and routinely stereotype and demonize Muslim subjects as passive Others (Abu-Lughod 2015; Morey and Yaqin 2011). We need to move away from the focus on women's veiling and men's beards that is still so prominent in official and media discourse (see fig. 1.1), and find new ways of thinking about Islam as it is individually experienced and expressed. Why did Bäkhtiyar hear this voice calling him to prayer? What personal transformations has it impelled? What are the wider effects of these new sensibilities on the local community?

Deborah Kapchan (2017, 5–6) has drawn attention to the burgeoning taxonomies of listening in scholarship: Anahid Kassabian's (2013) "ubiquitous listening" that structures the consumer experience; Pauline Oliveros' (2005) notion of "deep listening" that leads to states of profound absorption and transformation; practices of "tactical listening" to effect pedagogical and political change. Kapchan notes that all these genres of listening distinguish themselves by orienting the listener in particular affective directions, thus performing different aesthetic and political work. Denise Gill's (2017) discussion of *muhabbet* (love) and masculinity among classical musicians in Istanbul, develops this theme by attending to the gendered nature of affective listening practices. Of particular relevance to the processes engaged within Islamic revivalist movements is Charles Hirschkind's (2006) delineation of traditions of ethical listening in Islam. Hirschkind highlights the links between the cultivation of ethical sensibilities and listening practices such as listening to recitation of the Qur'an, reciting zikr, or listening to recording sermons, specifically in revivalist practice and also more broadly in Islamic traditions of religious practice. A substantial body of literature has developed in response to this approach, which I discuss in more detail below.

In this book, I argue that attending to the politics of voice and place may help us to cut through the highly polarized political debates about Islam and create new narratives about the nature of religious practice and ideology. In the equally fraught context of the Israeli-Palestinian conflict and the highly contested site of Jerusalem's Western Wall, Abigail Wood (2015) uses this strategy productively, arguing that "a shift in sensory modality might productively refocus and complicate our readings of the Western Wall plaza, showing how normative narratives are produced, jostled, negotiated and undermined by the individuals who use the site" (56). Listening in on the complex interactions at this site impels a focus on the politics of presence, proximity, and voice: how they are built into the physical space and how they are creatively enacted and contested by the people who come there to pray. In this kind of approach, there should be no disjuncture between anthropology's concerns with agency, subjectivity, representation, and power and the more sonically focused study of vocal practices that are traditionally more central to ethnomusicology. A soundscapes approach requires keeping these concerns together; as Amanda Weidman (2014) argues, "attending to voice in its multiple registers gives particular insight into the intimate, affective, and material/embodied dimensions of cultural life and sociopolitical identity" (37).

Although it is "not music," Wood (2015) shows the productivity of taking a musically trained ear to vocalizations at the Western Wall. She describes an Israeli Memorial Day service during which a prayer sung by the Jewish chief cantor was unexpectedly juxtaposed with the Muslim muezzin's call to prayer from the nearby al-Aqsa mosque, creating a vocal duet. Online commentators in Israel expressed profound unease over this event. Wood suggests that the sonic convergence created unease because it disrupted the normative narratives of Othering: the two voices—both unaccompanied solo male voices reciting a religious text in a mode characterized by augmented seconds—were so similar that it was hard to tell which was which; hard to distinguish Self from Other. In this book, I bring a musicological ear to the question of Qur'anic recitation (*qira'at*) in village rituals, considering how and why reciters adopted new modal and stylistic recitation practices and how these practices were absorbed into existing religious practice.

Is It Music?

As Sakakeeny (2015) neatly puts it, "Music is an idea, not just a form, and like any idea, music is a problem" (112). Although ethnomusicologists are familiar with the idea of working on sounded practices not locally understood as music, we may still be productively challenged by approaches that do not assume a privileged status for music within the wider soundscape. Thinking more broadly about sounds impels us to think about the meanings accorded to them. As David Novak and Matt Sakakeeny (2015) argue, metaphors for sound construct the perceptual conditions of hearing and shape the territories and boundaries of sound in social life. They term this a "feedback loop of materiality and metaphor" (1). For these scholars working at the intersections of sound studies and ethnomusicology, it is crucial to explore how the apparently separate fields of perception and discourse are entwined.

What terms are used to denote sounded practices in contemporary Uyghur Islam, and what metaphors are used in the debates that surround these practices? Qur'anic recitation (qira'at) is an important term for religious professionals, invoked in debates about the correct way to voice the Qur'an. *Musiqa* is sometimes invoked in debates around permissibility: the ethics of listening to certain kinds of sounds as part of a good Muslim life. Räyhan revealed how these debates create fault lines within families:

> Once, we were sitting drinking tea, and there was a Hindi film on television with singing, and my grandson said, "Grandma, please turn that off, it's not allowed." I asked my son, "Did you teach your children that music is *haram*?" I said to them, "There's nothing wrong with listening to music. I want to listen to it," and then they shut up. I know he told his son that music was *haram*. . . . If someone has a good heart, and believes in Allah truly, and they listen to music with good intentions, then there is nothing wrong with that. . . . Music is a kind of medicine for spiritual illness; it's essential to life. Beautiful songs are good for the soul. (Räyhan, Bishkek, August 2016)

Räyhan draws on a discourse rooted in Sufi traditions of *sama'* (listening) to support her desire to listen to Hindi film songs: a debate on the permissibility of listening to beautiful voices that has echoed in Central Asia for at least five hundred years (Papas 2015). These forms of listening are maintained by numerous groups of women and men across Central Asia, who meet weekly to practice a form of zikr, to recite the Qur'an, and to cry. For them, this form of listening to aesthetically beautiful sounds has powerful affective qualities and produces tangible spiritual and social benefits.

Another salient term in the contemporary debates is *song-and-dance* (*nakhsha-usul*), a more specific notion referring to folkloric types of public performance that are central to the representations of minority peoples in both the Soviet Union and China. Many Uyghurs listen to these kinds of performances as joyful expressions of national identity and pride, but many pious Uyghurs reject song-and-dance on both religious and political grounds, hearing such performances as an act of submission to Chinese hegemony, both a betrayal of nation and a form of religious sacrilege. All these categories of sound may be heard variously by different actors in this region as sacred sound, as an essential expression of identity, or as dangerous noise.

At a 2017 mass rally at Xinjiang University, officials called for the mobilization of the masses in the ongoing "People's War on Terror," and the elimination of all forms of "noise" (Ch. *zayin*) in the Xinjiang region. What did these officials mean by noise? As a metaphor in sound typically used in opposition to music, noise has emerged in the scholarly discourse as a productive site of inquiry. It is helpfully characterized by Douglas Kahn (1999): "We know they are noises in the first place because they exist where they shouldn't or they don't make sense where they should" (21). Noise often denotes the sounds of the Other: black noise, or low-class noise. Noise is also subversion: the sounds of punk or street protest. It raises "essential questions about the staging of human expression, socialization, individual subjectivity, and political control" (Novak and Sakakeeny 2015, 133). Noise as a metaphor has also been engaged in the sphere of political science. Davide Panagia (2009) argues that although democratic politics is first and foremost a politics of noise, political debates typically create hierarchical distinctions between those who have the authority of the word and those who are "just making noise" (50). In contemporary Xinjiang, as in certain sectors of Europe and the United States, the resurgence of the sacred sounds of Islam is heard by many non-Muslims and state officials as Muslim noise: backward and oppositional, a threat to state projects of modernization and development and essentialized dreams of nation. As I will argue, this conflict in metaphors in sound, or sonic imaginations, is also a conflict over territory.

Thinking about Soundscapes

Since the term was coined in the 1970s by Murray Schafer (1994) the field of soundscape studies has burgeoned, even though Schafer's writing and his subsequent World Soundscapes recording project have been extensively critiqued: for the way that his project classified and judged discrete sounds, objectifying sound rather than treating it as experiential, and for the way that it excluded all sonic traces of Canada's First Nation peoples.[5] Perhaps a more productive early influence on the field is Alain Corbin's (1998) work on church bells in nineteenth-century rural France, with its emphasis on sound, territory and identity. Corbin argued that the emotional impact of church bells helped create a territorial identity for the individuals who lived within range of their sound, a sense of being rooted in space. The village community was enclosed in a space structured and sacralized by the sounds emanating from its center. Church bells also organized the community's temporal markers, marking the hours and ensuring the simultaneity of prayer, which thus shaped the habitus of a community, a habitus of the senses. These ideas on the role of sound in ordering time and space have been further developed in studies of Islamic soundscapes with reference to the *adhan* (call to prayer) in more complex modern urban environments. Hirschkind (2006) describes the adhan in Cairo: "as thousands of mosques broadcast the call to prayer (adhan) over externally mounted loudspeakers, five times a day the city is engulfed in a sort of heavenly interference pattern created by dense vocal interlayings" (124). In Jakarta, Anne Rasmussen (2010a) hears "a multi-voiced tapestry of loose free-meter heterophony emanating quasi-simultaneously from numerous sources including mosques, radios, and televisions at set times" (38). Like Corbin's study of church bells, these studies of Islamic soundscapes note the power of the adhan to demarcate and sacralize space and to serve as a temporal marker. Unlike Corbin's village bells, these are urban soundscapes, where sounds are multiple, densely layered, heterophonic, and often mediated.

In officially multicultural societies such as Singapore, where Islam is not the state religion, the adhan is often banished from the public soundscape out of concerns over noise pollution, and instead is carried to the pious via dedicated radio stations (Lee 1999). In contemporary China, the place of the adhan in the soundscape depends on the local environment and politics. In 2013, we visited the town of Linxia in northwest China, a historical center of Chinese Islam popularly known as China's Little Mecca. Here, a rich tapestry of adhan filled the streets of the Muslim old town five times a day, emanating from a plethora of mosques linked to different Islamic groups, from Sufi orders to Salafis, each one following a slightly different timetable.[6] In rural Xinjiang in the same period, the adhan was rarely heard on the streets; instead pious Uyghur villagers downloaded an app to set alerts on their smartphones. A few years later, even these subterranean sounds were designated a sign of religious extremism and were more thoroughly erased from the soundscape.

David Samuels et al. (2010) define the soundscape as "a publicly circulating entity that is a produced effect of social practices, politics, and ideologies while also being implicated in the shaping of those practices, politics, and ideologies.... Similarly, as landscape is constituted by cultural histories, ideologies, and practices of seeing, soundscape implicates listening as a cultural practice" (30). The emphasis on ideologies of listening and the culturally inflected production of space is a key to much of the recent soundscape literature. It is a dynamic approach to soundscapes, which pays attention to forms of emplacement that are particular, contingent, and unstable, and it answers earlier critiques that portrayed soundscapes as immobile, fixed, and passive (Ingold 2007). Also important in more recent approaches is the focus on embodied relationships with sound, placing practices of sounding and listening within a fully sensory experience of time, space, and self. Hearing Islam in the soundscape strengthens identity through the ability of sacred sound to activate kinesthetic memories: the motions of prayer or the daily rhythms of religious life. Andrew Eisenberg (2009) argues that listening to the adhan "defines the spatial parameters of the community, and serves in the production of a broader—global—Muslim identity, both localizing and globalizing" (98). In Mombasa, as in many other societies where Islam is the dominant religion, the adhan is received by pious Muslims through a set of ingrained comportments such as the automatic adjusting of headscarves, or hushed conversations. Islamic soundscapes thus entail ways of listening, temporal and spatial properties, and embodied practices.

The New Islamic Soundscape of Erdaoqiao

Between 2009 and 2012, a remarkable transformation occurred in the soundscape of the Uyghur neighborhood in Ürümchi, the regional capital of the Xinjiang Uyghur Autonomous Region. The transformation was not obviously modern in the way of the Han Chinese–dominated soundscape of the public squares, but it clearly indexed an alternative form of modernity.

In the nineteenth century, under Qing imperial rule, the area lay south of the city gates and was little more than a shantytown for Uyghur traders. In the 1950s, it became the hub of Uyghur cultural and intellectual life, housing the cultural troupes and, just up the hill, Xinjiang University. By the 1990s, it was home to the city's main mosque and a sprawling Uyghur market. In 2002, the market was knocked down to make way for the new Big Bazaar: a tourism and high-end shopping development with a fake minaret modeled on the classical Central Asian Islamic architecture of Bukhara, adorned with huge advertisements for Kentucky Fried Chicken. In 2009, this was the area through which Uyghur students marched to protest against killings of Uyghur workers in factories in southern China. It was where some of the worst interethnic violence ensued after armed police broke up the demonstration (Millward 2009), and an afternoon of shouted protest gave way to a night of explosions and extended bursts of automatic gunfire. In the months that followed the violence, the existing segregation of the city grew much sharper as Han residents moved out and Uyghurs from the Han-dominated northern part of the city moved in. As the government began to impose tighter restrictions on religious practice in the rural south, pious Uyghur businesspeople moved to Ürümchi. In the wake of these changes, a striking Islamization of the Uyghur part of the city occurred.

The changes were visibly marked by women's choice of dress. Numerous young women could be seen on the street fully covered in what Uyghurs called the "Arab style" of dress or *jilbab*, some in full-length black robes, including the *niqab* facial veil, others following alternative fashions, their heads swathed in fake Burberry checked scarves (see fig. 1.2). Such clothing choices were not unknown a decade earlier, but before 2009 women who chose to fully veil in this manner formed a tiny minority and stood out against the traditional light headscarf and the many women who went about uncovered. Now they were the clear majority (Leibold and Grose 2016).

Fig. 1.2. Woman in jilbab beside an Ürümchi bus station in 2012. Photograph by Aziz Isa.

The changes were visible in other ways. Stallholders on the street were selling privately produced Uyghur-language books and pamphlets to teach the basics of daily prayers and Qur'anic recitation alongside an array of Islamic talismans and charms, prayer beads, and blue glass discs to avert the evil eye, mainly imported from Turkey. Cigarettes had disappeared from the roadside kiosks, and most restaurants had stopped selling alcohol, whereas before, Uyghur men had sat openly smoking and drinking strong Chinese liquor. "They take up space for too long and fight, and it is against our religion," said a restaurant owner. There were rumors of murders: a drunk had been set on as he staggered home one night, and his mutilated body was dumped in front of the main mosque.

Before, Uyghur pop songs and traditional *dutar* melodies had dominated the soundscape, but now imported DVDs of popular *anashid* religious songs sung in Arabic could be heard emanating from the restaurants. On Friday at noon, the sound of the sermon from the mosque was carried by loudspeakers out into the surrounding streets. The mosque was full to overflowing, and its garden was crowded with men bent in prayer. On the pavement outside, boys sold prayer mats and surreptitiously showed interested customers an array of religious media: videodiscs adorned with admonishing images such as a glass of beer overlaying the flames of Hell, or two kneeling skeletons, their bony arms upraised in ecstatic prayer.

Some studies have interpreted Islamic soundscapes as form of resistance, a force that runs against the grain of state messages and Westernized modernity (Rasmussen 2010a). Certainly it would be easy to read this new Ürümchi soundscape as a form of resistance, a political as well as a religious shift, driven in part by the violent state response to the 2009 demonstrations. Although some commentators view the rise of new ways of being Muslim primarily as a consequence of mobility and greater access to global Islamic debates, others have argued that the rise of new forms of Islam among Uyghurs should be read primarily as a response to state policies—in particular, a strategy for buttressing Uyghur ethnic identity in response to policies of assimilation. Joanne Smith Finley (2013) contends that religious revivalism in Xinjiang was driven by the failure of state development policies to provide equitable opportunities for Uyghurs and that economic and cultural marginalization were the principal drivers that led many Uyghurs to seek out the forms of personal transformation afforded by religious piety. This reading joins a significant body of thought that interprets religious revivals as a response among marginalized and deprived people to the upheavals brought about by the introduction of globalized capitalism: "a defensive reaction against the fear of a violent uprooting of traditional ways of life" (Habermas 2003, 32). The benefits of development are unequally distributed, and the sounds of development are heard differently according to the position of the listener.

Contested Soundscapes

This book is focused on the soundscapes of Uyghur Islam, privileging the ethnic group as a site of investigation rather than the geographical region. This focus might at first glance seem counterintuitive if we equate soundscape with landscape in a straightforward way, but if we understand soundscapes as culturally inflected sets of sounds and listening practices, then in this ethnically divided region soundscapes are also ethnically marked. A whole range of sounds are differently perceived by different ethnic groups, and indeed many sounds of key importance to one group may be barely audible to others. Equally, ethnic groups are not homogeneous, stable entities either analytically or in lived experience. Throughout China and

Central Asia, there is considerable variation across time and space in imagining and articulating what it means to be Uyghur, or Kyrgyz, or indeed Muslim (Reeves, Rasanayagam, and Beyer 2014). The notion of a Uyghur Islamic soundscape should not be taken to suggest a coherent set of sounded religious practices but rather a "discursive tradition," a set of processes and struggles through which local actors attempt to define what constitutes true Islam and a good Muslim within relationships of power.

Contemporary studies of urban soundscapes are often studies of contestation and highlight ethnically or racially marked practices of listening. Matt Sakakeeny's (2010) study of the New Orleans soundscapes takes as its subject the sound of a New Orleans brass band performing in a funeral parade as it passes under a concrete bridge. This is a study of African American New Orleans soundscapes, and the ways in which the sounded practices of New Orleans' black communities work to transform the (often racist) built environment of the city. Unlike Schafer's pastoral conception, Sakakeeny offers a view of industrial technology as soundscape and an understanding of soundscape that emphasizes positionality and experientiality. The brass bands under the bridge shape the soundscape for the black community, and through this act of music-making they reclaim and resignify the built environment that so often works to exclude and disempower them.

This capacity of sounded practices to reshape the urban environment is also emphasized by Hirschkind (2006) in his study of the Islamic revival in Cairo. Here, he argues, the practice of playing Qur'an or sermon tapes in cafes has reshaped the moral architecture of such places, introducing norms of sociability associated with the mosque. The pious soundscape plays a powerful role in determining the boundaries and characteristics of public space, producing effects of insiderness and outsiderness (Eisenberg 2009, 121). Eisenberg urges that we go beyond a simple methodological exhortation to listen, to focus instead on what he terms the "acoustemological disjuncture" of complex urban environments; that is, the different ways in which public space may be experienced and enacted and the struggles between contrastive understandings of space (Eisenberg 2013). As Jim Sykes (2015) notes in his study of Tamil street processions in Singapore, the religious soundscapes of modernity are inherently plural; characterized by negotiations between governing powers who seek to control and order public space and religious communities who remain invested in producing sacred sounds (efficacious religious technologies) and allowing them to resonate in public space.

In the cities of China, Islamic sounds and cultures of listening must contend with a host of other sounds and attitudes to sound, and we can observe ongoing processes of negotiation between local authorities, religious bodies, and individual citizens to find ways of accommodating these competing claims on the soundscape. Kashgar's Heyitgah mosque, built in the fifteenth century, is an enduring symbol of Uyghur religious faith. In 2009, the city authorities built a new plaza and tourist area around the mosque and placed a huge television screen directly in front of the mosque. Many Uyghurs complained about the religiously inappropriate sounds and images being brought into this sacred space through the television, and the authorities responded (minimally) to these complaints by turning the television sound off during prayer times (Huang 2009). Further east, in the province of Gansu, the Linxia town government built a new public square in 2010 "to facilitate mass cultural activities."[7] Unfortunately, they chose to situate the square right next to a major Sufi shrine, a complex housing the tomb of the founder of the Qadiriyya order—the first of the major Sufi orders to be introduced into China in the late seventeenth century—and an important site for pilgrimage and worship. Two months after the opening of the square, local Hui Chinese Muslims mounted a protest and submitted a formal complaint against the noise of the new square to the town authorities. The authorities responded positively to the protest, placed a ban on the use of amplified music on the square, and required event organizers to consult with the shrine keepers about noise levels, which temporarily silenced the square. But the desire for forms of sociality involving "heat and noise" (*renao*) among the wider community of Linxia gradually prevailed, and Muslims were by no means insensitive to this desire. When we visited in 2014, we found young *talib* (religious students) merrily roller-skating across the square to the pumping strains of techno during their afternoon off after Friday prayers. Our accounts of contested soundscapes need to be nuanced in terms of the oppositions they draw; we must consider time as well as space and take into account different perspectives and standpoints within the wider community. One important aspect of this variability is gender.

Gendering the Contested Soundscape

When we were young, there was a big tomb in the graveyard. They said it belonged to Karakol Ata [the father of the town]. People used to go there and recite the Qur'an. Now the imam says that women shouldn't go to the graveyard, so we don't go anymore. The hajis say that if you walk over a grave it's like you are walking through blood. They say if women go there the spirits of the dead will tremble, and on the Day of Judgment they will come to take account; it is *namahram* [it violates rules of modesty]. (Jännät Hajim, Karakol, July 2016)

It is surprising that questions of gender, given their now mainstream status in academia and beyond, are only recently beginning to feature in contemporary approaches to soundscapes. But if approaches to the soundscape encompass attention to the diversity of practices of listening, then clearly there is a gendered dimension to soundscapes that needs to be explored. As Jännät Hajim's testimony suggests, changing attitudes to religious practice in Central Asia have both a gendered and a territorial aspect. Women like Jännät Hajim resented the attempts of revivalists to impose new gendered restrictions on access to religious sites, but other groups of women used the revival to stake new territorial claims by establishing women's Qur'an reading groups in the previously male space of the mosque.

Still listening in at Jerusalem's Western Wall, Abigail Wood (2015) offers an instructive case study in gendering the contested soundscape. The Women of the Wall was a Jewish women's group who campaigned for the right to pray aloud and read from the Torah at the Western Wall. Strict Orthodox opponents objected on the grounds that voices of women should not be heard by men at prayer, and they disrupted the women's prayer meetings aggressively with shouted insults or by holding amplified prayer services nearby. This was a sonic contestation of space, religious practice and gender norms that aroused strong passions, which the Israeli state found it hard to mediate.

Roshanak Kheshti (2015) provides another interesting discussion of the gendering of the soundscape in her study of the 2009 protests in Iran. After the disputed elections of that year, numerous residents of Iran's major cities climbed to the rooftops at night to chant Allah-o Akbar. The collective chanting of Allah-o Akbar has long been a part of the Iranian public sphere—it was a rallying cry of the Iranian revolution, and it commonly featured in anti-American protests. But in 2009 it was deployed against the Iranian government for the first time. The sounds of this protest were broadcast around the world via social media as young Iranians, including significant numbers of young women, used their smartphones to record themselves from their own rooftops, listening to the protests and offering their own commentaries on events. The site of this sonic protest was significant. Kheshti (2015) argues that Iran's urban rooftops functioned as a liminal space, situated between the masculine public sphere and the feminine domestic sphere: "The demarcation of the public as the site of political agency and the feminized domestic sphere as the space of social reproduction is here disrupted by the seemingly simple political act of crying out from the rooftops. . . . Rooftop chants of 'Allah-o Akbar' performatively enact political possibilities that breach gendered spatial binaries" (53).

Both these studies offer accounts of women's voices that challenge patriarchal hierarchies of sound and space. Mainstream accounts of Islamic revivals, on the other hand, typically offer narratives of women being forced into positions of invisibility and voicelessness (Abu Lughod 2015). The account offered earlier by Jännät Hajim might serve to reinforce such perceptions, but the situation in Uyghur communities is not so straightforward. While some of the Uyghur women I knew certainly did feel the revivalist trends in their communities as an encroachment on their freedom and agency, others—perhaps the majority—embraced the movement, and they used it to create new forms of women's sociality and to make new territorial demands. In Bishkek in 2014, we found that Uyghur women had instituted a new form of social gathering that they termed *din chay*: religious tea parties. These gatherings, usually organized by women who had studied abroad in Turkey or Egypt, served to disseminate and discuss ways of being Muslim and to forge new community structures. In Bishkek's Uyghur district of Pokrovka, a large number of women were attending classes in the local mosque to learn to recite Qur'an. Previously, women had not been permitted to enter the mosque, but Pokrovka had recently become the proud possessor of a large new mosque, financed by the community. On its completion, a group of women went to see the imam and successfully petitioned to be allowed to use a room in the old mosque to hold their classes. This, to be sure, was a modest claim on shared space, but such developments suggest an alternative picture of these religious transformations, one that entails new forms of agency and new forms of voice for women.

The Networked Village

This book takes as its point of departure the religious experience and practice of rural Uyghur women—farmers and small traders—in a small village in southern Xinjiang that I will call Yantaq village, where I conducted fieldwork over several years. The religious practice of these women is of particular interest in the project of listening beyond text (De Certeau 1998;

Panagia 2009). New forms of Islam arose and developed among different sectors of Uyghur society in different ways. Rural women represent one of the most marginalized sectors of Uyghur (and indeed Chinese) society, distanced from power in terms of religious and political institutions, least able to speak within the context of mainstream discourse. The ways in which they do speak are easily dismissed by elites as ignorant, superstitious, and backward. As Magnus Marsden (2007) argues, if we seek critical insights into the popular politics of marginalized members of society, rather than privileging rationalism and reasoned debate, we need to shift our focus to embodiment, affect, and the ways in which persuasion, debate, and difference making may proceed by other means.

Rural Uyghur women are typically portrayed in the Xinjiang media and in Uyghur popular culture as idealized repositories of tradition and passive nostalgic symbols, or alternatively as "backward" (*luohou*) and lacking in "civilized" qualities (*suzhi*). In fact, many of the women I worked with were highly networked individuals who exercised considerable social and political agency, and their ritual activities were strongly responsive to social change. For anyone who has experience of village life in Central Asia, this responsiveness should be self-evident. As Kandiyoti and Azimova (2004) have argued, participants in village rituals experience the economic, social, and religious components of associational life as a seamless whole. The lives and religious expression of these rural Uyghur women who welcomed me into their village with great warmth and relentless hospitality are at the heart of this book. I focus in particular on the *khätmä* ritual that they performed for the dead. My approach is centered on their individual experience of and engagement with religious and political transformation.

An important theme running through the book is the circulation of religious media in Uyghur society and the ways that their sounds were absorbed, understood, and reproduced within Uyghur society. Recordings of Qur'anic recitation were dominant, especially major twentieth-century Egyptian reciters such as Abdul Basit and contemporary reciters from the Arab Gulf states such as Mishary Rashid Alafasy, but other sounds also entered the mix. They included recorded sermons, horror-film sound effects, and sung religious poetry called anashid, which were produced in Turkey and circulated in Xinjiang via social media platforms. The circulation of these sounds provides insights into the global-local dynamics of religious ideologies and practices, their changing meanings as they enter new contexts, their affective impact, and their power to persuade and transform. In many ways, this book is an ethnography of culture in circulation. Although its starting point is the religious practice of a group of women in a small village in southern Xinjiang, it is not in any way a study of an isolated local culture: their soundscape encompasses transnational networks of circulation entailed by their religious practice. The spiritual geographies surrounding local practices of pilgrimage to the tombs of saints that were central to Uyghur Islam in the nineteenth century have largely been curtailed by state policies on freedom of movement and association, but these women were mobile and networked in new ways. This book explores the spiritual and political geographies they inhabited, moving outward from the village to trace circuits of connection with Mecca, Cairo, Istanbul, Bishkek, and Beijing.

Mediated Listening and Transnational Flows

Uyghurs in Xinjiang and across the border have been accessing and learning about Islam since the 1980s via a succession of media forms: cassettes and videodisc recordings, the internet, and social media platforms accessed on mobile telephones. By the 1990s, China's state media was frequently highlighting concerns about the influence of Islamic media imported from outside Xinjiang, and the authorities made extensive efforts to control its circulation. Such media items were typically portrayed as dangerous polluting influences, ones that purveyed religious extremism, damaged interethnic harmony, and promoted terrorism. Such generalizations are implausible; mediated flows of religious experience and knowledge often follow surprising paths. One of the most influential forms of Islamic media to penetrate society in Kyrgyzstan in recent years was the Brazilian telenovela O Clone (The Clone), which followed the fortunes of a Muslim young woman from Brazil who resettled in Morocco. O Clone became a big hit in Kyrgyzstan in 2004. It led to a new fashion in headscarves (the "Clone look"), and popular debates in marketplaces and on street corners about how a Muslim woman should act, and what it meant to be a wealthy Muslim with two wives (Montgomery 2016, 120).

Studies of popular music are particularly helpful for thinking about these forms of circulation, for there are many points of intersection between the circulation of popular music styles and the circulation of Islamic media. Just as commentators feared that the rapid postwar expansion of popular music threatened a "cultural grey-out" (Lomax 2009) and the collapse of distinct music cultures into a homogeneous global mass, just so contemporary observers fear the spread of global Islamic radicalism and the destruction of local religious traditions. In fact, in the case of popular music, the opposite has occurred. Cultural difference feeds back into musical circulation and globally circulating popular music has become integral to contemporary senses of place and identity, serving to remediate local identity in all its myriad forms in dialogue with other new projects of listening, performance, emplacement, and selfhood (Novak 2013). Musicologists have argued that it is the special capacity of music to move between and mediate both a globally dispersed, virtual community and a localized copresent public—its oscillation between deterritorialization and place—that gives it particular power as an agent for identity formation (Born 2005, 29). In similar ways, we can see globally circulating mediated forms of Islamic sounds in dialogue with local embodied practices, synthesized to create new forms of practice, which facilitate powerful affective experiences of faith and remediate local religious identities and are cast back into circulation in continual loops of feedback.

The Islamic soundscape resounds not only in spaces but also in the sensibilities of listeners. Listening to such media is an essential part of Islamic revival movements, a daily practice for millions of Muslims, part of a complex ethical and political project that promotes social responsibility, pious deportment, and devotional practice. Hirschkind's (2006) influential study explores how new practices of listening ushered in by new Islamic media forms—in particular the cassette sermon—transformed the political geography of the Middle East and played a pivotal role in the new arenas of religious discourse and practice that underpinned the new "Islamic counterpublics" that developed across the region.

As I have argued, the act of listening is crucial to any discussion of sound, and the singing (or reciting) voice possesses great potency because it forges powerful experiences of religion. Writing on the revivalist movement in Turkey, Martin Stokes (2013; 2016) argues that the sensory order of the secular Turkish republic was overturned by new forms of popular cultural mobilization developed in the 1990s. Questions of aesthetics played a central role in this political realignment: the act of listening to and reflecting on the beauty of the voice in recorded popular religious songs drove the new forms of ethical self-fashioning that underpinned the emerging political order. In Turkey, as elsewhere, internet and small-media technologies helped to shape the new ethical and religious dispositions by enabling new forms of spiritual, ethical, and aesthetic connection and by creating a sense of participation in the new aesthetic and political community.

The use of religious media also may serve to translate established modes of listening and reproduce them within transnational networks of circulation. Writing on the circulation of recorded religious songs between South Asia and Mauritius, Patrick Eisenlohr (2018) notes how Mauritian Muslims have reshaped technology according to a genealogical form of Islamic authority centered on the safeguarding of textual and performative transmission. For Eisenlohr's interlocutors, recordings ensured the authenticity and the power of ritual performances by maintaining these chains of transmission and circulation.

Circuits of Affect

The powerful emotions released during religious rituals manifest the intersections of morality, aesthetics, and memory in ways that reveal lived social orders and embodied cultural norms. Circuits of affect move along lines of power, within social and gendered hierarchies. The Uyghur women immersed in their khätmä ritual in Yantaq village were engaged with a widespread, centuries-long tradition of religious practice, textual and oral transmission that includes instructions for the techniques of reciting the Qur'an, commentary on the Qur'an and its emotional impact, Sufi traditions of writing and practice, and debates on the permissibility of musical sound in Islam.[8] Yet their access to, interpretation, and embodiment of this rich tradition were particular to time and place, their social class, and their gender.

Sarah Ahmed's (2004) study of the sociality of emotion—what she has termed "economies of affect"—has helped frame my approach to this topic. Ahmed argues that rather than being situated on the interior of individuals, emotions circulate between bodies. Emotions take shape through the repetition of actions over time, as well as through orientations toward and away from others, accumulating over time and accruing forms of affective value. For Ahmed, the objects of emotion take shape as the effects of circulation. As sites of personal and social tension, these objects become "sticky": saturated with contagious forms of affect. In this book, I am interested in how the emotions that feature in local traditions of religious practice are taken up and revitalized through engagement with contemporary flows of aesthetics and ideology. Certain named emotions—which are integral to

Central Asian literary traditions of Islam and which also permeate contemporary Uyghur culture—appear as recurring themes in this book, notably the twin themes of *ishq* (divine love, passion), and *dard* (suffering).

In chapter 2, I discuss the khätmä rituals of reciting the Qur'an and forms of zikr performed by a group of rural Uyghur women, in which I participated during the summers of 2009 and 2012. The participants in these rituals—as they explained to me repeatedly—listened to the word of God and experienced ishq, which they expressed through weeping. As Hirschkind (2006) argues, the act of listening to recitation of the Qur'an is central to ethical and therapeutic practices in Islam. For these women, as for the many Muslims worldwide who can neither speak nor read Arabic, the experience of the Qur'an is primarily through its sound, not as text. But this lack of textual reference does not mean that the sounds are rendered meaningless. They are imbued with affective power that produces culturally embedded meanings with the ability to act within social life. Ishq played a crucial role in village society in Yantaq: an emotional state that must be produced through collective rituals in order to atone for the individual and collective sins of the community and to prepare their souls for the Day of Judgment.

These rituals were in no sense remnants of the past but were in active dialogue with global flows of religious ideologies and social and political change within Xinjiang. The women's practice was carefully muted: shielded from male ears according to gendered rules of modesty and carefully hidden from the ears of state agents. In these rituals, we find radically opposing ways of listening to the same sounds. State agents listened to the sounds as indexes of potentially violent resistance (see chapter 5), antithetical to projects of modernization and development; the women in Yantaq village saw the rituals as developing their religious traditions by absorbing and synthesizing the new models of sounded practice that circulated around the region in various mediated forms. Stigmatized in the national discourse as superstitious and backward, they developed their own understanding of modernity as nonsecular and as non-Western, and they strategically deployed new styles of recitation to sound out their modernity and to strengthen their ishq.

Chapter 3 focuses on another core aspect of village religious practice: the *hikmät*—Turkic-language prayers attributed to the early Central Asian Sufi sheikh, Khoja Ahmad Yasawi—that Uyghur village women sang with extraordinary affective power in their ritual meetings. Their listening to hikmäts impelled meditation on the impermanence of life, the inevitable embrace of the grave, and the meaninglessness of worldly gains. Listening to hikmäts provoked grief but also awe of God's power. In chapter 3, I consider the relationships between textual traditions of scholarship and orally transmitted traditions of affective ritual performance. Hikmäts existed in oral and written circuits of transmission. They were handed down within local networks of face-to-face transmission aided by handwritten copybooks (*däptär*), and this oral transmission was cross-fertilized by transnational circuits of published texts. I argue that the complex interactions between text and performance were motivated, just like the impulse to learn new styles of Qur'anic recitation, by the desire to incorporate correct practice into ritual performance in order to increase the spiritual power of the ritual. This pattern of circulation moved on a Turkic language axis and linked the women to other parts of Central Asia and to Turkey. This axis also entailed the circulation of people, primarily through mid-twentieth-century patterns of Uyghur migration across the Soviet-Chinese border. Performing hikmät in the diaspora activated powerful memories of the homeland but also involved radically new styles of performance, adapting to new contexts and new embodied cultural norms.

Chapter 4 traces the patterns of circulation of Qur'anic recitation emanating from the Middle East and considers questions of musical style, religious ideology and authority, and the sense of separation from the source of Islam that Uyghurs commonly express. A common theme in many conversations with Uyghurs was their sense of being distant from the Islamic heartlands, a position that explained their failure to adhere to "correct" religious practice. In addition to their sense of distance from the geographical source of Islam, Uyghur migrants in Central Asia (Kazakhstan and Kyrgyzstan) also experienced a feeling of temporal rupture. Older people often linked their sense of their own inadequacy as Muslims to the antireligion campaigns of the revolutionary period in Xinjiang and the secular ethos of the Soviet era. Their personal projects of religious reconnection often drew on memories of childhood religious lessons "back there."

In chapter 4, I focus on practices of listening to and reciting the Qur'an; the introduction of the sounds of the Qur'an into new spaces, the spread of Qur'an classes, and the debates about styles of Qur'anic recitation. What happens when Middle Eastern styles of Qur'anic recitation are reproduced in Central Asia? What does it mean when a rural Uyghur woman, conducting a Sufi-inflected ritual, imitates the recitation style promoted by Salafi preachers who are strongly, even violently, opposed to Sufi practices? The case studies in chapter 4 reveal the complexity of the interactions between local systems of meaning and experience and global forms of religious transformation. Where listening practices are so powerfully implicated in embodied ways of being, it is not surprising that (musical) style is also a site of contestation. When new ways of reciting the Qur'an displace local styles, they challenge embodied norms and sound out new ideologies of correct religious practice. They serve not simply as an aesthetic symbol of the new religious norms, they also usher in a new set of dispositions—embodied responses to sound, and processes of subject formation—which underpin the creation of the new Uyghur Muslim counterpublic.

In chapter 5, I focus on the ways in which Uyghurs related to and through specific media platforms and the affective impact of religious media in daily life, aiming to understand how the most marginalized sectors of society engaged with rapidly changing religious ideoscapes and soundscapes. I consider the circulation of specific media items such as "miracle" videos, Uyghur language sermons, and sung anashid. I discuss an internet meme circulating in Uyghur society in 2012: a video depicting the taxidermized remains of a snake, attached to the body and head of a monkey wearing a blond wig, accompanied by a horror soundtrack of animal cries and pulsing synthesized beats.[9] Around this grotesque and terrifying meme accrued a powerful web of meanings that centered on fear of God, forms of piety, and correct ways of being a Muslim woman. Drawing on Panagia's (2009) ideas on the politics of the utterance, I argue that we need to pay close attention to the affective impact of this kind of media item; we need to listen attentively to the noisy, messy world of rumors in a context of rising violence and fear if we are to understand the changing nature of Uyghur Islam in this period.

Chapter 6 traces the circuits of connection with Beijing, situating Uyghur Muslims as citizens of the People's Republic of China and considering the impact of state policies of development, education, and security. Here, my focus is on questions of embodiment and representation: tropes of professional folkloric performance in China and the symbolic potential of the smile. As we have seen, a focus on embodiment is central to many readings of the Islamic reform movement in the Middle East. Saba Mahmood (2005) draws attention to debates about performative behavior, arguing that forms of bodily practice (such as veiling, daily prayers, or reciting the Qur'an) do not simply express the self but also shape the self that they are supposed to signify. The anti-religious extremism campaign that has dominated life in Xinjiang since 2014 sought to expunge these new pious forms of embodied behavior and to replace them with forms of embodied behavior developed during China's Cultural Revolution, staking the state's claim on the Xinjiang soundscape through organized mass song and dance. One side effect of the campaign was to create a sense of deep alienation from formal musical performance among Uyghurs, in that what had formerly been prized as national culture became branded as a tool of state oppression. I read the anti-religious extremism campaign as a form of sonic territorialization (Yeh 2013; Daughtry 2015) aimed at reclaiming Xinjiang as an integral part of the territory of the People's Republic of China and reshaping its inhabitants as secular and patriotic citizens. Ultimately, I argue, it was the new, broad-based Muslim counterpublic in Xinjiang that the anti-religious extremism campaign and the subsequent extreme policies of securitization imposed on the region sought to crush and expel from the Chinese body politic.

The concluding chapter 7 brings the account of the anti-religious extremism campaign up to date at the time of writing with a discussion of the techniques of reeducation used in Xinjiang's mass internment camps, questions of rhythm and repetition, and attempts to reengineer human beings. I reflect on the narratives of cultural erasure and trauma that have come to dominate foreign media discussions of the camps and draw on recent writing on postcolonial movements in the Americas in order to historicize and contextualize these campaigns and offer the possibility of a narrative of a more hopeful future.

*   *   *

In this region, coercive forms of discipline and state power condition the experience of everyday life and shape the politics of the possible. Access for researchers is limited, and the dominant media representations offer distorted views of on-the-ground realities. Thinking across soundscapes may help us to think through these representations and create new narratives about the nature of religious experience, power, and resistance. Sounded and embodied practices, ways of listening, and ways of embodying spiritual power play crucial roles in producing Muslim subjects and in producing Muslim citizens. By listening in on the new religious modalities that circulated transnationally and within Uyghur society, and by paying attention to how people listened to them, we can begin to perceive how they helped to construct new ways of being Muslim in Uyghur society. A soundscapes approach to the Uyghur Islamic revival allows us to think about sound and space in ways that encompass conflicting projects of self-fashioning that involve bodies, desires, habitus, and emotion. It encompasses transnational flows of religious ideologies and practice, mediated listening practices, and debates about appropriate and inappropriate sounds, sound and architecture, gendered divisions of space, and processes of territorialization. A soundscapes approach allows us to explore the disjuncture between types of embodied listening practices and to understand the ways in which different ways of listening may influence the landscape, either in the creation of new ways of inhabiting the landscape, in the production of state territory, or for other ends.

Notes

1. I am grateful to the UK Arts and Humanities Research Council and the Leverhulme Trust for their support of this research. The project's activities can be explored through our website, www.soundislamchina.org, which includes conference paper summaries, fieldwork reports, and a sound map of Islam in China that holds numerous audio and video recordings.

2. Wahhabism is a conservative branch of Sunni Islam, which preaches a return to the fundamentals of Islam. Wahhabism was a popular revivalist movement instigated by the eighteenth-century Saudi theologian Muhammad ibn Abd al-Wahhab, who criticized the moral decline and political weakness in the Arabian Peninsula and condemned popular cults of saints and shrine visitation. It has become the dominant form of Islam in Saudi Arabia and is widely promoted around the world, supported by the political and financial power of the Saudi government.

3. Sunna is the way of life prescribed as normative for Muslims on the basis of the teachings and practices of the Prophet Muhammad and interpretations of the Qur'an.

4. In Uyghur custom, *näzir*s are held on the third, seventh, and fortieth day and one year after death. If the family is rich, then the whole mosque community is invited for food and to listen to recitation of the Qur'an, which builds up religious merit on behalf of the deceased. Families often go to considerable expense to mark the status of the deceased.

5. See Helmreich 2010; Mitchell Akiyama, "Unsettling the World Soundscape Project: Soundscapes of Canada and the Politics of Self-Recognition," *Sounding Out!* September 17, 2015. https://soundstudiesblog.com/2015/08/20/unsettling-the-world-soundscape-project-soundscapes-of-canada-and-the-politics-of-self-recognition/.

6. For recordings and further commentary see the project website, *Sounding Islam in China: A Multi-Sited Ethnographic Study*, http://www.soundislamchina.org/.

7. See Wei Yukun and Xiao Mei's conference paper summary, "The Public Soundscape of China's 'Little Mecca,'" with video illustrations, http://www.soundislamchina.org/?p=1033.

8. Faruqi 1985 and Nelson 2001.

9. A recording can be found on the project website: http://www.soundislamchina.org/?p=394.

Interlude 1

RABIYA ACHA'S STORY

I WAS BORN IN MAY 1948.[1] THAT YEAR they were digging out the Liberation River (Azad Därya). They called my father home from digging the river to do my naming ceremony. We were seven children, five girls and two boys, and when I was one year old my mother died. Seven children with nobody to look after us, so thirty-eight days after she died my father remarried. Then four years after my mother's death, my father fell sick as well. People told him, "If you give away something that you can't bear to part with, then you will get well." So they invited all the community elders to our home and served them food. My father was sitting in the middle of the group, and he called me to him, and then he handed me to one of our relatives and said, "Please give her away to someone," and so my relative took me and placed me in the arms of another woman.

Every week I peeled hemp and sold it to support my new brother's school fees. If I collected a kilo, I could make two *yuan*, enough for one week's fees. My new stepfather was the village head. He was in charge of three brigades at that time, and he was a party member. Then he lost his job: they accused him of stealing 3,600 sheep from the village, and they gave him criticism (*pipan qildi*). This was in the Cultural Revolution. At that time, I'd just got married. I finished school in 1961 and got married in August 1963. I gave birth to eleven children, and I had three miscarriages. When I got married, they built us a mud-brick house. My mother-in-law gave me an old cracked pot to cook with, a cloth for preparing dough (*supurgha*), and a mosquito net (*pashliq*). Then the Chinese started stealing our apples and we had to sleep in the orchard to protect the crop. It got really cold outside, and so I tried to run away, but my husband caught me and brought me back.

On the day I gave birth to my second son, another campaign started; it was called "catch the black strings" [people with links to foreign countries]. They called my stepfather to the village office and locked him up. After a while they released him, but then one night some men came to our home and they took him to the threshing ground. When he came back he was in a bad way. He got weaker and then he died.

Then I started work for the commune. There was not a single thing in the commune, no hoe, no yoke, that I didn't know how to use. We had to go to the other side of the village before sunrise. We carried good soil to the salty fields. They measured how much soil we brought each time, and we had to work until we'd brought our quota. Then, later, they found another kind of work for us, cutting bushes and pounding them to make fertilizer. There was no food, and so we secretly took some grain on the way back from the fields and ate that. In winter we had to weigh the wheat, and we would fill up our pockets with grain and make bread from it when we got home.

Going to work, we had to carry the hoe in one hand and Mao's portrait in the other. It was very difficult. When my daughter was born and my sons were bigger, I couldn't carry them all with me when I went to work in the fields. I used to put out the fire so they couldn't burn themselves; I left the felts on the brick bed (*kang*), with two pots of soil for them to go to the toilet, water for them to drink, and bread to eat when they were hungry, and I left my two little boys and baby girl locked inside the house.

In 1982, they disbanded the commune and every family got their own land. We started planting and tried to rebuild our lives. After they redistributed land and we held it privately, we planted lots of wheat and finally we had our own grain. The first time we brought home a whole sack of grain we stood and stared at it and said, "Is that really ours?" We were afraid and said to each other, "Will they take it away after a few months, or are we allowed to eat it?" In the end, they didn't take it away, it stayed in our home, and we planted the fields again the next year.

We opened up some wasteland and planted crops, but they didn't grow well, and we got into debt. We worked every year on the land, but it was never enough; all the money went on water fees, land fees, taxes. My husband said, "We have to have land! We have so many children, what will they do when they grow up? If they don't have land they will become thieves or go astray." So we kept the land for our children even though we never had any profit from it.

I made yogurt, and I sent the boys to sell the yogurt in the bazaar. Sometimes I planted sunflowers and sold the seeds in the bazaar. We also had a date tree, and we harvested the dates and sold them. I planted a lot of garlic and sold that too. Apart from my oldest daughter, I sent all my children to school, and then I sent them to learn a trade. When the big mosque was built in the village, I sent my oldest son there to learn to read the Qur'an. Then I sent him to be a chef. He worked hard and managed to open his own restaurant.

These days, if you attend too many religious events, they'll classify you as a political criminal. It started after the Saddam incident (i.e., the Iraq war). Where do these young people die? Behind the black gate (i.e., in prison camps), and you never know the cause. Five or six years ago they even dared to play Qur'anic recitation on the village loudspeakers. Now they say it is religious extremism.

Apart from prayers at funerals, people are afraid to gather and pray as they used to. The government controls gatherings very tightly. If anyone is found leading communal prayers, they'll be arrested, especially if there are schoolchildren there. In our village, only the Damolla can lead prayers or teach children because he has special permission. Every week he's called to a meeting by the government. For everyone else, they say it's illegal religious activities. Usually they don't care much if older people pray in the mosque, but they do care if people start disagreeing about how to pray. The government is afraid of these kinds of discussion among young people, people dividing into different factions.

Nowadays, mainly I just do my prayers at home. I don't do much other than that. If you do, you will have lots of trouble. But I never miss a funeral. I go and gather with the other women in our community. When someone dies, you have to recite *la illaha illallah* seventy-two thousand times. When we've finished seventy-two thousand times, then it is complete, and then we pray and we get up to go. Many of my cousins and relatives became *mulla* or *büwi*, but I never had an education. I was brought up by a stepmother, and so I never had the chance. A büwi is a woman who believes in Allah and follows all Allah's rules and understands the whole Qur'an and can recite the whole Qur'an and always thinks about life after death. That woman is a büwi.

Note

1. This account is an edited version of a recorded interview made in Yantaq village in August 2009. Translated from the Uyghur by Aziz Isa and Rachel Harris.

2

AFFECTIVE RITUALS IN A UYGHUR VILLAGE

In the summer of 2009, in a small village that I call Yantaq, sixty women squeezed themselves into the guestroom of a village house. In a three-hour-long ritual, they recited from the Qur'an (*khätmä*), they sang *hikmät* lyrics attributed to the twelfth-century Central Asian saint Ahmad Yasawi, they chanted *zikr*[1] and performed a slow, circling *sama*[2] dance, and they wept copiously and demonstratively (see fig. 2.1.). They were led by Märyäm, an elegant woman in her sixties, a senior *büwi* ritual specialist who sat in the place of honor at the center of the back wall flanked by her apprentices (*shagit*). The other women arranged themselves around her in roughly concentric semicircles. In this all-female gathering, Märyäm drew back her sequined face veil and directed the proceedings, almost as an orchestral conductor directs an orchestra. She also led the performance, giving the opening solo section of recitation herself and leading the other women in repeated rhythmic chanted zikr, which included phrases from the Qur'an and well-known Arabic language prayers (*du'a*). She called on her apprentices to perform longer sections of individual recitation and shepherded the whole group through emotional peaks and troughs toward the climax of the ritual. After around an hour, she led the group into a new chanted zikr: *subhan'Allah wa bihamdihi, subhan'Allah il adhim* (glory and praise to Allah, glory to Allah the supreme).

The women gradually settled into a regular rhythmic pulse, repeating the text to a short, falling melodic phrase. Many of them began to rock backward and forward. After two minutes, when the rhythm was established, Märyäm called out, "Come close, hold hands. Speak at the same time together, as if with one voice." The women shuffled forward and began to rock more energetically. Their chanting took on a new urgency, though

Fig. 2.1. Women gather around a *dastkhan* before beginning their khätmä. Photograph by the author. All images of my interlocutors have been textured to protect their anonymity.

the effect was hardly one of unity. Sixty voices overlapped, reciting the same phrase, slightly out of sync and slightly off pitch, forming a wash of sound. After another minute, one woman began to cry out and jerk her body, crying, "Woy Allah! Woy Allah!" The others maintained the chant under her though they were by now very scattered. The trancing woman called out a rhythmic "Woy! Woy!" not keeping to the rhythm of the chant. Other women restrained her and fanned her to cool her down. Many women were weeping loudly.

Emotion, Circulation, Performance

The most striking aspect of the ritual for the uninitiated observer was its emotional intensity, manifested in the women's copious weeping, the rhythmic wash of voices, and the spasmodic movements of the trancing woman. As a cultural outsider sitting in the room, I was also deeply affected by it; the rhythm was hard to resist, and the affective charge was highly contagious. How might we understand the emotional response of participants to this ritual?

The everyday language of emotion is based on the presumption of interiority, what we might call the "inside-out" model: emotions are part of an individual's inner life, and they burst forth into the world, separate from and opposed to conscious, rational thought. Classic anthropological approaches to emotion, drawing on work by the early sociologist Émile Durkheim, emphasize instead its culturally rooted social nature: "Just as thought does not exist in isolation from affective life, so affect is culturally ordered and does not exist apart from thought" (Rosaldo 1984, 137). For Durkheim—writing on crowds—emotion is not what comes from inside the individual body but what holds or binds the social body together, what we might call the "outside-in" model. In this tradition of thought, an emotion such as shame in European societies may be expressed through the involuntary response of blushing. This indicates the internalization and the embodiment of social values. Emotions play an important role in shaping action: as Catherine Lutz and Geoffrey White suggest, "emotions are a primary idiom for defining and negotiating social relations of the self within a moral order" (1986, 417). This Durkheimian tradition also remains central to contemporary approaches to religion and emotion: "The emotional lives of people—thought by some to be part of an inaccessible interior of self—are in fact socially dictated performances, social scripts, as it were, grounded in shared understandings about the meaning of social events and actions. . . . An emotion in this sense is given by culture, that is, made normative through 'feeling rules' that dictate the proper linkages between social experiences and emotional states" (Corrigan 2004, 11). Sara Ahmed argues against this "outside-in" model. She collapses the rigid dichotomy between inside and out, suggesting rather that emotions create the very effect of the surfaces and boundaries that allow us to distinguish an inside and an outside in the first place: "the surface of bodies 'surface' as an effect of the impressions left by others" (Ahmed 2004, 10). Emotions then are crucial to the very constitution of the psychic and the social as objects. Ahmed's approach is rooted in the ideas of feminist philosopher Judith Butler, who argues that social forms—civilization, gender, nation—are effects of repetition. It is through the repetition of norms that worlds materialize, and boundary, fixity, and surface are produced (Butler 1993, 9). Through this understanding, we can read emotion as a form of cultural politics or world making, and by paying attention to emotions, we can see how subjects become invested in particular ideological and political structures. This approach works against the distinction sometimes made between affect (as the raw stuff of the subconscious) and emotion (as the culturally processed product of affect). For Ahmed, it is important not to assume separation between the physical and embodied, and the conscious and intentional. Instead, she calls for attention to "the messiness of the experiential, how bodies unfold into worlds, and the drama of contingency, how we are touched by what comes near" (Ahmed 2010, 574).

Ahmed's primary site of analysis is text-based discourse. Discourse helps to shape experience and inflect emotion but—as I have argued in chapter 1—it is not the whole picture. Rather, we can think about a dialectical relationship between discourse and experience, between the ideological and the embodied. Discourse both inflects and is inflected by corporeal experience, including the heightened experience of performance in ritual contexts. A focus on embodiment helps us to question the dualism that pits bodily experience as natural and subconscious against the cerebral sphere of language and thought. Approaches to music and trance suggest a focus on the body as the site of personal experience, understanding the body as a physical structure in which emotion happens, and understanding the experiencing body as intimately linked to the environment. Attention to the voice in ritual performance helps us to understand the interface between sound, environment, body, and emotion. When we vocalize, we pull air into the lungs and push it out again through the mouth, manipulating our vocal chords in order to control the quality of the sound. Thinking about this process gives us a sense of the direct and embodied nature of the relationship between sound, environment, and bodily tension and release. Ritual performance is also fundamentally about bodily movement. Spiritual energy, place, self, ritual interactions, and relationships are all mediated through movement. The reason rhythmic performance is central to so many forms of ritual observance and public gathering is that it has potential to create a sense of collectivity in the course of performance through synchronized movement.

The sense of collectivity experienced in musical performance is sometimes explained as a form of entrainment and sometimes as a shared groove.[3] But—as Clayton, Dueck, and Leante (2013) argue—the entrainment that people experience during musical and ritual performance is not simply a question of "falling into time" with one another. Playing in time with the music also involves aligning one's comportment to broader ideologies of what is musically, or ritually, appropriate and effective. Musical experience can establish and reinforce senses of collective selfhood and otherness in embodied ways; the experience of being in a rhythmic groove is closely tied to feeling a sense of belonging (Clayton et al. 2013). Many studies have drawn attention to the connections between musical performance, coordinated action, heightened emotional experience, and the construction of community. Likewise, we can argue that community is experienced and constructed through religious ritual. Deborah Kapchan (2009), for example, describes zikr as a means of building community. Community, she argues, is created in acts of worship and in performance by virtue of submission to God and also through practices of sounding and listening: prayer, chanting, and singing. The processes of entrainment or falling into a shared groove that lie at the heart of many kinds of musical experience are also at work in the ritual gathering described at the beginning of this chapter, and I argue that they lie at the heart of its role within the village community.

Islam in the Village Community

I came late to the women's sphere of Uyghur society, after ten years researching the masculine world of Uyghur music: the "classical" *muqam* suites and the Uyghur pop industry. During this earlier phase of my research, I associated with male scholars and problematized issues of ethnicity and nationalism and the politics of representation, but I rarely concerned myself with the politics of gender. As a masculinized foreign scholar, I was distanced from the wives of my urban Uyghur colleagues. When I got married to a Uyghur man, relations with other Uyghur men became more distanced; I was invited into the feminine sphere, and I finally began to understand the necessity of attending to questions of gender. In 2006, we spent a long summer in Yantaq village in southern Xinjiang. Here it was the men who appeared as marginal figures in a woman-centric world. I took my place in the heart of the women's sphere, with my own small child in tow, attempting to participate in the work of housekeeping and hospitality: fetching the water from the well and lighting the fire for tea, nursing babies, feeding animals, baking bread in the *tonur* brick ovens, preparing dough for noodles and dumplings, and chopping carrots and onions ready to throw into the big communal cooking pot where an older woman was heating the oil.

The women of the family were immersed in a perpetual cycle of reciprocal hospitality and mutual aid that upheld the dense networks of community life (Bellér-Hann 2008). Our visits to the village were a catalyst for the renewal of community bonds. It began with the killing of a sheep: a visceral spectacle carried out by our brother-in-law in a corner of the yard. Sheep's blood was believed to have healing and strengthening properties, and my sister-in-law hitched up her skirt and bathed her legs in the jet of hot blood spurting from the animal's throat. The women of the immediate family arrived to assist with the preparation of an immense pot of *polo*: the celebration dish of braised mutton, carrots, and rice. The management of such an occasion required intimate knowledge of village society. The guests were arranged in hierarchical order around the *dastkhan* tablecloth laid on the large raised brick bed of the guest room. The polo was served on home-baked rounds of *nan* flatbread. Each guest received a piece of meat of a size appropriate to their social status, discreetly covered by another flatbread. Guests would eat a little of the food and then wrap the remainder in a cloth and take it home for the rest of their family.

After this opening gesture, the return invitations began. Every morning a friend or relative would arrive at our hosts' house to announce that food was prepared and we were expected. The village network was large, and the visits continued for two weeks, sometimes five or six times a day: rich pickings for the ethnographer but exhausting for guests and hosts, particularly for the women. Such patterns of reciprocal hospitality were by no means extraordinary; they governed village life. The summer months were devoted to weddings, each of which involved three separate rounds of hospitality and large numbers of guests. In winter, there were more funerals and memorial gatherings (*näzir*); wealthier villagers might also celebrate their sons' circumcisions. Ramadan was another important period for nightly gatherings to share the *iftar* meal at dusk. Religious custom was a normal and integral component of this reciprocal hospitality: the muttered prayer as the sheep was slaughtered, the obligatory silent prayer as people rose at the end of a meal, the scheduling of meals around the requirements of daily prayers (*bäsh waqit namaz*) that an increasing number of villagers were observing in this period, and the especially large piece of fat meat and bowl of fresh yogurt—hastily borrowed from a neighbor—placed before the imam of the town mosque as he arrived on an expensive motorbike to pay his respects: a real honor for the family.

In this rural Uyghur village, moral propriety and communal responsibility were intertwined with being a good Muslim (Waite 2006; Bellér-Hann 2008). Regular attendance at Friday prayers in the mosque for men and participation in funeral and other religious rituals for women were markers of respectability and affected their family's standing positively. Although the anti-extremism campaign has now curtailed this practice, in 2009 most families wished to send their children to a büwi or an imam to learn their basic prayers and to recite a few simple surahs of the Qur'an. Completion of this most basic form of Islamic education permitted young men to be addressed as Qari, which denotes manhood rather than any serious engagement with Qur'anic recitation. Completing the hajj was an aspiration then within the reach of only a select few well-connected and wealthier villagers. Becoming a haji provided a major boost to social status but also entailed a requirement to observe more stringent standards of religious observance.

Projects of Uyghur Womanhood

Weeping as part of ritual practice in this region is certainly not confined to women. Outpourings of emotion and the experience of spiritual ecstasy are also central to men's zikr in Xinjiang (Liu 2010; Mijit 2015), but, as I will argue, women's ritual emotional expression is understood and enacted in particular gendered ways. Cindy Huang (2009) notes a persistent theme in the oral histories she collected from Uyghur women for her PhD research: being one who is *japakesh*, one who perseveres through difficulty and suffers with a moral purpose. Huang argues that japakesh is a gendered ethical project of being a good Muslim woman in Xinjiang: "Uyghur women offered it as praise for one's hard work and empathetic recognition of one's troubles. Japakesh does not signify the opposite of love and joy; at times, it is the very vehicle for their deepening fruition. Given the shifting demands of the recent past and present, being japakesh entails different sacrifices and challenges for each generation" (vi). Young women in Yantaq village demonstrated japakesh daily. They shouldered a punishing workload that encompassed child rearing; cooking; baking; cleaning; maintaining the home, garden, and livestock; planting, weeding, and irrigating the fields; harvesting the wheat, corn, and cotton; collecting wood for the fire; making yogurt; picking fruit and seeds to sell in the bazaar; and, of course, taking on the lion's share of the labor of reciprocal hospitality. They demonstrated japakesh in its most extreme form during Ramadan, which fell in the summer months during our visits to the village. The long hours fasting were not taken as an excuse to lessen their daily labor in the beating sun, and the young women also were responsible for rising around 2 a.m. to prepare the morning meal to be consumed before sunrise, when fasting begins. This schedule took its toll, and the local women found a novel solution. Once we went into the local town and saw the doctor's clinic packed with young women with needles in their arms hooked up to bags of fluid dangling from portable metal frames. They were getting transfusions of blood plasma—a risky practice because of China's poor record on infected blood supplies in rural areas but one that at least gave them an excuse to sit down in the shade and rest for a few hours.

Tears were also a common sight. Years earlier, as a student in the Uyghur region, I had been struck by the frequent appearance in Uyghur pop music videos of weeping women, primarily weeping mothers. I thought then that there was an element of nationalism in it—tears for the motherland—but more lay behind it. Weeping was also a regular public act for women off-screen and an accepted part of daily life. Once I accompanied a male Uyghur colleague and his wife to visit their relatives in southern Xinjiang. As we approached the relatives' door, four women came running to meet us. They formally embraced my colleague's wife, and then without warning, all five women began to sob. My colleague caught my expression and laughed, clearly not partaking in any way of this emotional outpouring. "Are you wondering what's going on?" he asked. "Someone in the family died a while back, and they haven't seen each other since it happened." Another Uyghur woman told me how she used to play at visiting and crying with her friends when she was a young girl. "I would open the door, and we would lean on each other's shoulders and go *ber, ber, ber.*" Women's tears were also deployed with a kind of moral force, typically to persuade men to part with money. They were also used as a tool against male violence, both in the domestic sphere and sometimes in the public sphere. In the aftermath of the 2009 interethnic violence in Ürümchi, a group of weeping Uyghur mothers staged a demonstration that was, in an exceptional case, caught by the foreign media. Surrounded by Chinese riot troops, they wept and demanded the return of their children, victims of the mass arrests of young Uyghurs that followed the violence.[4] These images upended the perception of victimhood in international media reports of the incident and highlighted the social and political force of Uyghur women's emotional expression.

Rabiya Acha's life story, relayed in the interlude preceding this chapter, gives a powerful demonstration of japakesh. She wept during our recording session as she recalled memories of her father handing her over to another family and leaving her small children alone at home all day while she went to work for the commune. Rabiya's story is a performative expression of identity, which has much resonance with Benedicte Grima's (1992) account of Pashtun women's ritualized sharing of life stories. Grima argues that, through their stories, Pashtun women created self-images based in *gham* (sadness or suffering; a term also used in Uyghur). Women who were considered to have the best stories had undergone the greatest hardship and were able to move their audience to tears. Pashtun women earned respect and enhanced their moral reputation through narrative performances that demonstrated the amount of hardship they had suffered and endured with God's help. This analysis of gendered performative weeping fits certain tropes of Uyghur womanhood well.[5] None of this, of course, should be taken to suggest that the Uyghur women of Yantaq village did not frequently laugh, joke, relax, or dance. They did all of this. But these tropes of womanhood—and of Uyghur identity more broadly—are significant, and, as I will argue throughout this book, they are also played out in the ritual sphere where they are repetitively performed through sounded ritual practice. In Yantaq village, women's understandings of weeping in the ritual context drew strongly on the concept of *ishq* (love), an emotion with transformative power in the construction of both the individual and the community.

Rabiya Acha's story also is an important reminder of the recent history of the village and how this history continues to reverberate in contemporary life. The older generation of women spent their youth under the commune system and the subsequent chaos of the Cultural Revolution; its violence reached even these remote villages. The structures of revolutionary China remained very much part of villagers' imagination, even after these structures were long gone. When older village women named local places, they used the old Maoist terminology: the local town was still termed *gongshe* (Chinese: commune), the village was *bizning dadui* (Uyghur: our; Chinese: work team). When Subinur—a local büwi who taught me some of the basics of their practice—emphasized to me the importance of ritual washing and prayer in daily life, she said, "so that your children will grow up to be clean people (*pak adäm*), useful/competent (*yaramliq*), like township leaders (Chinese: *xiangzhang*)." Rabiya Acha was also well aware of how international politics affected the life of the village. "It started after the Saddam incident," she says, linking the US declaration of a "global war on terror" directly to China's declaration of its own religious extremism problem in Xinjiang and to the subsequent disappearance of young Uyghurs "behind the black gate" of the local prison camp.

Being a Büwi

Ritual gatherings like the one described in this chapter were led by ritual specialists, variously called büwi, *qushnach*, or *hapiz* in different regions of Xinjiang.[6] Gatherings typically involved between ten and twenty pious women from the local community. They were usually held in the guest room of a family home. Women are largely excluded from the mosque in Uyghur Islamic custom, and so the büwi tradition provides the main channel for women's religious association, instruction, and expression. Researchers have documented hundreds of informal women's groups like this, in communities right across Xinjiang, serving a cluster of villages or a small town (*bazar*) or a suburban neighborhood (*mähällä*: Zhou 1999; Anwar 2013). Many groups met weekly on Fridays before noon prayers. Part of the role of the büwi in Yantaq was to prepare the bodies of deceased women for burial, and they gathered for a vigil (*tünäk*) at the home of the deceased (roles carried out by the imam of the local mosque for men's funerals). They were invited to people's homes to recite the Qur'an and pray in order to dispel misfortune or illness, and they performed large-scale rituals at key points in the Islamic calendar. The büwi's ritual practices continued, though often underground, right through the social and political upheavals of the commune period and the Cultural Revolution: the mid-1950s to the late 1970s.[7] From the 1980s, they were able to practice more openly, and, in the 1990s, the number of women attending these meetings was swelled by the general rise in piety in Xinjiang. As part of the more recent crackdown, as I discuss in chapter 6, the Xinjiang authorities have sought to limit and control their practice, and by 2014 these practices—along with virtually all forms of everyday religious practice—had been criminalized and suppressed.

Muslim women in many parts of the world gather in groups to perform rituals related to healing and spiritual benefits.[8] Their gatherings have many things in common: they may involve reciting the Qur'an, spoken and sung prayers, zikr and ritual dancing, and they are often emotionally saturated, but the specific form and meanings of the rituals vary considerably in different parts of the Islamic world. Women's rituals generally do not form an exclusive tradition; they draw on shared Islamic practices, and they are often structurally similar to all-male ritual gatherings, though not always in straightforward ways. Groups of Uyghur men also hold regular meetings to perform khätmä and forms of Sufi sama' ritual locally termed *hälqä-söhbät*, and their gatherings—like those of the women—are embedded in community life (Kadir 2010; Mijit 2015). The büwi's practice is also intertwined with institutional Islam; several of the büwis I interviewed had studied Qur'anic recitation with an imam from an officially approved mosque. Many aspects of their practice suggest links with Naqshbandi traditions of Sufism that formerly dominated the political and religious life of the region and that, at least up to 2010, were still practiced in a few officially sanctioned *khaniqa* (Sufi lodges) in the towns of southern Xinjiang (Zarcone 2001, 2002; Anwar 2013).

The Uyghur büwi tradition is most closely related to that of the *otin*s in Uzbekistan's Ferghana Valley. Kandiyoti and Azimova (2004) describe the otins they met in the 1990s as informal religious practitioners educated in Islamic religious texts and classical literature who officiated at women's gatherings (births, marriages, and deaths) and religious feasts. They also served as teachers, giving religious instruction to young girls. Historically, they were the sole providers of women's education before the rise of the Jadidists in Central Asia in the early twentieth century. Many otins were the descendants of imams, but they maintained chains of transmission of their own ritual knowledge resembling the *murshid/murid* (master/apprentice) relation of Sufi orders. As among the Uyghurs, parts of Uzbek zikr rituals suggest strong links to the Naqshbandiyya and Qadiriyya Sufi orders. This close relationship between Sufi traditions and women's community-based practice is also found in other parts of Uzbekistan. Ritual specialists in Khorezm known as *halpa* also draw on Sufi traditions in their ritual practice and—like the women of Yantaq village, as I will discuss in chapter 3—they recite the texts of Yasawi and other Sufi saints and poets during their rituals (Kleinmichel 2000; Sultanova 2011).

Märyäm, the leader of the ritual described at the beginning of this chapter, was based in a neighboring village. She had been practicing for more than forty-five years and was the senior büwi in the locality. She explained to me their annual and weekly timetable: "We seek blessings [*sawaplik*] during Ghäjäb [Rajab, the seventh month of the Islamic calendar] and Barat [the fourteenth day of Sha'bān, the eighth month] and Ramazan [Ramadan, the ninth month, the month of fasting] and on *äzinä kuni* [the day of the call to prayer: Fridays]. On Thursdays or Mondays, we recite for people who request it. If you do a khätmä in your home, it will dispel the danger that comes from the seven sides, and your wishes will come true."

Aynisa, a tall woman in her late thirties with an air of authority, who was already regarded as a büwi of exceptional power, described their role serving individual clients, detailing some of the types of illnesses and misfortunes they might be called on to heal:

> We say *chätnäp kätti* [similar to the evil eye]. If a child gets the evil eye then the doctor's medicine is no use. You have to use Allah's power and pray for the sick child using the Qur'an.... We recite *ay ishpar* [moon cure]. This is a special medicine for the weak and ill; it's Qur'an medicine.⁹ ... If someone is jealous of you and prays against you, then you can get sick. We call that *ayat ichiwaptu* [drinking a verse of the Qur'an; often used against rivals in love]. If this is a problem, I can do *ay ishpar* for you or *yandurar* [send back the curse]. I have to repeat it seventy-one thousand times.

Nisakhan, a middle-aged büwi based in the local town, emphasized their role in providing spiritual protection for the wider community:

> We büwis have many duties; we have to work in the home and outside too. We wash the bodies of the dead, and we recite khätmä every week in summer between 11 a.m. and noon on Fridays. We recite when our children are sleeping, but we don't rest. We recite for the sake of our children and our husbands and our home.... Khätmä means reciting the Qur'an and praying. It is like a bullet fired from a gun. It is powerful. It helps people. If someone is sick, we do a khätmä to cure them, if someone dies, we do a khätmä to ask forgiveness for their sins. We recite khätmä for peace in our land [*yurtimiz amanlighi*], to prevent disasters coming on our town. For example, it often hails in spring and destroys the cotton crops, so we do a khätmä to prevent it. In Yantaq we rely on cotton and corn. The government helps us when there are disasters ... but they can't do everything.

These explanations of the büwi's role emphasize both their spiritual power and the highly social nature of their practice. Their rituals respond to everyday needs within the community, both individual and communal, and their recitation is brought into play for calendrical and life-cycle rituals as well as sickness or misfortune. Nisakhan's testimony is of particular interest. Alert to the rapidly worsening political climate and the frequent depiction of büwi activities as "illegal religion" or "feudal superstition," she argues cogently for the possibility of coexistence between the büwi's communal ritual role and the structures of the state, a counternarrative to the prevalent national discourse of "spiritual civilization" that inevitably situates the büwi at the tail end of the march of progress.

The role of büwi was often said to be attached to the wives of male religious clerics. Certainly that was the preferred model by the local authorities, for it enabled tighter governmental control over the women's sphere of religious life, in the absence of a formal religious institution for women, through the patriarchal model of the officially appointed imam taking responsibility for his wife's activities (Harris 2013b). In practice, the role required too much specialized knowledge and skills to be taken on without lengthy family or community-based training. The four women I worked with during fieldwork were married to peasant farmers or small traders. Many büwis, like Nisakhan, had inherited the role from their mother or other female relatives and expected to pass it on to their own daughters: "My grandmother was also a büwi; I am the seventh generation. If my daughter does it, she will be the eighth. I wanted to teach my daughter the Qur'an, but the government wouldn't allow it, and so I sent her to train as a nurse in Qumul. When she completes her secular education, I hope she will get the chance to learn and be a büwi."

Others found their own path toward the role of ritual specialist. Aynisa explained her own development in terms of a physical crisis marked by a dream encounter:

> After I had my second child, I was not well, and I had no time for my prayers for a few years. Then, one morning, around 3 a.m., I had a dream. An old man with a beard came toward me from the sky sitting on a carpet. I was in a graveyard. He lectured me about the Qur'an. I was very afraid. I had developed a liver illness, and I thought I would die. At that time, my youngest child was only six months old, and I was so scared. When I woke up, I understood myself. This was twelve years ago. Since then I have been praying and reading the Qur'an.

In Soviet and Chinese traditions of scholarship, this kind of experience is often linked to Central Asian shamanism. Such dreams, however, are widespread in Islamic culture, and they form an important part of religious experience and the management of physical and spiritual illnesses. They also frequently form a central part of conversion narratives.[10]

Märyäm's path to becoming a büwi was described to me by the women of our family in slightly different terms: "Märyäm became a büwi after seeing ghosts. She is a real *bakhshi* [a ritual healer]." They also commented, "When she was young, she was wild, she had a lover. Even now she likes to talk and laugh." This type of gossip echoes the popular Uyghur saying "When a slut gets old, she becomes a büwi" (*jalab keri bolghandin keyin büwi bolidu*), which points to the problematic social status of such women who permit their voices to sound out in powerful, albeit semihidden form and who possess the authority and charisma to lead large rituals.[11] But such gossip was muted, and, within village society, büwis were largely respected and feared for the role they play in dealing with sickness and death. Their significant role in the community provided them with elevated social standing and extensive networks of reciprocity to draw on, as Nisakhan explained: "People respect büwis. We wash their bodies when they die, we teach their children, and we teach them. I taught 30 percent of the women in Yantaq to read the Qur'an. I have thirty mu of land. I plant it with cotton; when the time comes in spring to clear the land, they all come to help me. Even party cadres come to help. It's the same when I plant the cotton and harvest it. When I invite guests to my house, they come to help too." Nisakhan's account underlines the central role of büwis in village society: in life-cycle rituals, in religious instruction, and in dealing with forms of sickness. Here again, we see the overlap and integration of official and communal structures at the village level: local government officials also were integrated into these social and spiritual networks of reciprocity.

Learning and Transmission

Nisakhan often emphasized the depth of knowledge that a woman needed in order to be recognized as a büwi: "It's a complicated thing. You have to be knowledgeable in Islam, you have to memorize thirty-four lessons to complete it, and you have to get permission [from a senior büwi] to recite khätmä. Not every woman can be a büwi." The transmission of Islamic knowledge and practice in the village was not exclusively gendered. Women or girls learned from fathers, brothers, or husbands within the home and brought this knowledge into the exclusively female sphere of the village khätmä rituals. Likewise, the religious knowledge and practice of the büwi was not entirely separate from institutionalized Islam. Although, as women, they were not permitted to study formally in the Islamic Institute, several büwis with whom I worked had learned Qur'anic recitation from a male religious cleric, either one working within the formal state religious structures or one attached to an underground religious school. Märyäm explained how she learned Qur'anic recitation from a male cleric and learned the practical tasks associated with funeral ritual from a senior büwi in the local area: "I learned the Qur'an with Timur Haji Mullam (a local religious cleric). For büwi work, I learned from a woman in the county town named Ishan Qushnach. She was famous throughout the whole county. I learned how to wash bodies with her. We washed the bodies together and then we wrapped them with proper material and got them ready for the funeral. She could recite the Qur'an, recite the *tählil*, explain the Qur'an, and recite zikr."

As Märyäm makes clear, büwis can perform all the required functions for the death of a woman that the local imam would perform for the death of a man, including preparing the body, reciting the appropriate prayers, and leading a vigil. Nonetheless, it is clear that masculine lines of transmission are given greater weight. For Nisakhan, association with a respected (male) cleric and his embodiment of institutional religion deepened a büwi's claim to authority and to possessing correct religious practice: "We learned from a proper teacher, a proper mulla. My teacher, Abla Damolla, was a famous religious scholar, respected across many counties. He was vice president of the Aqsu Religious Affairs Committee. We had weekly classes with him. He gave us things to memorize over the week, and then we came back to class and recited for him. Some women learn from here and there in the villages; they are not proper büwi. You can't recite khätmä without getting permission from your *ustaz*, or Allah will punish you."

Büwi as *Tärikätchi* (People of the Path)

Most village-based büwis did not identify themselves as Sufis and had no formal links to established Sufi lodges (*khaniqa*); indeed many of the women I worked with during fieldwork had little or no knowledge of organized Sufi groups and were hardly familiar with the term *Sufi* (Uyghur: *sopi*). The büwi's practice is, however, closely related to the ritual gatherings of organized Sufi groups in Xinjiang, and scholars have traced historical processes of transmission filtering outward from the Sufi khaniqa into rural communities. Some büwis identified themselves as tärikätchi (people of the "path," *tariqa*, Sufi orders). Nisakhan said, "We don't call ourselves Sufis; we are tärikätchi. The khätmä is the *tärikät yol* [literally, "the road/way of the path"].... These are people who wake up at two in the morning and pray, 'Allah, Allah!' When people keep reciting this through the night, their soul [*käläp*] becomes soft inside their chest."

Once, when we were listening to a recording of the khätmä, Aynisa commented on the links between their practice and the *tariqa*: "Educated religious people (*qarilar, kitap oqughan alimlar*) wouldn't understand this. Unless they follow the tärikät, they won't understand. Tärikät is like a secret movement (*mäkhpi suluq*). Religious scholars have a Jadidist understanding. They are two different paths. Only people who understand Islam well and know tärikät can understand this way."

Her account situates the büwi's practice clearly within the historical flows of religious ideology in this region, recalling the early twentieth-century tensions between the Jadidist Muslim reformists and the Sufi lodges (Brophy 2016) and the ways that Sufi groups in this region maintained their practice underground throughout the revolutionary period of the twentieth century (Zarcone 2016). What is especially interesting for the focus of this chapter is the way that Aynisa links her practice to embodied forms of transformation (the soul becoming soft in the chest) and ways of knowing that evade text-based forms of transmission.

Organized Sufism in Altishahr

In order to understand the genealogies of these women's practice we need to know something of the history of organized Sufism in this region. In the early modern history of the region—which in that period is more appropriately termed Altishahr (the "six cities" surrounding the Taklamakan desert)—the Sufi orders were far from secret movements. In the late seventeenth century, descendants of the Naqshbandi sheikh Makhdum-i A'zam, who are popularly known as the Khojas, came from the Ferghana Valley (in contemporary Uzbekistan) to the southern town of Yarkand (in contemporary Xinjiang). The ruler of the Yarkand Khanate patronized their teachings and allowed them to establish their order in Yarkand, and it spread to Kashgar, Khotan, and Aqsu (Zarcone 2002). The Khojas acquired significant political power, paving the way for the best-known leader of this lineage, Afaq Khoja, to establish direct rule over much of Altishahr until his death in 1694. During the eighteenth century, various branches of the Naqshbandis vied for power in complex and shifting alliances and rivalries (Papas 2015; Brophy 2018). The power struggles between Naqshbandi branches permitted—in the view of many contemporary Uyghur nationalists—the fall of the region into the hands of the Chinese Qing Empire, and Sufis are frequently vilified in Uyghur intellectual discourse (Thum 2014).

During the eighteenth and nineteenth centuries, there was considerable trade and religious exchange between Altishahr and parts of Central Asia and India. We know from historical accounts that communities of Kashmiris, Afghans, Badakhshanis, and Indians were all living in nineteenth-century Kashgar. The teachings and practice of the Qadiri and Chishti Sufi orders spread from India and became established in parts of Xinjiang, though they never achieved the widespread dominance that the Naqshbandi had, and, in many cases, these groups and their practices were subsumed into Naqshbandi traditions (Zarcone 2016; Mu 2019). There were long-standing links between Sufi lineages in Ferghana and those in

Altishahr, supported by the close linguistic and cultural ties between these areas. Naqshbandi sheikhs (also known as *ishan*) continued to move to and fro across the borders, either in ill-fated attempts to reclaim power in Kashgar or in fleeing persecution in Ferghana.

Overrule of the Xinjiang region by non-Muslim powers, under the Qing Empire and subsequently by Republican Chinese governors, meant that no government was imposing orthodoxy over religious practice, and little attempt occurred to formally regulate the Sufi lodges (*khaniqa*), which were sometimes able to develop large popular followings and amass quite considerable land and income (Bellér-Hann 2008). The Qing rulers of Xinjiang viewed these khaniqa as a constant threat to their authority, and, after periods of unrest in the region, they executed or exiled many Sufi sheikhs. The early twentieth-century Republican governor Yang Zengxin also closed down many Sufi khaniqa, fearing them as a potential focus of opposition to his rule (Zarcone 2016). With this unsettled history and with the frequent movement between neighboring regions, it is not surprising that Sufi orders in Xinjiang developed in a highly piecemeal fashion, with considerable overlap between recognized orders. Local groups, only loosely allied to larger orders, formed under the leadership of local sheikhs who built khaniqa attached to their own homes and developed networks that extended no farther than their own oasis. Sufism in this region has long been distanced from institutional teaching and sources of orthodoxy, and has become deeply rooted in local communities. In this way, the practice of zikr became widespread among community-based religious groups right across the region.

Interviews with religious practitioners conducted by Thierry Zarcone in the late 1990s suggest that a new wave of Naqshbandi Sufis arrived from the Ferghana Valley in the early twentieth century after the Soviet defeat of the Basmachi rebellion. They included two sheikhs (or ishan) who set up new lineages that came to dominate Sufism in twentieth-century Xinjiang, with networks of Sufi lodges (khaniqa) and followers (murshid) over the whole region. One lineage belonging to the Khufiyya branch of the Naqshbandis established a primarily madrassa-based style of Sufism, centered in Yarkand. This branch represented a form of "high Sufism" with an emphasis on learning derived (like the contemporary *dawah* movement) from the Indian Deobandi reformist tradition and opposed to saint cults and other popular practices. The other lineage belonged to the Jahriyya branch and established a network of khaniqa for the practice of zikr, including a major complex in Kashgar (Zarcone 2001, 2016). This branch has had the greatest influence on popular religious practices like that of the büwis in Yantaq.

The relationship between village women's practice and khaniqa-based practice in this region is thus very much an overlapping one. This context is unlike those in classic studies of women's ritual from the Middle East in that male orthodoxy is not opposed to marginal female practices: both are considerably marginalized, and, in fact, the büwi traditions are closely linked to men's practices. Early twentieth-century accounts of Sufi khaniqa in Xinjiang note the presence of spaces dedicated for women, and they describe well-attended women's ritual gatherings (Bellér-Hann 2008, 324). Some of the remaining khaniqa still operating in the first decade of the twenty-first century had retained these spaces for women's gatherings.[12] Village-based büwis, like the women I worked with, might take religious instruction from men who were more closely allied to Sufi lineages. Moreover, in the period of our fieldwork, there seemed to be no clear separation between institutional (state-sanctioned) and tariqa-based traditions in the region. Nisakhan presented her teacher as at once vice president of the religious affairs committee and tärikätchi: "There is a saying that after the Prophet Muhammad there will be no more Prophets, but if there were to be another Prophet, he would be like Abla Damolla. He was very tärikätchi [one who follows the Sufi path]. He was always very polite. If a woman came before him without a headscarf, he wouldn't shout at her, he would gently touch her head and say, 'Allah blesses you.' He was such a humble person."

Her use of the term *tärikätchi* in no way suggests a mystic or underground practice but rather a model of moral behavior. The role echoes early twentieth-century accounts of Sufi sheikhs in the region, who sometimes acquired a large popular following and were known for their (sometimes miraculous) acts of charity and intercession (Zarcone 2016).

Aynisa linked her practice, and her spiritual and emotional power, directly to the Jahriyya branch of the Naqshbandi: "People who follow tärikät, they don't control their love (ishq) for Allah. They hold a sword in their hands. From the people who follow the Jahriyya path, from among the wise ones, from them come the saints."

The links between the büwi's rituals and other Central Asian Jahriyya traditions of vocal practice are strong. The women of Yantaq name Bahauddin Naqshband in the course of their khätmä ritual, and they perform the *tahlil*: the repeated chanting of the *shahadah* (profession of faith), *lā 'ilāha 'illā llāh*, as a zikr, repeated and progressively shortened until the final consonant, the single syllable *hu* is repeated rhythmically, accompanied by dancing.[13] Among both men's and women's groups in Uyghur communities, the zikr consists of the rhythmic repetition of short phrases in Qur'anic Arabic, praising Allah and the Prophet. Over the group's rhythmic chant, a *hapiz* (reciter) sings a melodic counterpoint (*hikmät* or *talqin*), often set to a text by one of the major Central Asian Sufi poets.[14]

Reciting Khätmä

The local term *khätmä* is derived from the Arabic (*khatam*: literally, "sealing"), which more commonly describes a ritual reading of the complete Qur'an, divided into its thirty *juz*, either all recited simultaneously by different reciters or separately recited, one on each night of the month of Ramadan or during the single Night of Power, Layl al-Qadir (Graham and Kermani 2006). The practice is widespread in the Muslim world and is often related to funeral or memorial rituals. In Indonesia, memorial gatherings called *khatam al-Qur'an* involve the reading of the entire Qur'an by thirty reciters reading simultaneously in what Rasmussen (2010) describes as "a fast melodic patter" that creates a "wonderful cacophony" (1). In Uzbekistan, *khatmi qur'on* are held by older men as part of funeral ritual with the aim of transferring spiritual merit to the deceased. Here, the equivalent women's gatherings are called *bibishanba* or *mavlud* (Rasanayagam 2011). Among Uyghurs, the recitation of the whole Qur'an by the older men of the mosque community (*jäma'ät*) during Ramadan and *mäwlud* celebrations of the Prophet's birthday is common, but Uyghurs also apply the term *khätmä* to describe rituals involving solo sections of Qur'anic recitation interspersed with forms of zikr: rhythmic, repetitive, group chanting of Arabic prayers and short phrases from the Qur'an, accompanied by rocking movements, through which the participants work up states of heightened emotion that are expressed in weeping and sometimes by trance. Nisakhan explained, "When you recite khätmä, your whole body becomes soft. When you recite sorrowful verses of the Qur'an, your soul opens. When you feel sorrow and fear Allah, and devote yourself to Him, then you feel relief. This path is very well suited for women" (Nisakhan, Yantaq village, August 2012).

The women I worked with in Yantaq village performed slightly different forms of khätmä, based on a choice of prayers that depended on the ritual occasion, but all khätmä follow the same overall structure of a series of rhythmic chants interspersed with longer solo sections of the recited Qur'an, building through peaks and troughs to an emotional climax. The following description gives a detailed structure of a ritual performed in 2009 for the Night of Barat.[15]

* * *

The women recited unaccompanied, without reference to a written text. They began with a group recital of the short opening *surah* of the Qur'an, Al Fatiha, and then moved into the first five *ayat* (verses) of the second surah (Baqara, The Cow), which focus on the attributes of God, then skipped forward to verses toward the end of the surah. They continued with several popular du'a (prayers) from the beginning and end of the third surah.

After six minutes, Märyäm began to recite alone. She recited du'a drawn from various surah, all beginning *Rabbana!* (Our Lord!). A common theme of hellfire and the Day of Judgment linked the texts. Some of the women were already crying quietly. Märyäm concluded her solo section with the whole of surah 109 (Al-Kafirun: The Unbelievers), one of the shorter Meccan surahs toward the end of the Qur'an.

All the women then joined her for repeated recitation of surah 112 (Ikhlas: Purity), a short surah that is widely used in daily prayers, followed by the repeated phrase *Allahu Akbar* (God is great), the profession of faith (*la ilaha illa'llah*), and the final two surah of the Qur'an. They paused for silent prayer and then recited together prayers of repentance. The women were now twenty minutes into the recitation, and they moved into the phase of zikr: a series of short phrases and prayers in Qur'anic Arabic, repeated collectively on a rhythmic falling motif for a set number of times. Märyäm counted off the repetitions on her beads as they recited. The women began to sway from side to side, and the emotional atmosphere began to heat up.

From here they moved into another round of repetitions of surah Ikhlas, which they maintained for six minutes. A short prayer for the Prophet followed, and then another zikr, which also lasted for six minutes. They paused briefly and then resumed with surah Al Fatiha. This was followed by prayers for the Prophet and for Sheikh Bahauddin Naqshband. Many of the women were now rocking rhythmically from side to side and crying loudly. They moved off into another six-minute zikr in a curious asymmetrical rhythm. A series of short prayers glorifying God and the Prophet followed; then they settled into another six-minute chant on the attributes of God. With this chant on two rising and falling phrases, the atmosphere became less intense and distinctly more cheerful, and the women stopped crying.

Two short du'a linked this and the final zikr, *Subhan'Allah wa bihamdihi, subhan'Allah il adhim* (glory and praise to God, glory to God the supreme).

Described at the beginning of this chapter, this seven-minute chant marked the emotional high point of the ritual. Finally, Märyäm brought the excitement under control by pointing to Aynisa, who recited, with excellent pronunciation and musicality, surah 55 (Ar Rahman, The Most Merciful). As she recited, the women sobbed quietly in a sustained way, noticeably punctuating her phrase endings with louder sobs and sighs.

Märyäm concluded with a group prayer; then the women began to sing melodiously and spaciously, "*Allahu akbar! Allahu akbar! La ilaha illa-llahu wa Allahu akbar wa lillah'ilhamdu.*" The style of this song was very different from the rhythmic zikr. Here the women were performing perfectly in tune and in time, indicating a marked difference between what I gloss here as song and the chanting of the zikr, in which the text is supreme and melody is not overtly prescribed. This song marked closure of the ritual. For the next few minutes, they moved around the room slowly, shaking each other's hands and embracing each other, accompanied by copious noisy tears. After this conclusion of the ritual, the participants were offered food prepared by the women of the family, and they posed for a photograph before departing (fig. 2.2). Watching this part of the video recording, Hurriyät commented, "This is quite powerful. They are expressing spiritual closeness, solidarity. They are not crying because they feel weak; they are feeling close to Allah, feeling their enslavement to God, so free from enslavement to man . . . emptied out emotionally, spiritually filled, full of confidence. They feel their prayers have been accepted. They are free from sin. Matters will be resolved."

I have described this ritual in detail to give an impression of the complexity of the elements and the ways in which the Arab text of the Qur'an is brought to life in such varied ways in the course of the ritual, underpinned by contrasting rhythmic and melodic conventions that enable a powerful emotional experience.

Ritual Experience and Bodily Entrainment

In her rich study of time in sama' rituals in Pakistan, Regula Qureshi (1994) suggests that "any portion or facet of the text message [of the Qur'an] can become the focus of intense mystical engagement, to the point of ecstatic arousal. For such engagement to actually take place requires dwelling on the particular text unit so that the full impact of its meaning can be allowed

Fig. 2.2. A group of village women pose for the camera after a khätmä in 2009. Photograph by the author.

to unfold. This is achieved through repetition, so that the 'audible' present is filled with the single meaning of its message as in *zikr*" (507). Qureshi's exploration of the meaningfulness of repetition provides many insights into the intensity of ritual experience, but her emphasis on the lexical meanings of the text is perhaps overly cerebral. Especially in contexts of ritual practice where the Arabic texts are not well understood, we need to give greater weight to the links between experiences of sound, practices of listening, and the human body.

The practice of reciting and listening to the recited Qur'an is central to practices of self-cultivation, blessing, and healing in Islam. As experienced by Muslims over the past fourteen centuries, most of whom could neither speak nor read Arabic, the Qur'an is primarily sound, not script. This is certainly the case for the majority of Uyghur women with whom I worked. When she taught me the basic verses of the Qur'an used in daily prayers, Subinur offered neither translations nor even the rough lexical meaning of the sounds she imparted to me orally to commit to memory. For her, the lexical meanings were not important, which does not mean that the sounds were meaningless to her. Arguably, a key aspect of the efficacy of this ritual lies in the act of listening. Hirschkind (2006) argues that "audition is essential to the cultivation of the sensitive heart that allows one to hear and embody in practice the ethical sensibilities undergirding moral action" (9). The sounds of the recited Qur'an are imbued with affective power, which does critical work on the listener, enabling individual practices of self-cultivation and also reverberating through the wider community.

The experience of recitation, across many diverse Muslim communities historically and today, is preeminently emotional. Many hadith refer to weeping as an appropriate response to listening to the recited Qur'an. Classical treatises even collect the stories of those who have been "slain by the Qur'an," mortally overwhelmed by its sublime sounds (Dammen McAuliffe 2006, 6). Its aesthetic and emotional impact is an important part of its religious authority. The twelfth-century Sufi scholar al-Ghazali writes, "And when they hear what has been sent down to the Messenger, thou seest their eyes overflow with tears because of the truth they recognize" (quoted in Nelson 2001, 95). Within Muslim men's rituals in Mauritius, reciting in the appropriate performative style produced strong emotions in receptive participants, which helped them to become more pious. Participants described the ability to hear in a sensitive way as "hearing with the heart" (Eisenlohr 2018, 62). Such links between listening practices, emotional responses, and the cultivation of piety are common across the Islamic world.

Many of these sources highlight the multisensorial, embodied nature of listening to the recited Qur'an. Hirschkind (2006) describes such listening practices as a "moral physiology": the "affective-kinesthetic experience of a body permeated by faith (*iman*)" (75). To listen properly is to engage in a performance, the articulated gestures of a dance. "The word of God demands a range of ethical performances from the reciter/listener. She must not only seek to understand God's message, she must also make herself into an adequate 'host' for the presence of divine words, by bodying forth the attitudes and expressions corresponding to the verses heard or recited. Through practice, she must make her body and heart into an instrument capable of resonating (re-sounding) the words she submits to" (81).

This body of literature lays emphasis on the active and acculturated role of the participants who mold their bodies in accordance with religious traditions of practice. The weeping participants in the khätmä are engaged in an embodied and ethical performance, bodying forth the attitudes and expressions proper to the ritual and resonating (resounding) the sacred phrases. But there is another dimension to the ritual; as well as thinking about active listening practices, we need to think about the ways in which sound itself—in particular the sound of repetitive rhythmic recitation—acts on bodies. The literature on musical entrainment, with its focus on the embodied experience of musical sound and the reflexive relationship between body and environment, provides useful insights into the role played by sound in ritual experience.

Classic explanations of rhythmic entrainment describe the way that the experience of external musical rhythms may influence some internal bodily rhythm of the listener (such as the heartbeat), such that the listener's bodily rhythm eventually "locks in" to a corresponding periodicity. An interest in entrainment runs through many studies of ritual performance in ethnomusicology. The early British ethnomusicologist John Blacking coined the term "bodily resonance" to describe the sensation or awareness of synchronizing with the physical movements of others during music-making. Blacking (1983) described this as the experience of "falling into phase" and suggested that bodily resonance is felt both as an emotional connection and as the physical sensation of coordinated motion (57). Judith Becker (2001), writing on cross-cultural links between music and trance, also draws on the notion of rhythmic entrainment to explain trance phenomena. Rhythmic entrainment for her encompasses "processes through which bodies and brains synchronize gestures, muscle actions, breathing and brain waves when enveloped in musicking" (153).

Rather than focusing on the interactions between individuals, Tia DeNora (2000) describes body-music interactions in which bodies latch on to and become entrained by musical devices. In her approach, the bodily movements that music profiles may lead actors to identify, work up, and modulate emotional and motivational states. In this understanding, the external-internal dichotomy collapses, and the human body is reconceived as an emergent and flexible entity, reflexively linked to the material-cultural environment and what that environment may afford. DeNora's approach echoes Sara Ahmed's (2004) critique of the inside-outside dichotomy in approaches to emotion and is particularly helpful in understanding the experience of the khätmä ritual. In the course of the khätmä, such body-sound interactions were most evident in the zikr phase, when the women began to move their bodies together, latching onto the rhythm of the chant. This is the auditory-bodily experience that the büwis Nisakhan and Aynisa identified as effecting a physical transformation on participants, which they described as the opening of the soul or the softening of the heart within the chest.

In this phase of the ritual, the women swayed from side to side or backward and forward as they recited, some more actively than others, physically locking into the rhythm. But there was a special quality to their synchronization. The repetitive chants began weak and scattered and gradually built in intensity as the assembled women latched onto the rhythm. They recited together but never in perfect unison; their voices were always slightly overlapping, and slightly out of sync. Deborah Kapchan (2009) also notes this overlapping in the women's zikr gatherings that she experienced in France, noting that "the longer we chanted, the more each of us swirled into a unique tempo and tonality that nonetheless manifested an awareness of and response to all the others" (19). Writing on music making at Sufi shrines in Pakistan, Richard Wolf (2006) comments in a similar vein that the primary groove of the drummers (*dam-a-dam-mast-qalandar*) enables dance, but the best drummers are those who can eventually break the bonds of the beat. This slippage between agents who are cooperating but not keeping precisely together in time may be a symbol of successful spiritual union. These diverse examples give special ritual resonance to Charles Keil's (1987) well-known theory of "participatory discrepancies" in live ensemble music making, in which he argues that the "best music"—that which has the greatest affective power—must be full of discrepancies: ever so slightly out of tune and ever so slightly out of time. Thus, I argue that practices of cooperating but not keeping together in time are more than a symbol of spiritual union but actually enable and empower spiritual experiences of community.

Ishq (Love, Passion)

Listening, in the sense of "spiritual audition" (samaʻ) is also, of course, central to Sufi traditions of practice, including the textual traditions directly transmitted in the Uyghur region. The practice of the women of Yantaq is situated within a particular set of local traditions surrounding listening, passion, and the redemption of sin. We know something of the early textual understandings of samaʻ in this region from the Persian-language *Treatise on Audition* (*Risāla-yi samāʻiyya*), written by the sixteenth-century sheikh Makhdūm-i Aʻzam, who was the founder of the first Naqshbandi lineages to arrive in Xinjiang. In this treatise, samaʿ is defined as "listening to fine voices" (*āwāzhā-yi khūsh*). Makhdūm-i Aʿzam writes that when Sufis became tired in body and mind, their Sufi masters encouraged them to listen to sweet voices, harmonious lyrics, and exciting poetry because these things could inflame mystical desire and remove lassitude and produce the hidden qualities that put mystical love in motion. Thanks to this, the sheikh writes, the soul is opened to listening and remembers the pleasure of primordial words. The fire of mystical love being lighted, the bird of the soul can fly. In an instant, the disciple mounts several steps in spiritual progress that without samaʿ could not be crossed in several years.[16]

The text also reflects on and attempts to justify emotional responses to samaʿ, suggesting that lamenting does not always express sadness but may also express joy. Its cause can be fear, ecstasy, or desire. It gives examples of emotional Naqshbandi samaʿ gatherings where tears flowed in abundance, and it mentions famous reciters of the Qurʾan and mystic poetry who could provoke streams of tears among their listeners. The Prophet Muhammad is also cited as a model of emotional mysticism: when listening to one of his companions recite some verses, the Prophet fell into ecstasy, his mantle fell from his shoulders, and he tore it into pieces and gave them to his companions, who sewed the holy pieces onto their own garments.

In our conversations about their ritual practice, the büwis of Yantaq village echoed many aspects of the discourse of this early Sufi murshid, especially in the way that they interpreted and valued the shedding of tears. They consistently explained the act of weeping, and the emotional state that their tears expressed, through the term *ishq*. Ishq comes from the Arabic and is a core concept in textual traditions of Sufism, sometimes regarded as the key to the connection between humans and the divine (Schimmel 1975, 72; Abrahamov 2003). It appears in Makhdūm-i Aʿzam's treatise, describing the third and final stage of the Sufi's journey toward oneness with the divine. The term is also used widely outside religious texts and is found in languages across the Islamic world. It is central in Indo-Persian and Central Asian Chagatay literary culture, especially in poetic traditions of *ghazal*, where its shifting attribution of the beloved and the divine is deployed to great effect. *Ishq* appears in the ghazals that are sung within the Uyghur Twelve Muqam repertoire (Light 2008), and it is a common word in modern Uyghur, a familiar part of the lexicon of popular song.

The büwi's particular forms of engagement with these Sufi-inflected traditions of passionate listening were often expressed through metaphors drawn from their daily life. In particular, they employed ideas relating to cooking to convey the experience and the meaning of the ritual. On viewing the climax of a video recording of the ritual I described above, Aynisa commented,

> The oil is sizzling in the pot [*qazan kizip kätti*]. Their love for Allah is so strong that they can't stop themselves crying, just like the pot on the stove. When the oil is hot, you must throw in the meat otherwise the oil will catch fire. It's just like that. Then you must put in the vegetables, otherwise the meat will burn. So just like that the women cry a lot. . . . Their love [*ishq*] for Allah is like the hot oil in the pot, their love for Allah is so strong.

We know from various studies about the significance of cooking, and especially frying in oil, in Uyghur women's ritual practices. In Uyghur belief, the spirits of the dead are thought to be nourished by the smell of hot oil, and on the Night of Barat, women go to visit the graveyard, where they pray and lay fried cakes on top of the family graves (Bellér-Hann 2001). These explanations point to a highly localized and gendered interpretation and embodiment of traditions of emotion and faith. As Nisakhan explained, "You can't make yourself cry. When you have passion for Allah [*Allahning ishqi*], it comes out, you can't stop it. It's like hot oil. If your husband went away and left you alone you would miss him. It's just like that. They are missing Allah, and so they lose consciousness. Some of them are more passionate than others. Even if they say, I'm going to stop now, they can't. The emotion is so deep and strong, it floods out." Nisakhan folds the classic Sufi paradigm of separation from God into the everyday experience of family life. For her, it is the fundamental ethical sensibility of ishq that enables the emotion to overwhelm the participants in the course of the ritual. In this sense, they are acted on, but in another sense, they are actively harnessing the ritual experience, both for their own ethical cultivation and also in the service of the community.

Performing Community, Doing Emotional Work

Through their ritual practice, the women did spiritual work on themselves, cleansing themselves from sin and preparing themselves for death. This individual spiritual preparation was an important part of their practice, fully expressed in the hikmät that I will consider more fully in the next chapter. Here, though, I want to focus on the spiritual work that they did for the wider community through their ritual practice and by their weeping.

As one woman in our household explained to me, "They are weeping for our sins. When we die, we don't know if we will go into water or fire. That's why they cry.... [Büwis are] women who really believe in Allah, who really believe that Allah created us. If people doubt their faith and wonder if it is true or false, then they won't cry and the sin won't be relieved." One büwi told me a popular story about the Prophet, who once said that one cup of the tears of his followers could quench the fires of hell. For these women, weeping was a key part of the efficacy of their rituals and part of the emotional work that they performed for the community. They recited after a death as a form of intercession for the deceased's soul. The core meaning of their most important ritual—performed at a key point on the Islamic calendar, on the Night of Barat, when the sins and good deeds of all are believed to be weighed in the balance—was the alleviation of sin for the whole community.

Another layer to the women's explanations provides a sense of the instrumentality of this emotional state. Their tears were shed performatively, serving an active function within their conceptions of faith. Märyäm explained, "When we recite, our passion comes to the boil [*ishqi qaynap*]. Because in our lives in this world we can't always stick to doing good deeds; we live, and we don't know if we are doing good. We fear Allah. Allah created us, and when we die, we go to him, so we ask for mercy. We are sinful beings, so we cry to ask [forgiveness] for our sins." We can see similar perceptions in women's *mevlud* rituals in Turkey, at which weeping also did important work on behalf of others. Mevlud rituals were regarded as a way for the bereaved to help the soul of the deceased on the road to salvation or release by seeking Muhammad's intercession with God (Tapper and Tapper 1987). It is worth noting in passing that such emotional practices of intercession are not confined to Muslim societies. In Catholic Europe too, collective weeping in some communities has represented collective repentance and an appeal to God for forgiveness. The historian William Christian (2004), writing on public weeping in medieval Spain, argues that "weeping was of vital practical importance to communities, as well as of spiritual importance to individuals. Without it God would not be moved.... Emotions were serious business" (46).

The instrumentality of the women's emotional expression is closely linked to Uyghur beliefs and ritual practices relating to the Night of Barat, which falls on the fourteenth of the month of Sha'bān, the night when the büwis perform their largest and most significant rituals. According to popular tradition, the Night of Barat was when the tree of life was shaken. Each person has his or her name written on a leaf of this tree, and the leaves of those who were going to die in the coming year would fall to the ground. The fourteenth was also termed the Night of Forgiveness. This name reflected the local belief that for every person an angel sits on each shoulder, the angel on the right recording good deeds and the angel on the left recording sins. On the Night of Forgiveness the angels entered into the individual's book the amount of merit she or he had accumulated during the year. As Bellér-Hann (2008) notes, the Night of Barat had important spiritual dimensions rooted in local definitions of moral personhood and in notions of sin and judgment, good deeds and reward. These notions of love, sin, and redemption also play a central role in the ritual practice of the büwi, and they explain the central role of these rituals within village society.

In rural Uyghur society, reciting the khätmä and weeping not only is for alleviating one's own sin but can also serve as an act of intercession on behalf of the families of the deceased, or even for the whole community. Weeping, as a manifestation of ishq, is a key part of the efficacy of their rituals, a form of emotional work and a performance of the village community, including both the living and the dead. The embodied sound of their rhythmic, repetitive recitation is the cooking pot in which the oil of their emotion (ishq, love) is heated and bodied forth as tears, constituting in performance the community of the faithful.

Notes

1. I use the Turkic pronunciation and spelling of the Arabic *dhikr*: a practice associated with Sufi ritual; "the repetition, individual or collective, aloud or silently, with or without movements, of a divine name or a litany" (Dähnhardt 2012; see also Shannon 2004 and Papas 2015).

2. Usually translated from the Arabic as "audition," *sama'* forms a part of Sufi rituals across the Islamic world and often involves not only listening but also movement: formalized styles of dance, rocking, or circling movements. It is formally interpreted in textual sources as a means to achieve the ecstatic state of finding the divine (*wajd*) (Shannon 2004). In modern Uyghur, *sama'* refers specifically to the circling dance performed in rituals and also to a men's mass dance performed outside the Heyitgah mosque in Kashgar on festival days.

3. A body of theory arising out of the natural sciences that seeks to explain how autonomous rhythmic processes interact, for example, how two pendulum clocks on a shared base fall into synchrony or how human circadian rhythms are entrained to the twenty-four-hour cycle of light and dark.

4. Tania Branigan, "Woman's Lone Protest Calms Tempers as Uighurs Confront Chinese Police," *Guardian*, July 7, 2009, https://www.theguardian.com/world/2009/jul/07/uighur-protest-urumqi-china.

5. Ebersole (2000) defines performative tears as tears shed in rituals proper or in ritualized social situations that perform cultural work.

6. I use the term *büwi*, following the existing literature, e.g., Anwar 2013.

7. From 1958 until 1982, as Rabiya Acha recounts, village land could not be owned by individual families but was farmed collectively by the commune. In interviews, older women remember the early years of the commune as a time of hunger and hard labor.

8. See, for example, accounts by Elizabeth Fernea (1965) based on fieldwork in an Iraqi village; Eleanor Doumato (2000) on early twentieth-century women's healing practices in Saudi Arabia; Catharina Raudvere (2002) on zikr in late twentieth-century Istanbul; and Deborah Kapchan (2009) on French Moroccan zikr groups.

9. This ritual is described in chapter 3. It might be indicated for a persistent headache or for people recovering from illness. The büwis blow into a bowl of water during their ritual and then give it to the patient to drink as a form of medicine.

10. See, for example, Edgar and Henig (2010) on dreams and divination in Bosnia, Doubleday's biography of an Afghan healer (2009), and Rasanayagam's story of the dream conversion and cure of a ritual specialist in Uzbekistan (2011, 103).

11. This kind of personal transformation echoes van Nieuwkerk's (2013) account of the dreams and repentance of Egyptian belly dancers.

12. Anwar (2013) reports that two government-approved spaces existed for büwi gatherings in the Yarkand region, until the local government closed them down in 2010, and the büwi moved their activities to underground khaniqa.

13. See Michael Sells' study of Qur'anic meaning and emotion (1991, 251).

14. See the detailed descriptions of contemporary sama' rituals performed by Sufi groups in Uzbekistan (Pasilov and Ashirov 2007) and Xinjiang (Mijit 2015; Zhou 1999, 31–34; and especially Liu Xiangchen's 2010 film, *Ashiq*).

15. I worked with Hurriyät Nizamidin, a London-based Uyghur, a practicing Muslim, and an Arabic language graduate. We worked through the video recording trying to identify the texts: no easy task because of the overlapping voices and idiosyncratic pronunciation of the Arabic. Hurriyät caught snatches of Arabic and typed the transliteration into Google. Aided by the many websites devoted to the Qur'an and popular prayers (du'a) that the search engine brought up, we were able to piece together the complex jigsaw of the khätmä.

16. Ahmad Kāsānī Dahbīdī (honorific title Makhdūm-i A'zam), *Treatise on Audition* (*Risāla-yi samā'iyya*). Manuscript preserved in Istanbul University, translated with commentary by Alexandre Papas (2015).

3

TEXT AND PERFORMANCE IN THE HIKMÄT OF KHOJA AHMAD YASAWI

Hikmät as Performance

On another blazing hot day in August 2009, the women of Yantaq village gathered in the same guest room for a hälqä-sohbät ritual. Literally translated as "circle of companions," this is the local term for ritual gatherings based on forms of zikr in which recitation is progressively shortened until the final consonant *hu* is rhythmically propelled from the body on each outward breath. The collective rhythmic chant is accompanied by a solo reciter, usually called a *hapiz*, singing hikmät poetry. As the women recited, the atmosphere began to warm, and several of them rose to perform a rhythmic dance, stepping forward alternately to the left and to the right, their arms raised in arching, circling movements. Over the repetitive rhythm of the zikr, Märyäm sang a Uyghur-language hikmät. The words of each line of the verse tumbled out on a descending melody toward long, thrilling sustained notes. The atmosphere came to a boil, and the women began to weep and breathe heavily. Finally, Märyäm brought the zikr to a close, turned to one of her younger apprentices, and signaled to her to recite another solo hikmät (fig. 3.1):

> *Äy—ng—ng—äy*
> Of those who enter this life, none can avoid death.
> People living in this world never value each other.
> *Äy—ng—ng—äy*
> There is no escaping from mourning in this world.
> If you understand this, then do not attach yourself to this world, for it is faithless.
> *Äy—ng—ng—äy*
> Look down beneath your shoes to where you will lie alone in the dust.

Fig. 3.1. Transcription of a hikmät recited by Subinur, Yantaq village, 2009.

You never imagine yourself in such a position.
Äy—ng—ng—äy
But you will lie in the grave not knowing whether it is summer or winter.
Your son, your daughter, your friends cannot look after you then.
Äy—ng—ng—äy
After your death, your children will take your wealth.
Nobody will know how you pass your time underground.

Äy—ng—ng—äy
Qayghu janliq jahan'gha kälsä akhir adäm ölmäy qalmas.
Tirikliktä khalayiq bir birlirining qädärigä yätmäs.
Äy—ng—ng—äy
Äjäb matämsära dunya irub bayani yoq.
Buni bilsäng kisän bu dunyagha märghul bolmaghil härgiz wapasi yoq.
Äy—ng—ng—äy
Ayaghing astigha baqin himmät tupraq ichidä pinhandur.
Män häm shundaq bolarmän däp sening bir yading kälmäs.
Äy—ng—ng—äy
Lähät ichidä yatarsän yaz wä kishining ötkänini bilmäy.
Oghul qiz yar dosting bir kuni sändin habar almas.
Äy—ng—ng—äy
Sän olgändin son hämmä pärzäntliring malingni alghaylar.
Sening halingnichu kechkäy, qara yär astida bilmäs.[1]

Subinur sang these lines of poetry on a syllabic, stepwise, falling melody. The words of the text fell quickly, contrasting with the long, drawn-out *äy—ng—ng—äy* that began each couplet, seeming to mimic a wail of mourning. Her voice was nasal and strained; the sound of the sustained notes sent a shiver down my spine. The assembled women responded to the affective force of this hikmät with quiet but sustained sobbing. After the motion and excitement of the zikr, this moment was about attentive listening to a text whose textual meaning—unlike the Arabic of the Qur'an—they could directly grasp. Its message was the impermanence of life and the need to meditate on and prepare for the certain approach of the grave.

The Islamic concept of *huzn* goes some way toward capturing the affective and spiritual work done by Subinur's performance. The state of huzn is based in the awareness of the human state vis-à-vis the creator. In huzn one experiences true humility, awe of the divine, and full awareness of human frailty and mortality. It indicates vulnerability—a softening of the heart—to the experience of religious truth. Huzn is sometimes glossed as being "God-fearing," especially associated with fear of the Day of Judgment, and it is an emotional state often invoked in discussions of listening to the recited Qur'an (Nelson 2001). Subinur's explanation of hikmät suggests the same set of dispositions:

> The meaning of hikmät is that God and the Prophet are our guides . . . these are "words of wisdom" (*hikmätlik söz*). . . . Sometimes I recite them at home if I'm feeling frustrated, and then I feel better. When we die, we leave behind our money, our possessions . . . [she cries]. When we think of death, then we remember Allah. . . . Allah is our creator; he makes us and he claims us. We will go to the grave and lie in the earth, but our souls will stand up before Allah and he will ask, "Have you read the Qur'an? Have you said your prayers? Did you sit around the tablecloth with the learned and the pious? Have you done good deeds or bad deeds?" (Subinur, Yantaq village, August 2012)

For Subinur, hikmäts express the temporary nature of life on this earth, the sorrow of death, and the importance of preparing the soul for the Day of Judgment. She also suggests the affective work that they perform; the acceptance and contemplation of these spiritual truths provides the listener with comfort and relief from everyday troubles.

In the wider literature, huzn is a moral state and a felt emotion, but the term can also refer to an aesthetic quality. Huzn denotes not only the emotional state of affective awe produced by contemplation of the divine, and expressed by weeping, but also a quality, even a technique, of reciting that reflects and produces that state (Gade 2004). The term is often used with reference to reciting the Qur'an, but it is also relevant to other types of recitation. Reciting with huzn is especially emphasized in Sufi literary traditions, where it is described as a technique of self-cultivation and a form of moral and spiritual development that comes with the contemplation of impending judgment. The medieval philosopher al-Ghazali links its aesthetic aspect directly to its affective aspect, noting that the reciter affects huzn in order to effect sincere huzn in himself and others (Nelson 2001). Likewise, Uyghur reciters of hikmät make it clear that an effective performance requires musical skills. Only a skilled reciter can produce the aesthetic and affective qualities that provoke strong emotions in listeners and furnish the spiritual benefits that flow from these emotions. In the hälqä-sohbät in Yantaq village, Märyäm admonished Subinur before she started to recite, "Recite it beautifully!" (*chirayliq oqung*). Uyghurs attending hälqä-sohbät gatherings have been known to complain bitterly about a reciter's poor sense of rhythm and failure to stay in tune.[2] These musical qualities are an essential part of the affective and spiritual work performed by hikmäts; they unlock and enliven the spiritual power contained in the texts.

The sung performance of hikmäts is firmly embedded in Uyghur community life, playing a part in rituals of mourning and healing and as part of regular spiritual practice in both men's and women's gatherings. It is an integral part of what practitioners term the *tärikät yol* (the way of the *tariqa* or Sufi orders). Hikmät are maintained and transmitted through performance traditions that are widespread across Uyghur communities, passed down from master to apprentice (*ustaz-shagit*) in continuous chains of transmission through families or ritual specialists. The Uyghur tradition of reciting hikmät is linked across space to traditions maintained in Uzbek communities in the Ferghana Valley. All these traditions are believed to derive from a collection of texts attributed to the medieval Central Asian Sufi sheikh Khoja Ahmad Yasawi, whose shrine lies in the town of Turkistan in southern Kazakhstan. These texts, gathered together in collections named the Diwan-i Hikmät, circulated in manuscript form across Central Asia well into the twentieth century, and they have more recently circulated more widely in printed book form, released by publishers from Istanbul and Ankara to Kazan, Tashkent, Almaty, and Ürümchi.

In this chapter, I trace the patterns of circulation of hikmäts, considering the ways that these Turkic-language prayers link the women of Yantaq village to other parts of the Turkic-speaking world. I draw on recent debates on the relationship between orality and literacy, and consider how they help us to think about hikmäts as they are performed in ritual contexts in Uyghur communities. I ask to what extent, and in what ways oral traditions of hikmät transmission and performance interact with the textual circulation of hikmät. It has traditionally been assumed that these oral practices were passed down through linear chains of transmission, taught directly from teacher to pupil. If written texts were involved, they were assumed to be equally localized, written by individual learners to serve as personal aides-memoire (Light 2008). I challenge the common assumption that the hikmäts performed in ritual contexts in Uyghur communities are isolated, locally maintained, discrete traditions. Instead, I argue that these Uyghur traditions of ritual performance encompass more diverse and complex forms of circulation that bridge the oral and textual spheres and traverse international borders. Contemporary Uyghur reciters of hikmät are rooted in the oral tradition, but they also engage actively with circulating texts, and they have reappropriated the transnationally circulating print tradition and revivified it within the performative context of their rituals.

My discussion in this chapter is based on work with several groups of Uyghur women who recite hikmäts. The first group of women, based in Yantaq village, was introduced in chapter 2. I also draw on recordings gathered in eastern Xinjiang by my research partners in Xinjiang University. Finally, I introduce a third group of women who met in 2015 to recite the Qur'an and sing hikmäts in a village in southeastern Kazakhstan. The women who belong to this third group were Uyghur migrants who came to Kazakhstan from the Ili valley of northwest Xinjiang in the mid-twentieth century. Their revival of the hikmät tradition allows us to think about other types of mobility across borders—not only the circulation of texts, but also human mobilities and diasporic patterns of contact and circulation.

Unlike the circuits of transmission of Qur'anic recitation or sung *anashid* which I discuss in later chapters, the transnational circulation of hikmäts that I describe here was not digitally mediated but purely text-based. Perhaps for reasons related to gendered codes of modesty, or perhaps because of their musical style, which strongly recalls laments, these hikmäts were rarely recorded or circulated in audio form. Instead, their circulation was conducted in ways that have been sustained over several centuries: through direct forms of oral transmission and the regional circulation of handwritten manuscripts, joined during the twentieth century by transnational circuits of print media.

Hikmäts in a Healing Ritual

One afternoon in late summer 2012, twelve women, including two büwi ritual specialists, paid a visit to a household in Yantaq village. Their purpose was to perform a khätmä for Hurriyät Hajim, who was recovering from a back operation. Her back problems had begun with a mule cart accident several decades earlier while she was working for the village commune. This was her second operation, which had involved a long journey to Ürümchi and several weeks in the hospital. The major expense of this operation had been paid for in part through a medical insurance policy, in part through loans from the extended family. On her return home, Hurriyät Hajim spent several months immobile in bed while her daughter cared for her and managed two households. Now she was slowly moving around the home on crutches and beginning to take back some of the burden of household chores. She was a devout woman who had completed the hajj a few years previously, but she did not regularly participate in khätmä rituals. On this occasion, though, her sister-in-law, who was a keen participant in khätmäs, had arranged a visit from the büwis. It was quite normal for villagers to combine recourse to institutional medical support with religious rituals to promote healing.

This visit by the büwis coincided neatly with our presence in the village. The political climate in 2012 was already tense, and any home-based religious practice was at risk of being dubbed "illegal religious activities" or even "religious extremism." It was only through the steadfast enthusiasm of büwi Aynisa for our project that we were able to be present at this meeting and record it. A tablecloth was laid, tea was served, and Hurriyät Hajim's female relatives began the work of preparing a meal for the visiting women. The two büwis who led the ritual would also be paid—or rather thanked—with lengths of dress cloth and store-bought shirts for the men of their family.

The bulk of the khätmä ritual was devoted to the repeated recitation of short Arabic prayers and supplications and short ayat (verses) from the Qur'an.[3] After the completion of each cycle of prayers, the women blew noisily into a bowl of water, "Ffsheeuw!" This transferred the spiritual benefits and healing properties of the recitation into the water (*ayat su*), which would be carefully preserved by the sick woman and sipped regularly over the coming weeks. As the women recited the Arabic prayers, several "came to the boil" emotionally; they wept noisily, and one began to hyperventilate.

Fig. 3.2. Transcription of a hikmät led by Nisakhan, Yantaq village, 2012.

After around an hour the women moved into spoken Uyghur-language prayers for Hurriyät Hajim's recovery. This section of the ritual concluded with a surah from the Qur'an and finally a melodious and rhythmic hikmät (fig. 3.2), sung in unison by all the women present.

Aghzingning nimi qashqay, amin,	It will dry the saliva in your mouth,
Közum nuri öchkäy, amin.	Extinguish the light in your eyes.
Tupraq ichigä köchkäy, amin.	You will enter into the dust.
Wäyran qilur bu ölum, amin.	Be fearful of death.
Qul Khoj' Ahmäd sän oyghan, amin.	Awake Khoja Ahmad, slave of God.
Yoqtur bu sözlär yalghan, amin.	These words are no lies.
Tupraq ichidä qalghan, amin.	You will be left in the dust.
Wäyran qilur bu ölum, amin.	Be fearful of death.
Saraylirini buzup, amin.	Palaces will be destroyed.
Bostanlirini köchurup, amin.	Orchards moved away.
Hämimizgä barawär, amin.	It is the same for us all.
Kälgän ölum ämäsmu, amin?	Death will come, will it not?
Khotunlirini tul qilghan, amin.	Wives will be widows.
Gulzarliqni khar qilghan, amin.	Gardens will be abandoned.
Yitimlarni qakhshatqan, amin.	Orphans will weep.
Kälgän ölum ämäsmu, amin?	Death will come, will it not?[4]

The performance of this hikmät formed a great contrast to the overlapping wash of sound and the emotionally charged style of the preceding Arabic-language recitation. The women's voices sounded out confident and strong, easily keeping together to a strong pulse. The lyric structure here—with seven syllable lines, and an AAAB rhyming structure—is commonly found in hikmäts. Although the lyrics reflected on the inevitability of death and its power to erase all earthly things, the mood was not one of fear and apprehension but rather was confident and calm. Singing the hikmät seemed to serve the purpose of bringing the women back down from the excitement of the khätmä and providing resolution after the emotional upheavals they had experienced.

Khoja Ahmad Yasawi

The reference in this sung text to Qul Khoj' Ahmad denotes Khoja Ahmad Yasawi, the celebrated Central Asian saint who most likely lived in the late twelfth century.[5] Yasawi is popularly known throughout Central Asia as a Sufi sheikh and a mystic poet, author of the Diwan-i Hikmät. His shrine lies in the town now known as Turkistan in southern Kazakhstan. In the twelfth century, this was the town of Yasi, the place where Yasawi is said to have studied under the probably mythical figure of Sheikh Arslan Baba. Yasawi's shrine has been an important religious center and pilgrimage site at least since the monumental mausoleum was built on the orders of Amir Timur, founder of the Timurid dynasty, at the end of the fourteenth century, which still stands today. A smaller shrine to Arslan Baba lies outside the town.

Yasawi's biographical details are obscure and contested in the historical record, and even his relationship to the Yasawi Sufi order and what we know of its *silsila*, or spiritual genealogy, is not straightforward. The Yasawi as an organized Sufi order did not survive competition from the rival Central Asian Naqshbandi, which restricted Yasawi activities and later appropriated its legacy and subordinated it to Naqshbandi interests. But the Yasawi tradition has had lasting and far-reaching influence in the realm of popular religious practice and the shaping of communal identities across Central Asia, including contemporary Xinjiang. Its broader legacy includes many aspects of religious practice maintained today, including styles of zikr, aspects of shrine veneration, and narratives of the spread of Islam in the region. It also had lasting influence on notions of communal identity. The Yasawi tradition's political and social role was not expressed through a conventional Sufi order, but through intimate bonds with local communities. In this tradition of social organization, whole villages or nomadic communities were formally recognized as disciples of hereditary sheikhs linked with the Yasawi tradition, and they regarded their affiliation with such lineages as a central feature of their communal solidarity and identity (DeWeese 1996a, 1996b, 1999, 2006).

These local traditions of social and religious organization intersect with the tradition of veneration of Yasawi, the circulation of stories about his life, and lyrics attributed to him. Yasawi's shrine has continued to serve as a major pilgrimage destination for Central Asian Muslims. According to a detailed ethnographic study of Turkistan in the 1990s (Privratsky 2001), hereditary sheikhs who were addressed as khojas and who claimed descent from the Prophet served as guardians of Yasawi's shrine. They officiated over large-scale zikr rituals until Stalin's purges of the 1930s, when they fled to Tashkent, and religious specialists were lost to Turkistan. Pilgrimage revived in the 1990s, and Muslims from across Central Asia began to visit the shrine in order to access the saint's miraculous powers. Popular versions of the Diwan-i Hikmät in Kazakh, Uzbek, and Turkish languages were sold at the shrine, and oral stories about the life and miracles of Yasawi circulated and were retold at the shrine.

The term *Diwan-i Hikmät* refers to manuscript collections of Turkic-language Sufi mystic poetry attributed to Yasawi, which have circulated, historically and today, in multiple forms from Turkey to Xinjiang. The oldest manuscript collection is believed to date to the seventeenth century (Azmun 1994). There are significant divergences between extant versions of the Diwan-i Hikmät in terms of content, number of poems, and aspects of wording and style. Larger collections contain more than a hundred hikmäts; shorter collections include around thirty. They are identified with Yasawi through the inclusion of his name within the poem in the manner of Central Asian poetry. The name appears in various forms, primarily *Kul Khoj' Ahmad* (Ahmad, servant of God) or *Miskin Ahmad* (poor Ahmad).

Typically, the opening series of hikmäts in the written collections recount in highly formulaic fashion the life of Yasawi, listing his spiritual achievements in every year of his life verse by verse up to the age of sixty-three (the age of the Prophet at his death), after which he retires to an underground existence in a cave. Of the collections I have viewed, a nineteenth-century manuscript collection of hikmät from Kashgar and one recorded performance from Turpan, as well as various versions published in Xinjiang, all adhere closely to this narrative structure. According to legend, Yasawi lived on to the age of 125. In popular belief, and in much of the relevant scholarship up to the late twentieth century, it was uncritically assumed that the Diwan was actually the work of Yasawi (DeWeese 2006, 2011). But some hikmäts are panegyrics, obviously written by Yasawi's followers; there are anachronistic references to Yasawi's tomb, and scholars have now generally accepted that the Diwan dates from after Yasawi's lifetime and was likely composed by his disciples and later followers of the Yasawi tradition. Variations in the signature, the style of poetic meter, the type of Turkic Chagatay language used—particularly its extensive inclusion of Persian vocabulary—and the late date of surviving manuscripts all suggest that the Diwan-i Hikmät is a compilation of poetry postdating Yasawi and probably was composed by multiple authors over a substantial period of time (Light 2008).

Hikmät in Circulation

Traditions of hikmät as a living performance practice have been maintained in Xinjiang to the present day, and they occur in diverse contexts. Ethnographers in the 1990s and early 2000s documented numerous groups performing hikmäts in both women's and men's hälqä-sohbät gatherings in rural Uyghur communities right across the region (Liu 2010; Mijit 2015).[6] Aynur Kadir (2010) notes that Uyghur followers of the tärikät yol regarded Yasawi as a saint, and they recited hikmät as part of their gatherings. Some of these performances of hikmät, associated with rituals of Sufi groups around Kashgar, were absorbed into sections of the canonical musical repertoire of the Uyghurs, the Twelve Muqam, and recorded in twentieth-century anthologies of Muqam poetry (Light 2008). Hikmät texts are also found embedded within the performances of *dastan*: sung tales of lovers, religious figures, and warriors from the Central Asian narrative tradition, performed in bazaars and at shrines by acknowledged bards (*dastanchi*) who accompany their sung narratives on stringed instruments (Kadir 2010).

In terms of their lyric structure and content, hikmäts are also diverse. The repertoire overlaps with other sung forms, such as monajat or mäshräp, but there is an identifiable core style, with a stepwise melody descending to a sustained note corresponding to a single line of the text (as can be seen in the transcription, fig. 3.1), syllabic delivery and strong pulse (illustrated in figs. 3.2 and 3.4). As the translated texts show, they typically feature themes of death and judgment and often are identified within the text by reference to the putative author, Khoja Ahmad Yasawi. Crucially, their performance should be affectively powerful and capable of provoking weeping. This affective force is especially centered on the long, sustained notes at phrase ends and the thrilling timbre in which reciters deliver them.

The oral circulation of hikmäts is not confined to Uyghur communities in Xinjiang. We know that hikmäts are also sung as part of contemporary Sufi meetings of Uzbek men across the border in Uzbekistan's Ferghana Valley. Pasilov and Ashirov (2007) describe a ritual they observed in 2004, noting that "at the end of every *zikr* they say in the manner of a sing-song or only sing the moral-ethical verses of Yassavi (d. 1162), Mashrab (d. 1711), Khazini, or Mazdub Namangoni, with the purpose to give moral forces to participants of the zikr" (172). Hikmäts also form part of the contemporary practice of Uzbek women ritual specialists (*otin*) in Uzbekistan's Ferghana Valley. We can trace these performance traditions to the early twentieth century through the accounts of travelers and early ethnographers. The Russian scholar Troitskaya described regular women's rituals taking place in Tashkent in the 1920s:

> The Ishan-bu, wife of an ishan, recited in a loud voice the zikr qadiri (jahari-yya) accompanied by her assistants Haifa and Otin, dressed in white. Every zikr ritual followed a precise structure, beginning with the first surah of the Quran and the salavat for Ghavsuli Agzam (praise for a Muslim scholar), followed by zikr based on the chorzarb ("four beat"), rhythmic repetition of the profession of faith, "La ilaha illa 'llah." Then the women dance in a circle to the poems of Mashrab and Ahmad Yasavi, before reciting from surah 112 to end the ritual. (Troitskaya 1928, 176–88, cited in Sultanova 2005)

The brief notes on style and meaning contained in these quotes highlight the similarities between practices among men's and women's groups in different parts of Central Asia across a period of more than a century. The "moral force" noted by Pasilov and Ashirov parallels my description of the affective work done by reciting hikmäts. The metric formula for zikr (*chorzarb*, or four beats) noted by Troitskaya is also found among Uyghur groups. Chorzarb describes the regular four beats of the recited declaration of faith, which begins the zikr: *LA—i—LA—ha—IL—la'll—AH*. This is followed by the *duzarb* (two beats): *IL—la'll—AH*, and the gathering culminates with the *yekzarb* (one beat): the repeated exhalation of the syllable *HU* (Zhou 1999).

We have even earlier explorers' accounts of listening to hikmäts in the Uyghur region. The German explorer and archaeologist Albert von le Coq recorded a hikmät in Qarakhoja town near Turpan in 1904.[7] He wrote that it probably derived from the region of West Turkistan, now the territory of contemporary Uzbekistan and Kazakhstan, perhaps making the link to the shrine of Yasawi (Von le Coq 1911, cited in Bellér-Hann 2000). In fact, the patterns of circulation are more complex than von le Coq imagined. Manuscript and more recently print versions of the Diwan-i Hikmät

Text and Performance in Hikmät of Ahmad Yasawi | 81

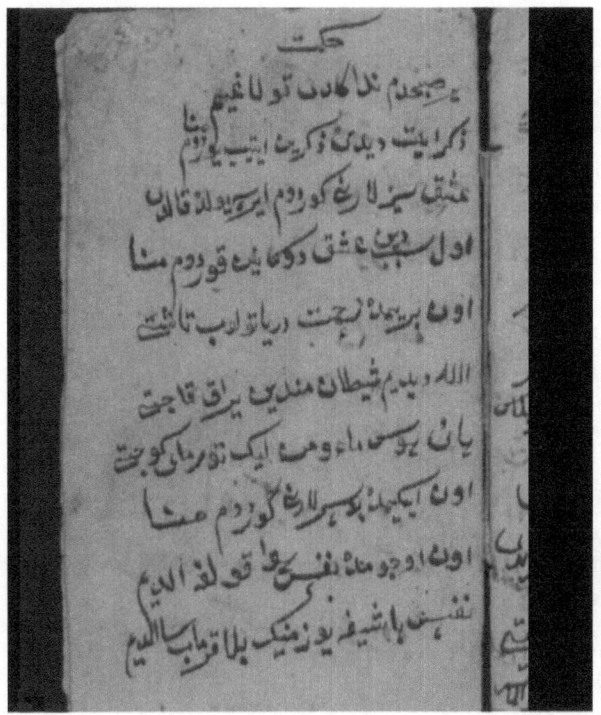

Fig. 3.3. Opening lines of a nineteenth-century manuscript copy of a hikmät. Jarring Collection at Lund University Library. Courtesy of Lund University.

circulate transnationally, part of a rich tradition of hagiographical Central Asian literature relating to Yasawi (DeWeese 2006). In the Uyghur branch of this tradition, manuscript copies of the Diwan-i Hikmät were common. At least seventeen copies of the Diwan are held in the Ürümchi archive,[8] and a nineteenth-century manuscript collected by Gunnar Jarring in Kashgar resides in the archive in Lund,[9] suggesting that the Diwan was one of the most widely circulated texts in the region, next after the Qur'an. Unofficially published collections of hikmäts still circulated in Uyghur bazaars in the 2000s, and many men and women who participated in khätmä or hälqä-sohbät rituals kept their own notebooks in which they transcribed or copied versions of the hikmäts that they wished to learn or remember.

A nineteenth-century manuscript in East Turki (the precursor of modern Uyghur) collected in Kashgar and preserved in the Gunnar Jarrings Archiv at the Lund University Library provides a vivid example of premodern manuscript versions of the Diwan. (See fig. 3.3.) This version adheres to the core narrative structure of the Diwan-i Hikmät, with its verse-by-verse description of the spiritual advances made by Yasawi in each year of his life. More than any modern published version I have seen, this manuscript version is steeped in concepts and terminology drawn from philosophical traditions of Sufism, and it represents the life story of Yasawi as a Sufi journey toward unity with the Divine. Ishq (love or passion for the divine) is a central concept in these verses, as it is in contemporary khätmä rituals in Uyghur communities. In these nineteenth-century hikmäts, ishq is represented as the key to the spiritual journey of the Sufi follower.

> *Bir subhdäm nida käldi qulaghim.*
> *Zikr et dedi zikrin äytib yürdüm muna.*
> *Ishqsizlarni kördüm ersä yolda qaldi.*
> *Ol säbäbdin ishq dukkanin qurdum muna.*

> One morning at dawn the call came to my ears.
> Remember God [recite zikr], it said, and I began to remember Him.
> I saw those lacking in love [*ishq*] left behind on the road [the Sufi path].
> For this reason I built the shop of love.

> *On birimdä rähmät därya tolub tashti.*
> *Allah dedim shäytan mändin yiraq qashti.*
> *Hay u häwäs ma'u mänlik turmay köchti.*
> *On ikimdä bu sirlarni kördüm muna.*

> At the age of eleven, my mercy brimmed over like the ocean.
> I spoke the name of Allah and Satan fled far from me.
> Ah, worldly desires, together as one we pass them by without pausing.
> At the age of twelve I saw these secrets.[10]

The emphasis on spiritual love and secret knowledge displayed in this text is notably lacking in the modern print tradition of Yasawi. In fact, there is a yawning gulf between the meanings ascribed to Yasawi and his poetry in the world of print and their meanings in the oral performative tradition. Turkish scholars have shown great interest in Yasawi and the Diwan-i Hikmät since the early twentieth century, seeing in him a literary forefather of the Turks: the first known poet to have written in a Turkic language. Several versions of the Diwan derived from diverse sources from Central Asia have been published in Turkey, often with translations into modern Turkish.[11] Much of this work fell into the Turkic nationalist framework established by the early twentieth-century work of the influential scholar Mehmet Fuad Köprülü (2006). Köprülü's life project was to establish a grand narrative of the shared cultural heritage of the Turkic peoples, and he situated the roots of Anatolian literature in these early Central Asian traditions. In Köprülü's understanding, the Diwan-i Hikmät was a piece of Islamic missionary literature, which promoted a simplified form of Sufism to suit the simple needs of the Central Asian Turks. In this Turkic literary genealogy, Yasawi served as a precursor for the more sophisticated work of later Sufi poets such as Yunus Emre.

The twentieth century brought a series of unlikely twists in this literary history. The figure of Yasawi also acquired symbolic power in the writings of the Jadidists, the Central Asian Muslim modernizers of the late nineteenth and early twentieth centuries, who depicted him as a nationalist and a proletarian, and even as a socialist poet. During the early Soviet period, Yasawi's name became linked politically and ideologically to the Jadidists, and when Stalin's persecution of the Jadidists began, Yasawi also fell out of favor and was officially labeled a feudal bourgeois and an apostle of reactionary dogma. Yasawi's reputation was subsequently revived in post–Soviet Central Asian scholarship, but in these rereadings, the religious mysticism of the tradition was downplayed in favor of a strongly nationalist and religiously diluted interpretation better fitted to the political ideologies of the new Central Asian nations (Zarcone 2000). Privratsky's (2001) ethnographic study of post-Soviet Turkistan traces the effects of these developments. He notes that modern pilgrims at Yasawi's shrine did not link Yasawi to the notion of Sufism; the term was discouraged in the Soviet period, and the Yasawi legacy in 1990s Kazakhstan was quickly being subsumed into projects of ethnic nationalist identity.

Modern Uyghur scholars also were interested in Yasawi's hikmäts. Not long after the end of the Cultural Revolution, an important and influential version of the Diwan-i Hikmät, edited by Nijat Mukhlis (1985), appeared in the pioneering literary magazine *Bulaq*. It is remarkable that this edition— and all the subsequently published versions available in modern Uyghur translation—are not based on the living traditions of hikmät practiced in Uyghur communities but on nineteenth- and twentieth-century collections of hikmät texts previously published in Turkey. The 1985 *Bulaq* version is based on an 1879 Ottoman publication (Kadir 2010), and the most recent collection published in Uyghur (Yessewi 2012) contains translations into modern Uyghur by Abdureshid Jelil Qorluq of 101 hikmäts from various published versions of the Diwan-i Hikmät from Turkey and Uzbekistan. The Uyghur intellectuals who promoted Yasawi were much more interested in the Turkic nationalist, Jadidist vision of Yasawi—forged in circulation between Ankara and Tashkent, which portrayed Yasawi as literary forefather of the Turks—than they were in the oral traditions of the tärikät yol with its performative enactment of huzn being practiced right under their noses. This divergence of interpretation did not, however, stop the followers of the tärikät yol from subsequently reappropriating and revivifying the print tradition of the Diwan-i Hikmät within their performative ritual practice.

Text and Performance

If we want to understand the relationship between these textual and performative traditions of hikmät, it is instructive to consider the wider scholarship on literacy and orality. Recent reassessments of the study of European traditions of oral poetry have thoroughly problematized the notion of a discrete oral tradition. As Karl Reichl notes: "When Milman Parry decided to exclude from his recordings in former Yugoslavia all singers who had learned from printed or manuscript texts, he did so in order to make sure that the recorded heroic songs were firmly based on oral tradition, and could therefore also be analysed as representatives of oral poetry. As it turned out, this clear separation between poems transmitted orally and transmitted in writing was not always easy to make" (2015, 21–22). In their seminal work on the oral origins of Homeric epics, Parry and Lord developed a model for the study of what they understood as "purely oral" performance traditions, arguing that oral tradition involves the (re)creation of a text in performance by drawing on a stock of metrical or melodic and rhythmic formulas held in the memory of the performer. The structure of the resulting text reflects and enables the process of oral composition in performance. Therefore, they argue, the structure of an oral poem is fundamentally different from one composed with the help of writing (Lord 1960; Widdess 2014). Karl Reichl's comment, however, makes clear their theories encountered immediate difficulties when Parry tried to apply them in the field.

The influential body of work by Ruth Finnegan (2014) cautions against the binary division of the world into oral and literate societies with fundamentally different social and mental characteristics. For Finnegan, such a division is underpinned by technological determinism, and it fails to grasp the diversity of ways in which communication technologies (speech, writing systems, print or digital) develop in different historical circumstances. More recent studies generally accept that most literary performance traditions develop out of patterns of interaction between written texts and oral performance, effectively collapsing the opposition between the two modes of creativity. For this reason, the focus of many studies has shifted to a consideration of the nature of the interactions between these realms in specific traditions and under particular historical circumstances. In his discussion of orality and literacy as revealed in the *bada* (notebooks) belonging to performers of praise poetry in the Punjab, Christian Lee Novetzke (2015) asks us to consider what a text is for and how its intended function affects its form. Bada notebooks are texts that privilege performance. Bada are handwritten, loosely organized, and often hastily constructed, full of marginal corrections, lines crossed out, and other emendations; they record fragments of songs arranged for performative effect. In the bada notebooks we find examples of text subservient to the demands of performance: text as a tool, a means, not an end. They are not intended to fix and ossify, they are dynamic, meant to trigger and prompt a performance.

Ethnomusicologist Richard Widdess (2015) considers the same problem from the opposite point of view, arguing that we need to look beyond the binary of orality and literacy and focus more broadly on the whole performance. The traditions of ritual recitation on which he works in Nepal "escape conventional categories like orality and text, but are better understood as performance: a process in which text may be present, in written and/or oral form, but is subsumed by musical elaboration and the enactment of religious and social meanings" (245). For Widdess, it is important to consider how the reciters and listeners relate to the text in situations where its meaning may be obscure. Sometimes a single word of the text can act as a pointer to its entire meaning and hence to a network of associations and usage. Why, he asked the reciters, would you sing a text you don't understand all through the night? Because, they replied, we wanted to sing all night. For them, the process of performance was the important thing, and the text was a means to an end. As I argued in the previous chapter in my discussion of ways of listening to the recited Qur'an in a Uyghur village, the question then shifts away from the lexical meanings in the texts: what is the meaning of the performance, as distinct from the meaning of what is performed?

Text and Performance in Premodern Uyghur Practice

As the early twentieth-century Uyghur scholar Mohammad Ali Damollah explains, "When reading, the greatest thing is this fact that one has to put one's heart and soul into it and read with all one's heart. If one does it only with the power of one's eyes, little comes out of it. Many times, when someone's mind is somewhere else but his eyes are with the script, other words emerge from his mouth" (translated in Scharlipp 1998, 112).

Literacy in nineteenth-century Xinjiang—or Altishahr, as it is more appropriately termed in that period—was more common than contemporary European travelers knew, and certainly more common than the prevalent narratives of the liberation of the region by the Chinese Communist Party might suggest (Bellér-Hann 2008). Community schools (*maktab*) supported by charity and donations at shrines and mosques were widespread across the region, and they taught their pupils to read Qur'anic Arabic as well as Persian and East Turki texts. Madrassas provided higher learning in the form of Arabic-based Islamic education. Mohammad Ali Damollah's comments immediately suggest two important things about reading (*oqumaq*) in the Uyghur tradition: a deep-rooted respect for literacy and an assumption that reading generally meant reading aloud. Both these understandings are linked broadly to Islamic norms, and they are confirmed in the Uyghur tradition of hikmät. Mohammad Ali Damollah even cites lines attributed to Yasawi: "Paradise is assigned to the knowledgeable, Hell for the ignorant" (Proverbs 207.1.73, cited in Bellér-Hann 2000, 10). Furthermore, he says, knowledge becomes ripe (*pissiq*) only through discussion.[12] Similarly, when discussing their rituals, the village women I worked with always spoke of "reading" hikmät (*hikmät oquymiz*) in the same way that they always read the Qur'an (*Qur'an oquymiz*), regardless of whether an actual text is present or whether the reading is sounded or silent; there is no separation in Uyghur, as there is in English, between reading and reciting. For men in Yantaq village, a common marker that they had passed from childhood to adulthood was when they acquired the title *qari* (reader/reciter of the Qur'an), indicating that they had completed their basic religious instruction and were able to recite a few short surahs from the Qur'an.

A rich tradition of hand-copied manuscripts flourished in the Altishahr region from the eighteenth century up to the mid-twentieth century. The tradition continues in a more limited form today alongside, and to some extent cross-fertilized by, modern print traditions. The manuscripts that circulated in pre-twentieth-century Altishahr included the Qur'an, talismanic handbooks for trades or crafts (*risalah*), and—most numerous—the biographies of Islamic saints (*tazkira*), which were transmitted to Altishahr through Sufi missionaries during the sixteenth and seventeenth centuries.

Rian Thum (2014) describes numerous contexts for the performance of the written word in early twentieth-century Altishahr. Professional dastanchi storytellers recited poetry from written texts; there were regular public readings of Turki romances and epics at barbershops, in the bazaar, or at mäshräp gatherings; and religious Arabic and Persian texts were read daily at mosques. At the shrines of the Sufi saints, pilgrims listened to readings and purchased copies of tazkira manuscripts that recounted the life of the saint. In many cases, the oral performance of these texts was highly musical.[13] This account builds up a picture of texts whose primary purpose was to be activated in performative contexts, and that were thoroughly embedded in social relations.

Thus, we can say not only that there was considerable overlap between the written and the oral in Uyghur traditions but also that the written and oral traditions were and still are interwoven and inseparable. Consider Nisakhan's explanation of the hikmät tradition and her own place within it:

> Where do they come from? Long, long ago there lived a man who wrote a book called Hikmät Shärip. It was handed down from one person to another, and so it came down to us. I learned hikmäts from my mother. My mother had her own notebook (*hatärisi*) that she wrote hikmäts in. I used it when I learned, and I made a copy for myself. When the police raided our house, they took her book away. They said they would return it, but they still haven't. But I kept my own copy. With this book, we recite in a way that other people cannot. (Nisakhan, Yantaq village, August 2012)

Nisakhan traces the origins of her own performance tradition to an ancient written text, identifiable as the Diwan-i Hikmät, which has been transmitted hand to hand through the generations. Hers is a family tradition, transmitted from mother to daughter, and the notebooks that they carefully copy serve to enable their performance. Crucially, these handwritten notebooks help them to "recite in a way that other people cannot": to maintain and strengthen their own unique tradition of performance and the ritual and spiritual power that they use in the service of the community.

"For This Reason I Entered the Cave"

In summer 2009, another group of women gathered in a family home in a small town near Turpan in eastern Xinjiang. They were led by a woman named Hädichäm, who was given the title *khälpät* (from the Arabic honorific title *khalifa*). She sat on a spacious raised brick bed in the courtyard of the house, flanked by a small group of her followers. They were dressed formally in white headscarves and waistcoats over their dresses in the manner of older village women across the region. A small table was placed on the bed before them, covered with a tablecloth and laden with bowls of fresh and dried fruit, nuts, tea, and *sangza*: crisp, fried strands of dough arranged in spirals and piled high on a platter. As always, these ritual practices intersect with forms of hospitality. This particular occasion was a performance arranged for the camera, part of a carefully arranged documentation project by the Xinjiang University Folklore Unit led by Rahile Dawut. Hädichäm Khälpät recited in a low-pitched, nasal style with a forceful, ringing delivery. She established an insistent rhythm, rocking slightly forward and backward and slapping her knee to underline the regular duple beat. The other women began to rock in time with her. She sang a repeated five-line melody with a regular six measures per line, which descended consistently to the same sustained repeated note. Stylistically, this performance is clearly related to the hikmät recited by the women in Yantaq village. After the first verse, the women seated beside her began to recite the zikr. As the song unfolded, their chant became gradually louder, a deep, noisy inhaling and exhaling: "*ah—HUM—ah, ah—HUM—ah.*" They continued to rock back and forth but maintained a relatively restrained decorum, conscious of the camera.

Hädichäm Khälpät's performance has a close relationship with the textual tradition of the Diwan-i Hikmät. She began her hikmät (fig. 3.4), singing

> *Äya dostlar häsbi halim bayan äyläy.*
> *Shu säwäbtin häqtin qorqup ghargha kirdim.*
> *Chin därtlikte bu sözlärni bayan äyläy.*
> *Shu säwäbtin häqtin qorqup ghargha kirdim.*[14]

> Oh, friends, I will tell you about my situation.
> For this reason I withdrew from others and entered the cave.
> With pain-filled words I tell my story.
> For this reason I withdrew from others and entered the cave.

The core, repeated line of this verse, "For this reason I hid myself from others and entered the cave" (*Shu säwäbtin häqtin qorqup ghargha kirdim*), is, as we have seen, an important recurring motif in the Diwan-i Hikmät, denoting a key trope in the story of Yasawi's life: his retreat from the world at the age of sixty-three. This broad structuring theme is shared with the early

Fig. 3.4. Transcription of a hikmät recited by Hädichäm near Turpan, 2009.

manuscript version discussed earlier, but the religious sensibilities of this text are quite different. The Sufi mysticism of the nineteenth-century text has been replaced by an emphasis on daily prayer and the everyday duties of a pious Muslim. Hädichäm Khälpät's performance is closely related to recent published collections of hikmät. She recites:

Ghar ichidä keche-kunduz ta'ät qildim.
Neqli namaz oqup uni adät qildim.
Härnä japa chäksä anga taqät qildim.
Shu säwäbtin häqtin qorqup gharghga kirdim.

Inside the cave I worshipped night and day.
I recited my daily prayers regularly.
If I felt weary, I persevered.
For this reason I withdrew from others and entered the cave.

This oral rendition is a very close match with a 2012 collection that contains translations into modern Uyghur of hikmäts from versions of the Diwan-i Hikmät previously published in Turkey and Uzbekistan. The equivalent verse in the 2012 collection reads like this:

> *Ghar ichidä keche-kunduz ta'ät qildim.*
> *Tätäwwu namaz oqup uni adät qildim.*
> *Härnä japa chäksä anga taqät qildim.*
> *Ol säwäbtin häqtin qorqup ghargha kirdim.* (Yessewi 2012, 53)

Hädichäm's language is virtually identical with the print version, varying in some sections only where it substitutes everyday vocabulary for the more literary language of the published version and adds refrains (*hu-Allah*) to fit the rhythm of the zikr. It seems evident that she has based her performance on the 2012 published text. As I noted earlier, this published text deviates considerably from the nineteenth-century manuscript version from Kashgar that is so strongly imbued with Sufi ideals. In contrast, the 2012 print version is almost completely cleansed of esoteric themes and portrays Yasawi's spiritual journey principally in terms of adopting the regular practice of a pious lifestyle. This shift in emphasis suggests its debt to the twentieth-century literary history of Yasawi.

It is fascinating that Hädichäm Khälpät has directly adapted the cleansed print version and reinserted it back into a Sufi-inflected zikr ritual. This kind of readoption of modern, authoritative texts—often viewed even by ritual practitioners as examples of correct religious practice—and reinserting them into traditional affective ritual performance, is a recurring theme in this book. We will encounter it in the next chapter in the discussion of correct ways to recite the Qur'an; we find it in digitally mediated discussions of the proper ways to be a good Muslim, and we see it here in the adoption of an authoritative published version of the verses of Yasawi. It demonstrates that there is no simple opposition between tradition and modernity; these supposedly opposing poles are always in close conversation with each other, enabled by complex circuits of transmission involving manuscripts, print, and performance.

Hikmät in the Uyghur Diaspora

The road from Almaty stretches out eastward in a straight line all the way to the border town of Zharkent. In the Soviet period, it was known by the Russian name of Panfilov, and Uyghurs name it Yärkänd using the Uyghur pronunciation. Long mountain ranges, branches of the Heaven Mountains, shadow the road on both sides. When we took this road in summer 2015, there were frequent police speed checks close to Almaty, but regulation faded as we headed further east toward the Xinjiang border and our driver accelerated to 130 kilometers per hour over the cracked and pitted road surface. As the gravel flew, it became clear why so many cars on the road had cracked windshields. At regular intervals, I spotted small gravestones bearing the image of a young man. It took me a while to link the driving practices to the gravestones.

Closer to the border, a gleaming new road was under construction, a project financed and implemented by the Chinese government. We passed a newly built railway station, again constructed with Chinese expertise and money, anticipating greater cross-border economic activity impelled by China's Belt and Road Initiative. This economic stimulus was not overtly visible in Zharkent, which in 2015 was still an old-style Central Asian town. The streets were laid out in a grid pattern; most of the houses were single-story with sloping corrugated iron roofs and thick whitewashed walls, privately built and surrounded by small plots of land where people kept hens, sheep, and noisy guard dogs. Cows and donkeys wandered untended on the town streets. The majority of the cars on the road were the tiny, rickety Soviet-era Lada, many carrying astonishing loads of anything from cut hay and melons to furniture.

Just outside Zharkent town lay Pänjim, a former Soviet *kolkhoz* collective farm (like the communes across the border in Xinjiang), now a "pure" (*sap*, monoethnic) Uyghur village. It boasted a small mosque that broadcast the *azan* five times daily and two large wedding halls—one for summer weddings, one for winter—both of which seated up to 250 people. In this village lived a remarkable group of some twenty elderly Uyghur *haji* women. Most of them had arrived in Kazakhstan as children in the late 1950s. Some had come with their families from the town of Ghulja in Xinjiang's northwestern Ili valley during China's communization drive, fleeing persecution under the "four olds" campaign. The group leader, Adiläm Hajim, came to Pänjim from Ghulja in 1958, having already completed secular school education and trained as a nurse. Others told us that their families had come here thanks to a surprising deal, struck between the Chinese and Soviet authorities before the détente, to remove the entire population of the Uyghur village of Ching Pänzi, which lay on the Chinese side of the border, and relocate them in Soviet Kazakhstan.

Fig. 3.5. Uyghur women in Pänjim village pause for refreshments at a neo-khätmä. Photograph by the author.

The Chinese paramilitary Xinjiang Production and Construction Corps (*bingtuan*) then took over the sensitive border area where the Uyghur village originally lay.

Since the opening of the border in the 1990s, and the increase in trade between China and Kazakhstan, many Uyghur families in this area had profited from the opportunities for trade and haulage. The area had seen a corresponding rise in religious piety. These elderly women living in a remote village accessed by a single-lane road deeply pitted by potholes, many of them walking with some difficulty, were not one-off haji; they had all been on the hajj at least three times. As I sat with them and asked about their pilgrimage experiences, they shouted competitively across the room, "I've been four times!" "Me too!" "I've been *six* times!" They met weekly, taking turns hosting the gathering, to perform a kind of neo-khätmä. Like the women's groups in Xinjiang, they wore white clothing and gathered around a tablecloth heavily laden with food, but theirs was a reinvention of the ritual. (See fig. 3.5.) The familiar sequence of orally transmitted repeated short Arabic prayers had been replaced with reading from a published text: the Uyghur translation of the Qur'an. Gone was the musicality and emotional force of the khätmä as I had experienced it in Yantaq village, replaced by a dutiful engagement with the textual content of the Qur'an. It was a striking change.

After reading the translated Qur'an, and some personal prayers offered to the host of that week's gathering, Adiläm Hajim led the group singing a hikmät. This text was rather childlike—indeed one could imagine it being taught to young children—and its content and lyric structure was remote from the verses of the Diwan-i Hikmät, although it included the signature Qul Khoj' Ahmad. Musically, with the low pitch, strong pulse, and descending melody with extended melisma at end of the third line of each verse, it was clearly related to the group sung style of hikmät led by Nisakhan in Yantaq village, which I described earlier in the chapter.

Beshingdiki nimä digändä.	What is in your head, they say.
Taji döwlät digäymän.	The kingdom of glory, I say.
Qolungdiki nimä digändä.	What is in your hand, they say.
Äziz Muhämmät digäymän (häq Allah).	Beloved Muhammad, I say.
Közungdiki nimä digändä.	What is there in your eyes, they say.
Nuri Muhämmät digäymän.	The light of Muhammad, I say.
Buruningdiki nimä digändä.	What is there in your nose, they say.
Mish mish Muhämmät digäymän.	The snot of Muhammad, I say.
Aghzingdä nimä digändä.	What is in your mouth, they say.
Kelimä shahadet digäymän.	Surah Fatiha and the Shahadah, I say.
Qolungdiki nimä digändä.	What is in your hand, they say.
Heyri sahawät digäymän (äy Allah).	Charity, I say.[15]

Unusually among Uyghurs in Kazakhstan, the group's leader, Adiläm Hajim, had retained the ability to read and write Uyghur in the Arabic script as well as the Russian Cyrillic. When we asked her how she came to participate in khätmä rituals and recite hikmät, she gave a familiar litany of loss and grief: the persecution of her family in the 1950s, the disruption and hardships of migration, the deaths of loved ones, and personal illness: "We suffered a lot when we left there. We wept tears of blood. I have cried a lot: my parents died, many friends died, my husband, my younger sister. My health suffered because of it, so now I always try to attend the khätmä." Since the 1990s, she had gone back to visit Ghulja several times, and while there she sought out women's ritual gatherings: "I have very strong memories of them doing zikr when I was young. I liked it, and when we visited Ghulja, if I heard they were doing zikr, I would go there." But the zikr that Adiläm had adopted was a modified version, one that had been cleansed of excessive emotion: neither ishq nor huzn were manifest in their gatherings. Adiläm explained: "We used to recite Allah-hu. We would crawl on the floor and embrace and comfort each other and wish that the other's wishes would come true, but now we've stopped doing these things. We said to each other if people see us, it might be embarrassing. We were afraid. When you fully engage in zikr you can't control yourself."

Adiläm's words suggest the influence of reformist Islam on popular attitudes toward religious practice in this area. New attitudes had led this group of women to reject the embodied, emotionally saturated styles of religious practice that Adiläm remembered from her youth and to replace them with practices that emphasized textual meanings and emotional restraint. Even in the lyrics of the hikmät they recited, the emphasis was fully on the centrality of reading the Qur'an in religious practice:

Här kim oqusa bu Qur'an,	Whoever reads the Qur'an,
Rähmät anga parawan	They will receive blessing
Uchmaq ichidä qirawan.	Like a pheasant ready to fly.
Yar bolur bu Qur'an.	Let the Qur'an be your friend.
Qur'an tängrim hädisi.	The Qur'an is God's story.
Uchmaq bolur rolchisi.	It is a role model for all.
Isra'ät otäp kuchisi.	Its followers offer prayers.
Chiraq bolur bu Qur'an.	The Qur'an is a light.
Qul Khoj' Ahmad ghapilmän:	Glorious Khoja Ahmed:
Ghapil kishini tonurmän.	I know that victorious person.
Mundin artuq bähtim yoq	There is no other pleasure
Oqur bolsa bu Qur'an.	Than reading the Qur'an.

Here again, the name of Qul Khoja Ahmad makes a slightly incongruous appearance, a passing nod to forgotten Sufi traditions in this otherwise fully revivalist performance. This kind of close engagement with the recited Qur'an within the Uyghur Islamic revival is something I will explore more fully in the next chapter.

During her visits to Ghulja, Adiläm also collected hikmät texts. She brought to the gathering a lined schoolchild's notebook, with a series of prayers and hikmäts neatly copied in the Uyghur Arabic script. (See fig. 3.6.) "We read hikmäts; we copy them from other people's books, and we learn and recite them," she said. Just as we found in Hädichäm Khälpät's performance in Turpan, one hikmät copied in Adiläm's book was an almost

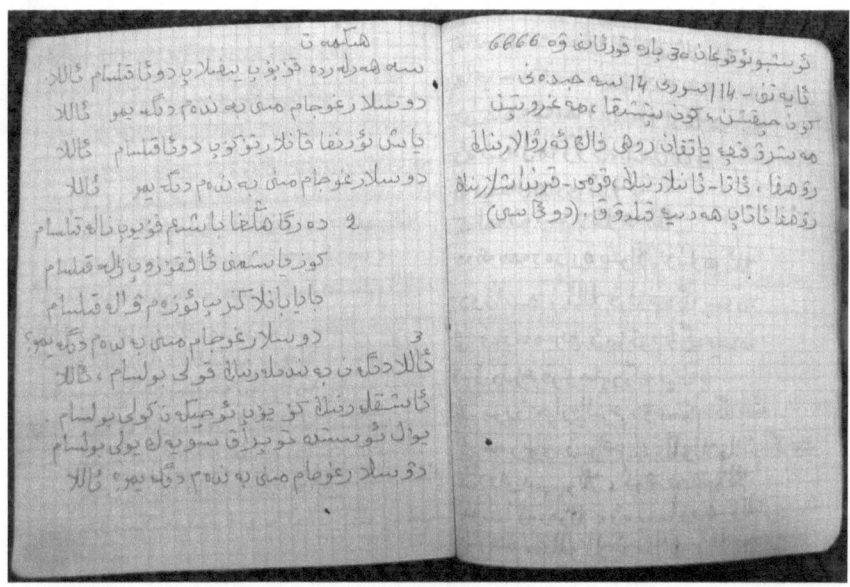

Fig. 3.6. Page from Adiläm's notebook containing the lyrics of a hikmät. Photograph by the author.

identical match to the print version of the Diwan recently published in Xinjiang (Yessewi 2012, no. 63). Just a few subtle differences suggested that Adiläm had not copied it directly from the published text and that it was a text that had been adapted for oral performance: the addition of the name of Allah at line endings and a few letters altered.

> *Sähärlärdä qopup yighlap du'a qilsam Allah.*
> *Dostlar khojam meni bändäm digäymu Allah.*
> *Yash ornigha qanlar tukup du'a qilsam Allah.*
> *Dostlar khojam meni bändäm digäymu Allah.*

> I rise at dawn and pray in tears.
> The Khoja is my companion.
> Weeping tears of blood I pray.
> The Khoja is my companion.

This correspondence between Adiläm's version and the published version offers more evidence of the close relationship between local traditions of copying and performance and the textual tradition that has traveled from Central Asia to Turkey and back. It seems likely that Adiläm has copied this hikmät from the notebook of another reciter in Ghulja who has taken a published text and adapted it for performance. Here again we find circulation and cross-fertilization between the textual and oral traditions, and we find the influence of revivalist approaches to religious practice: the emphasis on everyday pious practices of daily prayer and fasting blending seamlessly with references to the companionship of the saint.

Circuits of Transmission

It is interesting to consider this kind of movement from published texts back into locally maintained traditions of ritual performance in the light of existing literature on the twentieth-century canonization of Uyghur literary and musical traditions (Harris 2008; Light 2008). Nathan Light writes extensively of the work of twentieth-century Uyghur scholars who edited and revised the lyrics used by folk performers of the Twelve Muqam, both for publication and for use in stage performances by the new professional troupes. These lyrics were drawn from the Central Asian poetic tradition of writers including Ali Shir Nawa'i and Baba Rahim Mashrab: a tradition soaked in Sufi imagery and ideals, and one that frequently intersects with contemporary ritual performance practices (Kadir 2010; Harris 2017). But the process of oral transmission and adapting these lyrics to performance means that there is often a considerable gap between published and sung versions of these texts. Light highlights the anxieties of those twentieth-century Uyghur scholars as they considered the international scholarly reception of the muqam texts they intended to publish. How could they reveal to the world that the poetic texts as sung in their classical Uyghur tradition deviated from published versions based on other strands of the Central Asian literary tradition?

> The dominant perspective among institutionally trained "experts" was that illiterate "folk" performers had preserved the muqam tradition, but it was time to take it off their hands and return it to the entire Uyghur people, to whom it rightfully belonged. In the process the distortions introduced by the folk performers should be set right. The muqam tradition was thus being treated much like a manuscript tradition: scholars thought of it as fragile and easily lost through poor copying and limited distribution. Thus it was in need of editing to correct flaws and then publication of an authoritative edition to prevent further losses. (Light 2008, 225)

As I have discussed in this chapter, this notion of a correct or authentic version of an early historical text is widely acknowledged to be deeply problematic. Much of the poetry associated with the Twelve Muqam tradition is attributed to poets for whom we have no single authoritative source for their writing. In the texts attributed to Yasawi, as we have seen, multiple versions circulate transnationally, and they respond to the social and political climate in which they were adapted and performed. The historical evidence suggests that it is highly unlikely that their putative author had anything to do with them other than serve as inspiration for their creation, and indeed for their ongoing performance and re-creation.

What can the kind of ethnographic research presented in this chapter contribute to our understanding of the ways in which the oral circulation of hikmät interacts with the textual circulation of the Diwan-i Hikmät? Light (2008) argues that the oral tradition of hikmät differs profoundly from the written tradition ascribed to Yasawi. For him, the hikmät now found in the verses of the Muqam were more likely part of a discrete oral tradition maintained by Sufi groups in Kashgar and quite unrelated to the published textual tradition of the Diwan-i Hikmät. Other researchers diverge from Light's assessment that a gulf exists between oral and text traditions. Drawing on her extensive field research around the region, Uyghur ethnographer Aynur Kadir (2010) proposes a much more flexible Yasawi-based tradition. Hikmäts occupy such a large percentage of the Uyghur tradition of recited poetry, she argues, that they cannot all be attributed to one author. The early tradition established by followers of Yasawi formed the basis of a poetic style that continues to be extended and enriched by numerous anonymous poets whose creative practice has been subsumed under the name of Yasawi.

This view of a more diverse and flexible tradition is consistent with Thum's (2014) discussion of community authorship and textual drift in the Uyghur tazkira manuscript tradition. Thum suggests that through processes of copying—as copyists over a period of centuries edited, abbreviated, corrected names, misread, and added new praise sections into their texts—a great diversity of versions of the tazkira manuscripts accumulated. This process rendered these texts flexible and changeable over time to reflect the changing needs of a community of readers. I argue that in order to fully understand these historical processes of textual drift, it is crucial to take into account the complex interactions between text and performance. As the examples of Adiläm in Kazakhstan and Hädichäm in Turpan suggest, modern print versions of the texts also are fully integrated into these processes. Aynur Kadir provides evidence of the ways that another print publication has provided an important interface between the printed and oral circulation of hikmäts in the Uyghur tradition. She describes a fieldwork encounter with an elderly man in Turpan who claimed to have followed the tärikät yol (Sufi path) for fifty years. He told her that his strongest desire was to meet Nijat Mukhlis (1985), the man who had published the Diwan-i Hikmät in *Bulaq* magazine, a publication that had provided him with a rich resource for his own ritual practice (Kadir 2010).

Like the Qur'anic reciters whom I discuss in the next chapter, these *hikmätchi* (reciters of hikmät) craved correct versions of practice to strengthen their performance. They regarded the versions enshrined in the medium of print as possessing greater authority and therefore as having greater potential to release spiritual power in performance. Their appropriation of the published versions was enabled and facilitated by the living tradition of musical performance, which provided a framework into which performers could slot new texts, as long as these texts lay within the stylistic boundaries of the tradition in terms of their poetic form and structure. Instead of thinking of separate oral and written traditions, then, we should recognize the existence of more diverse, complex forms of circulation, crisscrossing the oral and textual spheres and crossing international borders. Hikmät performers refer to published versions as well as the handwritten notebooks of hikmäts they directly inherit, and they adapt the published texts to the musical frameworks that they have learned orally. The consistencies in lyric structure mean that the published versions are easily subsumed into the oral tradition and easily fitted to the musical framework of the performance.

We know that twentieth-century performers of the Twelve Muqam deployed texts in their performances in a highly flexible way (Light 2008). Although couplets formed the basic fixed units of memorized verse, sometimes singers used independent lines as filler material to extend the lyrics to reach the end of the musical phrase, choosing especially beautiful or meaningful lines to use in this way (Harris 2008). In the hikmät tradition too, a central part of the performance style is for performers to repeat and adjust the poetic lines to fit the melodic lines and to insert exclamations addressed to the beloved or to listeners addressed as friends (*dostlar*), and to God, often in the form of the zikr (hu-Allah).

The possibility of this kind of movement from published texts back into locally maintained traditions of ritual performance suggests that we need to revise our assessments of the process of canonization in Uyghur literary and musical traditions. It is pleasing to think that this work of canonization—far from being a final, authoritative sealing of tradition—may in fact be just one more link in the chain of oral transmission. We may more productively conceive of "feedback loops" (Novak 2013), in which traditions of manuscript copying and oral performance intersect and feed into each other in circuits of transmission. The advent of print versions fits seamlessly into these circuits, not in any way disrupting the cycles of movement between text and performance, but instead enabling faster moving and more far-flung loops of feedback, as Turkish scholars in Ankara rework manuscripts sourced in Turkistan, Uyghur scholars in Ürümchi translate these texts from the eighteenth-century Turki into modern Uyghur, and ritual specialists in Turpan and Ghulja adapt these translations into a form that fits the musical structure of their performance tradition. Texts that are meant by nationalist scholars to fix and ossify can in fact be revivified in the hands of performers who retain the framework of the performance tradition and be reanimated with the affective power of ritual performance. Thus revised and enriched, and enshrined in a reciter's notebook, the hikmät is then set in motion in a new cycle of transmission.

The consideration in this chapter of the interactions between the older forms of communication technology in Uyghur traditions of religious practice also informs the discussion to which I turn in the next two chapters: the circulation of religious sounds via digital media. In the next chapter, I turn to the digitally mediated circulation of the preeminent sounded practice in Islam, recordings of Qur'anic recitation, and the ways in which these recordings are incorporated into ritual practice, discussed, and debated and strategically deployed as part of the new Islamic soundscapes of Central Asia.

Notes

1. Some Uyghur colleagues have suggested that, stylistically, with its long lyric structure and rhythmic flexibility, this song should be classified as a *monajat* rather than a hikmät. I have decided to respect Subinur's own identification of her performance as a hikmät noting that the boundaries between genres of ritual song are often not clearly defined. Access the audio here: http://www.soundislamchina.org/?p=1660.

2. See, for example, the sequence in Liu Xiangchen's 2010 film *Ashiq: The Last Troubadours*, in which a group of *ashiqs* who have gathered at a shrine for zikr have a long argument about the poor musicianship of some of the reciters, which is spoiling the quality of their ritual experience.

3. In terms of structure and content, this is similar but not identical to the khätmä described in chapter 2; different forms of khätmä include sequences of phrases for the zikr that vary according to their ritual function.

4. From a hikmät sung as part of a khätmä, Yantaq village, August 2012. Singing led by Nisakhan. Recorded by Rachel Harris. Translated by Rachel Harris and Aziz Isa. Audio available here: http://www.soundislamchina.org/?p=1411.

5. There is no historical evidence to support the popularly cited date of his death (1166–67). Devin DeWeese suggests that the historical Yasawi most likely lived a half century later.

6. We have a comprehensive picture of performance style through the work of the musicologist Zhou Ji who recorded and transcribed performances of hikmät from dozens of locations around Xinjiang (Zhou 1999).

7. Le Coq is notorious in China for removing more than three hundred crates of priceless murals and artifacts from the Kizil Buddhist caves near Kucha.

8. Described in the catalog of historical manuscripts, Shinjang 1989, 31, 55–57, 65, 84–86, and 178–80. Thanks to Rian Thum for this information.

9. The Gunnar Jarring Collection of manuscripts from eastern Turkistan in the Lund University Library, Lund, Sweden, https://www.ub.lu.se/en/the-jarring-collection (last updated October 30, 2019).

10. See figure 3.3. From a manuscript collected by Gunnar Jarring, c. 1930, believed to be of nineteenth-century origin, source unknown. Full manuscript available as folio 7r in Gunnar Jarring Collection at the Lund University Library, searchable via the Alvin platform as Gunnar Jarring: Collection of hikmet and gazal: https://www.alvin-portal.org (accessed February 20, 2019). I am grateful to Iskandar Ding for his generous help with transliterating and translating these verses.

11. One useful Turkish publication (Azmun 1994) provides translations into modern Turkish and English, alongside transliterations and copies of the original manuscript, of a small compilation of forty-nine well-known hikmäts collected in the town of Turkistan in 1954, which may date to the late seventeenth century.

12. For further discussion of attitudes to literacy, see Bellér-Hann (2000, 19–23).

13. See the videos and audio recordings made by Rahile Dawut and her team at contemporary shrine festivals in southern Xinjiang, available on http://www.soundislamchina.org/?p=1521, and in the videos accompanying the chapter by Dawut and Anderson (2015): http://www.musicofcentralasia.org/Tracks/Chapter/24. See also musical transcriptions and discussion by Zhou Ji (1999).

14. Verse 1, recited by Hädichäm, recorded near Turpan in 2009. A section of the recording can be accessed here: http://www.soundislamchina.org/?p=1411. For comparison with a printed text, see Yessewi 2012, 53.

15. Hikmät led by Adiläm Hajim, recorded by Rachel Harris, Pänjim village, Kazakhstan, August 2015.

4

STYLE AND MEANING IN THE RECITED QUR'AN

Hearing the Qur'an in Arzu Style Restaurant

We were having lunch in a high-end Uyghur-owned restaurant on Togolok Moldo Street in central Bishkek. Outside, a thick pall of smoke and the smell of kebab greeted guests. Inside, the large dining room was fitted with air conditioning, comfortable banquettes, and a long bar along one wall. Russian pop music videos played on television screens hanging from the ceiling. Suddenly a resonant voice cut through the chatter and bustle of the restaurant, reciting the preparatory phrase that must be given before giving voice to the Qur'an: *A'ūdhu billāhi min ash-shaitāni r-rajīmi* (I take refuge from Satan in Allah). A prominent Kyrgyz imam was eating at the restaurant and, still seated with his party, had taken it on himself to recite from the Qur'an at the time for noon prayers. An immediate hush fell over the restaurant, and his voice filled the large room for ten minutes, the mellifluous Arabic words of the Qur'an followed eventually by a barked Kyrgyz language prayer. Everyone in the restaurant stopped their activity and sat motionless, heads bowed and hands cupped in prayer, until he had finished. The waiters too ceased to serve their customers and stood still, heads bowed and hands cupped. The music had been hastily silenced, but the videos continued to play incongruously, their scantily clad dancers still gyrating, suddenly an affront to the new ethical soundscape created by the voice of the imam. (Field notes, Bishkek, August 2016)

This 2016 encounter captures something of the ways in which sounded practices can reshape the urban environment. Charles Hirschkind (2006) describes how playing recordings of the Qur'an or sermon tapes in taxis and cafes in Cairo reshaped the moral architecture of such places by animating substrata of kinesthetic and affective experience in the people who occupied them. The performance of Qur'anic recitation in a public place calls forth mimetically the sensory elements of the tradition of ethical listening in Islam. The sound of the recited Qur'an acts on bodies; Muslims listening to its sound may unconsciously adjust their headscarves or shape their lips in the words of the prayer, adapting themselves to the demands of its "sonorous moral acoustics" (Hirschkind 2006, 124). Listening to the recited Qur'an sounding out in a Bishkek restaurant, we can understand how it has come to play an instrumental role in creating a new Muslim counterpublic in Kyrgyzstan.

The sacred nature of the recited Qur'an has the capacity to determine the boundaries and characteristics of public space. For this reason, it plays a powerful role when mobilized and sent forth to resound in public spaces normally marked as secular. Its sound marks certain styles of speech or comportment as inappropriate in that space and likely to draw censure. By recruiting a set of bodily practices and ethical norms, the sound of the recited Qur'an has the capacity to transform secular spaces into places belonging to an emergent Muslim public (Eisenberg 2009, 2013). The ethical transformation of Arzu Style Restaurant was a fleeting one, but repeated interventions such as this are likely to persuade the restaurant's managers that a change in the sonic and moral architecture is required in order to cater to the changing demands of their clientele. In this way—as we have already seen in the rapid transformation of the Erdaoqiao soundscape in Ürümchi described in the introduction—the transformation of sonic architecture can easily acquire greater permanence and solidity.

Hirschkind (2006) describes the Islamic counterpublic as a discursive arena that cuts across distinctions between public and private spheres. Within it circulate media that are geared to produce the embodied sensibilities and modes of expression that facilitate the development of Islamic virtues. During the twentieth century in the Middle East, everyday practices of pious sociability gradually came to inhabit a new political terrain, shaped by discourses of national citizenship and emerging forms of transnational religious association. As opposed to the standard emphasis on text-based forms of debate in the formation of the public sphere, in Hirschkind's conception it is the figure of the ethical listener—with all its dense sensory involvements—that founds and inhabits the new Islamic counterpublic. Islamic traditions of listening and affective experience form the basis for these emergent publics, through the deployment and mediated circulation of new styles of moral exhortation and religious sounds geared to the cultivation of pious sensibilities.

Recent decades have seen new publics, like that of Cairo, arising across the Islamic world. Turkey saw a progressive Islamization of the public sphere in the mid-1990s, as Islamist political gains and media deregulation allowed new forms of pious popular culture to flourish. Martin Stokes

(2013) has described the role of another form of Islamic sound production in the formation of a new public in Turkey. Popular religious songs became ubiquitous in the Turkish media and online platforms and subsequently achieved mainstream status with the rise to power of Erdoğan's AK Party and have become an essential part of municipal events. Stokes notes how the cultural managers of the Islamist movement in Turkey actively fashioned habits of listening through the verbal pedagogy accompanying music recordings and online. This top-down instruction elaborated the proper emotional and aesthetic states for listening to this kind of music and in this way helped to constitute the new public.

In the early years of the twenty-first century, Uyghurs in communities across Xinjiang, Kazakhstan, and Kyrgyzstan avidly consumed, listened to, and imitated recordings of the recited Qur'an, which they purchased as cassettes or videodiscs or downloaded digital files onto their smartphones. Uyghur women in Bishkek organized regular religious tea parties (*din chay*) to discuss ways of following a religious life, and young men in Ürümchi met in private rooms above restaurants to listen to recorded sermons and discuss their contents. Many people sent their children to a local imam or büwi to learn to recite their prayers and a few surahs of the Qur'an, and older people organized community recitation classes for themselves—to attend to their immortal souls before it was too late, as I was often told. Many people were aware of leading reciters from Egypt and elsewhere and had a keen appreciation of the aesthetic beauty and emotional power of their recitation. In this chapter, I consider how performances of the recited Qur'an—resounding in public spaces, circulating in the form of digital media, and embodied in daily practice—helped to constitute new Muslim publics in Central Asia, across the former Soviet states and in Chinese Xinjiang. In order to understand these processes, I pose a series of interlinked questions. To what extent, and in what ways, were these new publics linked in their listening practices and ethical formation to other Islamic revivals in the Middle East and elsewhere, and to what extent were they driven and shaped by the particularities of regional history, the sensibilities of local people, and the scope for the emergence of such publics in the political environment of the time?

Revivalism, Separation, and Longing

When Uyghurs in the Central Asian states and in Xinjiang spoke of their personal turn to Islam, their explanations were often framed by a narrative of the renewal of family traditions of faith, a sense of rediscovery, and sometimes explicitly of seeking their roots. Ali Shir, an Almaty-based publisher, told us, "My grandfather was a religious man, and my father was a scholar; he understood religion, and he taught us when we were young how to be good Muslims. Then we came here [Kazakhstan], and I went to Russian school. That was a strong influence, and I forgot many things: our history, our culture . . . it was as if I had fallen asleep. But when I reached twenty, I looked around and I remembered my roots and I decided I should follow Islam" (Ali Shir, Almaty, 2015).

Alongside this kind of return to family roots, there was often a parallel narrative of intense longing for, and emotional engagement with, religious practice and knowledge that emanated from "over there," from the Muslim heartlands in the Middle East. Their desire might be sparked by and nurtured through travel—most commonly the intense experience of going on the hajj—and sustained by engagement with media items emanating primarily from the Arab world. Predominant among these encounters were accounts of hearing the recited Qur'an:

> When I went on the hajj, I felt as if the pages of the Qur'an were opening to me everywhere. I felt so emotional! I thought, what kind of Muslim am I if I don't know the Qur'an, and I said to myself that I must learn the Qur'an. I am a human being, like everyone else, Allah gave me eyes, gave me a tongue, gave me intelligence, so why can't I read the Qur'an? When we got to Mount Arafat, whenever I heard the sound of reciting the Qur'an, I went and sat nearby and I cried. I spoiled my eyesight with crying, and since then I've had to wear glasses. (Gulnisa Hajim, Bishkek, 2015)

Gulnisa expressed an emotional register commonly found among Muslim revivalists in Uyghur communities in Central Asia and Xinjiang: their sense of separation from the source of Islam, a sense of being marginal Muslims, far removed from the religious centers of Cairo and Mecca, inadequately engaged in their faith, and with a tendency to deviancy that needed to be redressed. With this sense of deviance came a strong desire for the "true Islam" emanating from the Muslim heartlands. This desire was especially manifested in an emotional engagement with the sounds of Qur'an emanating from the Arab world, voiced by famous reciters like Abdul Basit 'Abd us-Samad, Mishari Rashid Alafasy, and Abdul Rahman al-Sudais. Their voices not only served as auditory symbols of true Islam, they also had the power to evoke powerful affective experiences of faith. People who engaged most passionately with the recited Qur'an had strong views on the formal and musical ways of giving voice to the Qur'an, and they lamented the way that local styles of recitation deviated from the "correct" pronunciation and style that was transmitted in the centers of Islamic learning in the Middle East.

The sounds of their Qur'anic recitation also offer clues to the connections between the village world of the büwi and wider trends in transnational Islamic culture. In this chapter, I draw links between this sense of religious separation and longing and discussions of the role of music in identity formation in a globalized world. These discussions are grounded in the perception that, under conditions of global modernity, no local identity can be purely constructed on grounds circumscribed by a bounded, defined locality; modern identities are forged across intensely interconnected worlds, often making connections across great distances. This approach draws on the now classic work of sociologist Anthony Giddens (1991), who argued that one of the defining characteristics of modernity is the lifting out, or disembedding, of social relations and individual experience from local worlds and their reconstitution across time and space. Music—and in this case the highly musical sound of the recited Qur'an—is a common way of mediating those relationships: a context and a conduit for appropriating and reconciling different worlds (Stokes 1994; Erlmann 1999).

Changing Habits of Listening

Beginning in the 1990s, and intensifying in the 2000s, new ways of listening swept across Uyghur society. The sound of the recited Qur'an permeated the soundscape, making sonic claims over new territories, as we saw with the imam's intervention in the Bishkek restaurant, and many debates took place over the correct way to give voice to the Qur'an. The upsurge in enthusiasm for the recited Qur'an was facilitated in part by the relaxation of restrictions in the 1980s and 1990s, which permitted the resumption of family traditions, and in part by greater access to wider trends in transnational Islam.

In Uyghur society, traditional contexts of recitation included Friday prayers and daily recitation of the complete Qur'an over the course of the thirty days of Ramadan in the larger Friday mosques. It was also recited during life-cycle rituals in the home, such as weddings, circumcision parties, and especially funerals. Families might mark Ramadan by inviting the mosque community of male elders (*jäma'ät*) to an evening meal (*iftar*) followed by a khätmä—in this case usually denoting a complete simultaneous recitation by thirty reciters of the thirty juz of the Qur'an—and the local mosque might organize the community to fulfill a complete recitation of the Qur'an in nightly sessions over the course of Ramadan. Similar rituals of hospitality and recitation were performed for *mäwlud* celebrations of the birth of the Prophet. Another context for recitation in the home was within the khätmä rituals conducted by women ritual specialists (büwis) for the purpose of healing or expulsion, women's funerals, or to mark the Night of Barat. Sufi groups also recited from the Qur'an as part of their hälqä-sohbät ritual gatherings.

These practices were driven underground, but not completely curtailed, during the revolutionary period in Xinjiang. The Qur'an became a target in the late 1950s under the "four olds" campaign[1] and during the Cultural Revolution, when Red Guards conducted household searches for religious literature and organized the ritual burning of Qur'ans and other religious texts in front of the town mosques. Edmund Waite (2006) recounts how a Uyghur imam was found to have recited the Qur'an at the birth of a friend's baby during this period. As a punishment, his face was blackened and he was paraded around Kashgar on a donkey. To a certain extent, the revival of practices around the recitation of the Qur'an involved a straightforward resumption of custom as soon as the political climate permitted, but it also went beyond that simple sense of revival.

In the post-Soviet Central Asian states, the lifting of travel and trade restrictions in the early 1990s facilitated people's access to Islamic knowledge and lifestyles. The loosening of policy permitted an influx of religious groups, literature and digital media, and consumer goods, including clothing and halal food brands. Islamic donors from various countries, especially Turkey and Saudi Arabia, funded mosques and religious schools for children and for training imams. Another significant source of new ideas and attitudes were the itinerant preachers known as *dawa'chi*, who were active across Central Asia. The majority were local converts loosely allied to the Tablighi Jama'at, whose roots lie in India and Pakistan. Recognizable by their long beards and adoption of the South Asian *salwa* chemise as an "authentic" form of Islamic dress, they preached simple messages of the need to return to an authentic, correct, and pure Islam, often using weddings as a platform for their preaching (McBrien 2006; Mostowlansky 2017). Wider travel for local Muslims, on the hajj and for study in Egypt and Turkey and elsewhere, was also an important factor in the spread of new attitudes to religion. Besides imported literature, there was a huge upsurge in locally printed publications in local languages, as well as a wide array of bootlegged compact discs and videodiscs on sale at mosques and

Fig. 4.1. "Look, my people, where are we heading?" An anti–religious extremism billboard dominates the landscape on the road to Karakol, in eastern Kyrgyzstan, 2016. Photograph by the author.

in markets. Market traders and food companies imported a wide variety of Islamic clothing and halal food items, most often from Turkey. The spread of text-based interpretations of Islam, new forms of religious digital media, and halal food also served to increase people's awareness of being part of a global community. Although their responses have been less draconian than those implemented in Xinjiang, Central Asian governments have also conducted periodic campaigns to crackdown on these trends (see fig. 4.1; Rasanayagam 2011; Kirmse 2013).

Many new mosques and madrassas were constructed in Kazakhstan and Kyrgyzstan in the 1990s, and the imams and teachers in these institutions familiarized Central Asian youths with their interpretations of correct religious practice and the sounds of correct recitation of the Qur'an. The young people trained in these centers spread these messages beyond the urban centers and right into local communities. We spoke with Shurbäk, one of these newly trained imams, in the border town of Zharkent in Kazakhstan in 2015. Shurbäk had studied Islam in a private school in Almaty before taking on the post of imam in a newly built neighborhood mosque, sponsored by an elderly, wealthy, and pious Uyghur couple. He recounted with pleasure the growing engagement of the local community with the mosque:

> The mosque is doing well; many people in the community are coming to pray regularly. This year during Ramadan, a lot of young people started to fast for the first time, and they came to the mosque to listen to the reading of the

Qur'an in the evening.² In previous years, it was mainly old people and regular attenders who came, but this year, even though it was very hot, many young people came and attended actively. It was very impressive. During Ramadan, they came five times a day to pray. (Shurbäk Imam, Zharkent, 2015)

This pattern of sponsorship of new community mosques by newly wealthy businesspeople, foreign-trained imams, and growing youth engagement with a pious lifestyle was one that we encountered repeatedly in the former Soviet states. In Xinjiang, the activities of foreign religious organizations have been much more limited than in the Central Asian states, and the circulation of religious media and literature, as I described in the introduction, was subject to strict controls and targeting by periodic campaigns. Even so, patterns of travel, mosque building, and avid consumption of religious media similar to those in the former Soviet states grew steadily from the 1980s, with a significant upsurge after 2009. By 1984, there were reportedly fourteen thousand mosques open in Xinjiang (Waite 2006), mainly supported by donations from the local community and wealthy individuals. The desire for the Qur'an, both by listening to recordings and learning to recite, was second in popularity only to the decision to start regular daily prayers and to observe the Ramadan fast, for men to renounce alcohol, and for women to adopt some form of veiling.

Self-study played an important role in the revival in Xinjiang. Edmund Waite (2006) recounts the personal journey of religious renewal undergone by the imam of the mosque in the community near Kashgar where he did his fieldwork. This elderly man had undergone a formal religious education, including Qur'anic recitation and interpretation, sharia law, and Persian poetic religious texts, in a madrassa in the 1940s. In the 1980s, as soon as conditions relaxed, he began intensively relearning the Qur'an and extending his religious education through whatever books and media he could acquire, even teaching himself to translate the Qur'an into Uyghur. This desire for religious knowledge was widespread. Numerous informal and underground schools sprang up during this period to teach children and adults to recite their daily prayers and a few surahs of the Qur'an. In the county town near Yantaq village where we did our fieldwork, the imam of the town mosque taught Qur'an classes for boys; his wife taught another class for girls, and many of the büwis also taught village children. In rural areas, people regarded this as the resumption of normal education and socialization for children.

Recordings of recitation, in the form of cassettes, videodiscs, smartphone apps, and other gadgets were sold in Uyghur bazaars both openly and covertly from the mid-1980s, and pilgrims returning from the hajj commonly gave cassettes of Qur'anic recitation as gifts to friends and relatives. By far the most dominant sounded practice in the religious media circulating in Xinjiang, prior to the recent crackdown, was the recited Qur'an. Recordings of Qur'anic recitation came from many sources, in many different styles, including short teaching videos produced by the Islamic Institute in Ürümchi, imported videodiscs from Pakistan, and locally produced discs of content downloaded from the internet. They included lengthy high-quality recordings in the ornate classical Egyptian style and the simpler but emotive Saudi style, thick with reverb. On the accompanying videos, the recitation was sometimes overlaid by gruesome images of death and decay—reminding listeners of the need to look beyond earthly concerns to the destiny of their immortal souls—but more often it was accompanied by images of blue skies, doves and flowers, or crowds of the faithful praying in the huge mosques of Egypt and Saudi Arabia.

Listening to the Qur'an: Sound and Emotion

> It was Friday morning, and we were waiting for Halmud outside a mosque on the potholed main street of Karakol, another border town that lies at the western end of Issyk Kul lake in Kyrgyzstan. He eventually pulled up in his tiny, beat-up old Lada, and laboriously extracted himself from the driver's seat. Halmud was a big man with a military bearing, a retired firefighter. Since his retirement a few years previously, he had rediscovered his Islamic faith and now worked as doorman for the local mosque. As the car door opened, a recording of Qur'anic recitation by the Kuwaiti sheikh Mishari Rashid Alafasy boomed out of his car. Its sound matched Halmud's prayer cap and suit of white cotton clothes, which give him a rather saintly air. He was preparing himself spiritually for Friday prayers. (Field notes, Karakol, July 2016; see fig. 4.2)

The Internal Music of the Qur'an

For Muslims, the Qur'an is divine revelation, the fixed speech of God as revealed in the Arabic language to the Prophet Muhammad. As I argued in chapter 2, the Qur'an as text is inseparable from its recitation as solo vocal performance. Reading the Qur'an most commonly involves reciting it aloud, and the experience of the divine text is therefore primarily auditory. The sense of the holiness, and the blessings (*baraka*) imparted by the sounded Qur'an—as the word of God—penetrates every corner of the Muslim world (Graham and Kermani 2006). Its power and spiritual

Fig. 4.2. Halmud (right) with Aziz Isa in Karakol, 2016. Photograph by the author.

function are quite apart from the understanding of every word of the Arabic text. In her seminal study of Qur'anic recitation in Egypt, Kristina Nelson argues that the role of the reciter is not only to transmit the meanings of the text but also to stir the hearts of listeners with those meanings (Nelson 2001).

Recitation of the Qur'an is governed by a set of rules called *tajwid*. Tajwid preserves the nature of the revelation and guards it from distortion by a comprehensive set of regulations that govern many of the parameters of the sound production, such as duration of a syllable, vocal timbre, and pronunciation. The science of tajwid is itself primarily transmitted orally, though supplemented by teaching texts, the student imitating and practicing the sounds produced by the teacher. The correct recitation of the Qur'an, as regulated by the rules of tajwid, clearly involves the correct transmission of the semantic message. But the unique sound of tajwid also signals a text and an event set apart from all other texts and experiences (Nelson 2001). Individual reciters may heighten the affective impact of Qur'anic recitation through their art, but the rules of tajwid serve to separate this heightened

Fig. 4.3. "Alif, lam, mim. This is the Book, about which there is no doubt." Transcription from a recording of Aynisa reciting surah al-Baqarah in Yantaq village, 2012.

experience from other aesthetic experiences. Moreover, much of the affective impact of Qur'anic recitation is inscribed into the text and fixed by the tajwid.

The stylistic and rhetorical features of the recited Qur'an, what Anna Gade (2004, 91) calls the "internal music of the Qur'an," create affective states of unanticipated tension. Qur'anic verse is characterized by abrupt shifts in the length of its lines and between regular and irregular patterns. Gade suggests that these moments of syntactic rupture, when the poetical and expressive patterns of the text are shattered and can no longer be anticipated, may be a constructive aspect of the emotive power and experience of Qur'anic recitation. These abrupt shifts are also inscribed in the tajwid. For example, in the popular opening section of the second surah, shown in figure 4.3, the first words are simply the vocalization of letters of the Arabic alphabet: *alif*, *lam*, and *mim*. The inclusion of this series of letters in the text is usually interpreted as one of the miracles of the Qur'an, as their meaning is unknown to any except Allah.

Sonically underlining this sense of mystery, the syllables *lam* and *mim* are recited with *madd* (indicated by the symbol ~ placed over the syllables), meaning that they should be lengthened to the duration of four syllables. The following phrase is suddenly contrastive and fast. This rhythmic structure underlines the textual message, which contrasts the mystery of the letters with the sure guidance provided by the Qur'an.

Another important aspect of the links between Qur'anic recitation and its affective impact lies in the vocal quality of the recitation, the grain of the voice, and in particular the use of nasality. In the recitation of the Qur'an, the use of nasality (*gunnah*) is prescribed by the rules of tajwid (Nelson 2001). The diacritic *shadd* (ω) over a letter prescribes a doubling of the consonant. It indicates stress and a nasalized delivery that has affective force. Consider

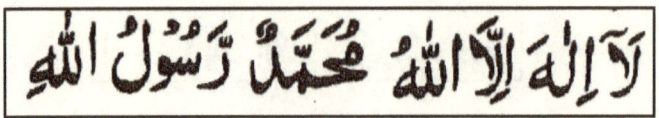

Fig. 4.4. The shahadah, Arabic text with tajwid markings: *lā ilāha illa'llāh, muhammadun rasūlu'llāh* (There is no god but Allah, Muhammad is the messenger of Allah).

the thick deployment of the shadd symbol in the declaration of faith (shahadah), which is often described as the most powerful phrase in Islam (fig. 4.4).

These formal aspects of Qur'anic recitation, inscribed within the text and in the rules of tajwid, underpin both the affective experience of listeners and the widespread discussions of correct recitation style that I encountered among Uyghur reciters.

Learning to Recite: Embodying Piety

"They say if you can recite the Qur'an well, according to the rules of tajwid, then you are like a lemon tree, always fresh and sweet and fragrant. . . . If you have intention to learn, then you are like a tree in bud, but if you aren't interested then you are like a poisonous plant and you smell bad" (Aynisa, Yantaq village, August 2012). Aynisa invokes a pious sensorium when she explains the importance of learning to recite the Qur'an. A similar sense of the necessity to reform themselves, to make their bodies fragrant and their souls fit to meet God through sustained engagement with the recited Qur'an, had provoked extraordinary levels of activity among Uyghur women in Bishkek, drawing them out of their homes and into the mosque for regular classes. Every weekday morning in summer 2015, between the regular prayer times (when the mosque was configured as male space, and women stayed away), Pokrovka mosque was filled with the sound of women and girls giving voice to the Qur'an. (See fig. 4.5.)

Spurred on by her experiences during the hajj, described at the beginning of this chapter, Gulnisa Hajim returned to Bishkek and threw herself into studying the Qur'an:

> I came back from the hajj, and I decided to study the Qur'an. I have a child who has learned the Qur'an since he was seven, first in a school here in the Bishkek Central Mosque, and then in Turkey. So I asked my son to teach me. He said, "No mama, you won't manage it." But I said, "You teach me the letters, teach me the pronunciation, and I will learn." Then he agreed and began to teach me the twenty-nine letters from *alif-be*. I learned how to pronounce

Fig. 4.5. A women's Qur'an class in Pokrovka Mosque, Bishkek, August 2016. Photograph by the author.

> them properly, and I practiced day and night. I couldn't get to sleep if I hadn't learned my lesson for the day. Sometimes I was so exhausted I had a pain in my head, but I didn't give up. I kept saying to myself, "I must read the Qur'an," and suddenly I was able to read it myself. So my Qur'an teacher was my own child. (Gulnisa, Bishkek, 2015)

Gulnisa subsequently began to teach other women and took on a leading role in the increasingly pious Bishkek Uyghur community. Her struggle to educate herself was followed by a struggle to carve out a space for women to exercise their voices:

> We started at first doing our class in our homes, taking turns to host, but we found that didn't work very well, so I thought maybe we can use a room in a mosque. I went to ask permission from the imam at the Central Mosque. He asked, "What are you teaching there?" And I said, "Qur'an recitation and translation." The imam said, "Bring the book to show me. You need to show the imam of this mosque your 'characteristics.'"[3] That stopped me short. I thought, how can I show my "characteristics" to a man? So then I went to the local imam. They were building a new mosque, and they said we could have a room in the old one when it was finished. When the women heard the news, they were happy. At the moment, we're working on copying the text of the Qur'an and on our reciting. Since we started the class, we've completed reading the whole Qur'an twice. Even if they don't recite well, they can still read it. They're not young, these women, it's not that easy for them, but they're doing their best. (Gulnisa, Bishkek, August 2015)

In 2015, twelve women were attending the class regularly, most of them over sixty years of age. Half of them had been on the hajj. They were mainly former shopkeepers or had worked in the local cloth factory that closed down in the 1990s. They all lived in the same neighborhood in Pokrovka, an eastern suburb of Bishkek where the Uyghur community was concentrated, and they all had family roots in the Ili valley in the northwest of Xinjiang. Only Gulnisa came from the southern town of Atush.

Gulnisa led the class; she started off by reciting the opening lines of the section they were learning that week and then encouraged each woman in turn to recite a passage. They tried to complete a surah a week, she said, but they broke down the longer surahs into shorter weekly sections. Each of the women had her own copy of the Qur'an, and they followed the text with a finger as they recited. Gulnisa thought it important to read the Uyghur translation and explication as well as learning how to voice the original Arabic text. Some of them were competent readers with a basic grasp of the rules of tajwid, and they approached the recitation with distinct musicality. After class, they cited the former imam of the Saudi Grand Mosque, Abdul Rahman al-Sudais, the mid-twentieth-century Egyptian star reciter Abdul Basit 'Abd us-Samad, and Mishari Rashid Alafasy as influences. In the second half of the lesson, Gulnisa presided over the group, reading selections from a book of questions and answers on Islam written in the Uyghur Arabic script and published in Turkey.

In addition to her role as Qur'an teacher, Gulnisa had also taken on a role as religious and community leader. She had taken on some of the tasks reserved for büwis in rural Xinjiang, including reciting the Qur'an and leading prayers for the female mourners at funerals. She would also take the opportunity to preach the requirements and benefits of a pious lifestyle: regular prayer and fasting, submission, and modesty. Gulnisa's leadership role had come by virtue of her charisma and her religious authority, which was based in part on her family history—her father had been a respected religious scholar in Atush—and in part on her own fierce engagement with religious practice. This was entwined, crucially, with her ability to read the Uyghur Arabic script, which she first learned (just like Adiläm, who led the women's group in Pänjim village in Kazakhstan) as a young girl in religious lessons within the family, even before she left Xinjiang in the 1950s. This ability gave her access to a wider range of published material in the Uyghur Arabic script—primarily books published by Uyghurs in Turkey—and it also facilitated her encounter with the text of the Qur'an. Her wider reading gave her a major advantage over the majority of these women, whose literacy was confined to the Cyrillic script taught in Soviet schools and whose engagement with the Arabic script was a more onerous task. I heard on more than one occasion an acid comment on the efforts of a less talented older student that she was "reading without her reading glasses." Texts—the printed verses of the Qur'an, translations, and text-based commentary—played a much more important role in the former Soviet states than they did in Xinjiang, but they were always a complement to sounded and listening practices.

One of the most enthusiastic students in the Qur'an class at Pokrovka mosque was Asiya, one of a wave of Uyghur migrants from Xinjiang to arrive in Bishkek in the 1950s. Recently retired, she had worked for thirty-eight years for the Kyrgyz state trade administration department. In 2016, she was struggling to pay the medical bills for her sick daughter and was deeply engaged in the life of the mosque community. Because money was tight and she was caring for her daughter, she could not contemplate the time and expense of going on the hajj, though she clearly longed to do so. She began learning the Qur'an in 2015, she said, and tried to read the Qur'an every day. She attended as many classes as she could, several times a week, and in the evenings at home she would go online to listen to recitation and check whether she'd learned it properly: "I'm learning because we will all die; we will all pass to the other world, and I don't want to go empty-handed. Our Qur'an; our religion; our prayers. When we were young we had fun, but now our time is coming. We won't live forever, so we should attend to our religion, and the Qur'an is the heart of our religion. How can we stand before Allah if we haven't learned our religion?" (Asiya, Bishkek, 2016).

There are close parallels between this movement in Bishkek and Saba Mahmood's (2003, 2005) discussion of the women's mosque movement in Egypt. Mahmood reads forms of bodily practice such as daily prayers and learning to recite the Qur'an as a bodily means to cultivate virtue, the outcome of a professed desire to be close to God. Such bodily practice is part of the larger project of becoming a pious Muslim in the entirety of one's life and a means to the training and realization of one's pious self. It is a kind of ethical self-formation, a form of habitus requiring constant work on the self—strengthening the desire to pray or to recite—and constant vigilance to hone the moral capacities in order to please God. Mahmood invokes the writing of medieval philosopher Ibn Khaldun to explain this kind of Muslim subject-formation as a type of habitus that is an "acquired excellence at a moral or practical craft, acquired through repeated practice until that practice leaves a permanent mark on the character of that person"

(Mahmood 2005, 136). This economy of bodily and moral cultivation had taken a powerful hold among Uyghur women in Bishkek, strengthened through regular gatherings to exchange religious knowledge (*din chay*) and cultivated above all through engagement with the recited Qur'an, through both disciplined regular practice and emotional, aesthetic appreciation.

Style and Meaning

Certain core aspects of Qur'anic recitation are governed by the rules of tajwid, and other aspects—primarily the more melodic and expressive aspects of recitation—are less fixed. Several recognized readings of the Qur'an, known as *qira'at*, form the basis for recitation. The readings are associated with prominent reciters of the eighth century and their students and were fixed in written form in the tenth century CE. All these readings can be rendered in practice in two styles, known as *mujawwad* and *murattal*. Murattal is associated with daily individual practice whereas the contexts of mujawwad are public and performative. Both adhere to tajwid, but the sound of murattal aims for simplicity and clarity suited to its instructional and devotional context, while mujawwad is distinctly and explicitly more musical: it requires a command of the Arab classical musical system, and it is intended to produce an emotional and spiritual effect on listeners (Nelson 2001).

In the Qur'an classes in Pokrovka, the women were engaged in learning the simpler murattal style, but they listened to recordings in the more musical mujawwad style in order to access the aesthetic and spiritual experiences they afforded. Experienced listeners can identify particular qira'at, regional styles of recitation, and even styles associated with particular reciters. During the twentieth and twenty-first centuries, particular styles of Qur'anic recitation have achieved global hegemony through systems of technology and political patronage, and they have become linked to particular Islamic ideologies. In the 1960s and 1970s, developments in recording technology permitted the global spread of what is now regarded as the classical Egyptian style, as Egypt's state-owned recording company SonoCairo produced a series of star reciters, among them Abdul Basit 'Abd us-Samad and Khalil al Hussari, for worldwide export (Frishkopf 2009). Renowned for their artistry, their recitation style featured dramatic melodic ornamentation and ecstatic techniques of repetition and modulation. In the audio recordings of their live performances—which are still massively popular on YouTube and other media platforms—murmurs, sighs, and shouts of appreciation from the audience are often audible.

In the 1980s, a new style of recitation began to compete with this established style in the Middle East via a new media form. Saudi forms of revivalist Islam were widely promoted at this time through cassette recordings of sermons and recitation. In contrast to the ornate Egyptian style, the Saudi style eschewed melodic elaboration and was typically more rapid, simple, and direct. This style was not the same as the traditional Egyptian murattal because it was intended not for private practice but for public performance. The heavy reverb used in its recordings indexed the acoustics of its most common live venues, the huge mosques at Mecca and Medina, and it was particularly associated with the nightly recitation of the Qur'an held in those mosques during Ramadan (*tarawih*). Michael Frishkopf (2009) has argued that this Saudi style of Qur'anic recitation was used in Egypt to sonically promote reformist-revivalist Islamic ideology. To play a recording of the Saudi style in Egypt in the 1990s was to make a public political statement about one's approach to Islam. The Saudi style of recitation expressed a direct relationship to God, one affectively colored by fear, awe, and repentance and linked to Salafi ideology. It opposed the traditional Sufi-influenced mystical-aesthetic values of Egyptian Islamic practice, which were represented by the classical Egyptian style.

In the next section, I consider what happens when these different Middle Eastern recitation styles circulate globally and the particular ways in which they filtered into Uyghur practices of Qur'anic listening and recitation. Did the ideological attachments they signaled in Egypt remain true for Uyghur listeners? Can the semiotic system that Frishkopf proposed be applied to the ways in which Qur'anic recitation is listened to, interpreted, and reproduced in Uyghur society, or did new meanings accrue, suited to the new contexts in which they now resounded?

Abdul Basit Comes to Aqsu

During a fieldwork trip to Aqsu in 2012, I discussed the changing styles of Qur'anic recitation with Damolla, a young imam who had trained in the Islamic Institute in Ürümchi before being officially appointed to a town mosque in southern Xinjiang. In the 1980s, China's Islamic Association began to reestablish relations with Islamic centers of learning in the Middle East. Up to that time, according to Damolla, the style or "voice" (*awaz*) of Uyghur recitation was local, but beginning in the 1980s, new styles—or the "Arab voice" as he put it—started to be introduced: "In our local area, my father's teacher was the first to introduce the Arab recitation style [qira'at] from Saudi Arabia. He studied for seven years in Mecca. Now the local style has gone. Everyone uses the Arab style. Why? It's better we lose our old style. The Arab style is good. The whole Muslim world is using it. The only reason we didn't adopt it earlier was because links were weaker, we didn't have so many opportunities to travel." Here is a clear articulation of the sense of disdain for local practice and need to conform to the "correct" style. Damolla marks correctness here as a specifically Arab phenomenon, perhaps a straightforward connection made with the Arabic language of the holy text, or perhaps because of his personal relationship with individuals who had traveled to Saudi Arabia. Yet Saudi Arabia was not the only source for Uyghur reciters to access "Arab styles." Damolla also waxed lyrical about the Egyptian classical style of Abdul Basit:

> We are all following Abdul Basit: Muslims in China, and across the whole Islamic world. It's fashionable to copy his qira'at, his tajwid, his voice [awaz]. No one has yet been born to take his place.... When he reads a verse, every word is in its proper place. His voice and breath last a long time. I don't know anyone better than him.... I'm also trying to follow his style at the moment. When I recite in his style, and I make my voice sound like his, people value it more; it strengthens my reputation. (Damolla, Aqsu, August 2012)

As Damolla suggests, a range of Middle Eastern styles were popular among Uyghur reciters in Xinjiang at that time; they were highly valued and were fast supplanting local styles of recitation, and trained reciters like Damolla possessed detailed knowledge of specific styles and individual reciters. Moreover, this question of style goes deep into questions of embodiment and vocal timbre: Damolla must literally inhabit the voice of Abdul Basit to cement his reputation has a reciter.

Voicing Mishari Rashid in Zharkent

Across the border in Kazakhstan, Shurbäk (the young imam in Zharkent whose mosque community was flourishing) was a regular listener to recordings of Qur'anic recitation from the Middle East. He was especially fond of a more contemporary star reciter who had achieved prominence and considerable wealth through the internet: the Kuwaiti imam Mishari Rashid Alafasy (see fig. 4.6). Unlike Damolla in Aqsu, who won praise for imitating Abdul Basit, Shurbäk was frustrated that the mosque community in Zharkent did not always appreciate his attempts to replicate Alafasy's style. He told us,

Fig. 4.6. Bootleg compact disk of Qur'anic recitation by Mishari Rashid Alafasy for the Russian-speaking market, on sale at the Dongan Mosque, Zharkent, 2016.

> I mainly listen to recordings from Saudi Arabia and Arab countries. In our family, we really like Mishari Rashid (laughs). One of my brothers is always listening to him, and he can copy his style exactly. . . . For many people here, it sounds a bit strange if you recite the Qur'an following tajwid . . . the old people want to hear it the way they're used to. If you do it differently, they say, "You've made it sound like singing a song" or "You've turned into an Arab!" Once I was reciting the proper style in the mosque, and some people got very unhappy and shouted at me! I was so embarrassed. They said, "Where did you go to study? What kind of Qur'an did you study? Our grandfathers never recited like this!" It's very difficult to explain to them that this is what the Arabic should sound like, because they don't understand what you're talking about. I say to them, "You have to recite the Qur'an beautifully (*chirayliq*). You have to recite it correctly (*drus*), because it is a blessing (*sawab*), so you have to follow every mark on the text." (Shurbäk Imam, Zharkent, July 2015)

The elderly mosque community in Zharkent were much less well disposed to "Arab" sounds than Damolla's listeners in Aqsu. They rejected the new style as alien and untraditional, unconvinced by Shurbäk's arguments that linked the accrual of religious benefits to correct practice and aesthetic beauty. Shurbäk would find a more receptive audience in the younger generation who began to flock to his mosque as part of the wider growth in pious practice during this period.

Mishari Rashid Alafasy, the imam of the Grand Mosque of Kuwait, was a constant presence in Central Asia in 2015 and 2016. By that time, Alafasy was already an established transnational public figure and media personality. His Qur'anic recitation was disseminated worldwide via his own television channel, Alafasy TV, as well as through compact discs and his website and via social media. He maintained a prominent presence on Facebook, Twitter, Soundcloud, and YouTube, and even had his own smartphone app to deliver his recorded recitation directly to smartphones. Although his style was broadly in line with Frishkopf's notion of the Saudi style, and he studied Qur'anic recitation at the Islamic University of Madinah in Saudi Arabia, Alafasy should not be understood as promoting Salafi ideology. As can be seen through the numerous advertisements on his channels for Alafasy-branded products and religious commentaries delivered on premium SMS services, Alafasy personified a new brand of commercialized transnational Islam (Osborne 2016). His recitation formed part of a global halal industry that grew exponentially in the early decades of the twenty-first century.

The expression of Muslim piety was in this period increasingly mediated through the production and consumption of material goods, styles, fashions, and expressive registers that circulated via transnational media and linked Muslim believers around the globe. A growing number of Muslims worldwide have felt compelled to pursue and express their religious convictions by relating to a globalizing market of religious media and halal goods. These practices of consumption and media engagement have sustained, expanded, and transformed conventional understandings of religiosity. Halal is at the center of a wider social and political narrative among those who have embraced the label as a marker of piety and Muslim identity. In a recent study of the halal industry, Faegheh Shirazi (2016) argues that consuming the halal brand was not only a marker of piety but also part of a search for identity and security in a global environment where dominant narratives cast Muslim men as potential terrorists and Muslim women as repressed. (See also Schulz 2006.)

The industry assumed particular importance among Muslims living as minorities in non-Muslim societies—in the West as well as in the former Soviet Union and in China—who used it to mark their difference from mainstream secular society and to connect to a wider global Islamic community. The rise of patterns of halal consumption was a notable aspect of the Uyghur Islamic revival, especially in Ürümchi, where two Uyghur-owned supermarket chains, Arman and Ikhlas, which featured halal food and products from Turkey, were hugely popular with Uyghur consumers in the early 2000s (Erkin 2009). The consumption of recordings of Qur'anic recitation can be linked directly to this phenomenon.

Re-Sounding Maqām Bayati in Yantaq Village

In chapter 2, I described a khätmä ritual performed on the Night of Barat, when the good and bad deeds of the dead are weighed in the balance. Led by Märyäm, the women recited a series of zikr, gradually increasing in intensity until they wept and some fell into a trance. At the end of the zikr, Märyäm signaled to Aynisa, who began to recite the surah Al Rahman. Her recitation was beautifully voiced and, unusually among the büwis in Yantaq, faithful to correct Qur'anic pronunciation and the rules of tajwid. She was also recognizably following the classical twentieth-century Egyptian style and reciting in the Arab mode of *bayati*. The assembled women answered her phrases with sobs and gasps.

The use of mode is a key aspect of the art of Qur'anic recitation and crucial to its ability to stir emotional responses in listeners. Kristina Nelson (2001) argues that the ability to relate the *maqām* of Arabic classical music to the meaning of the Qur'anic text is essential for a good recitation. She cites a remarkable appreciation of the recitation by the renowned Egyptian reciter Sheikh Rif'at: "I heard him once evoking *huzn* [sorrow and awe] in his reciting, and I heard the *nagamat saba* [which is famous among the Arabic modes for huzn] coming out of his throat as if it were drowned in tears. Then he came to verses that required zeal and enthusiasm in their execution, and suddenly *nagamat rast* burst out like the beating of drums" (al-Najmi, cited in Nelson 2001, 63). This Egyptian connoisseur's appreciation of an outstanding performer emphasizes that, in this particular context, Qur'anic recitation was an act of modal improvisation.[4]

The aesthetics of improvised performance and emotional listening span the sphere of Qur'anic listening and classical musical performance in Arab cultures. Ali Jihad Racy (2003) describes the production of *tarab* (ecstasy) in twentieth-century Egyptian music: The feeling of a "true *sama'*" event (note the incorporation of Sufi vocabulary into this musical sphere) rises and descends in an arc. The singer (*mutrib*) is a psychologist who gauges and plays with the mood of the audience. Light signal pieces or "musical aphrodisiacs" throw the audience into an instant participatory frenzy; repeated phrases with variations are especially likely to lead to tarab. But, above all, Racy places the musical evocation of emotion in the sphere of mode. Cadences are very important, he says, a test of skill; they may be calm or burning, provide closure or uncertainty. The experience of listening to modal improvisation is the most ecstatic, especially in the hands of a skilled performer who can manipulate familiar material or modulate in artful or surprising ways.

The art of tarab is closely associated with the great twentieth-century Arab singer Umm Kulthum, whose repertoire of vocal qualities was drawn directly from her training in Qur'anic recitation and religious song. Umm Kulthum deployed these qualities in secular songs to heighten emotion, conveying, for example, the feelings of an abandoned lover (Danielson 1997). Listening to Umm Kulthum's weekly radio broadcasts in the 1950s and 1960s was a defining experience in modern Arab practices of collective listening. These broadcasts sustained the tarab relationship—the affective synthesis of performer and listener—into the sphere of mediated listening and the circulation of sound in commodity form. This form of mediated tarab was taken up in the religious sphere by great twentieth-century Egyptian reciters like Abdul Basit and spread around the world.

If we skip from Egypt to Indonesia, we can see how the classical twentieth-century Egyptian style of recitation began to achieve dominant status in the 1990s, supplanting local styles. Anna Gade (2004) describes the Indonesian habitus of recitation in transition in this period. As the new sounds were becoming widespread, new ways of listening to the Qur'an were also being introduced. The older local style was labeled dull, sleepy, and gloomy; it connoted weak engagement with the Qur'an and poor religious knowledge. The Egyptian styles connoted correct practice, and with them came a whole new emotional system, one that had dynamic emotional modulation as a goal and strategy. This was a transitional moment in Qur'anic emotional history. New norms of performance adopted from recordings conveyed idealized affective norms of beauty, which reconstituted the ideal and instrumental aspects of Qur'anic emotion in affective, escalating engagement.

Anne Rasmussen's (2010a) more recent study of Qur'anic recitation in Indonesia focuses on a later phase in this transition. In her account, we can read how the culture of tarab had been thoroughly internalized by Qur'anic reciters and teachers in Jakarta, and we can feel their sense of longing for the sounds of the Arab world. Rasmussen describes how teachers in Indonesia's Qur'an institutes elaborated on the way that recitation should take shape, exhorting students to "read the Qur'an with Arab melodies or tunes." Through years of repetition, practice, and memorization, Indonesian reciters embodied the patterns of Arab music and learned to artfully manipulate the Arabic modes. Rasmussen's own recitation teacher would urge his students to infuse their singing with "Arab soul" and to listen to the "great singers from the Arab world: Umm Kulthum, Fayruz, Warda," describing their songs as "the music of the Qur'an" (Rasmussen 2010a, 35).

In rural Xinjiang in the early twenty-first century, I found a situation similar to that described by Gade (2004) in 1990s Indonesia: a spiritual aesthetic in transition, where local styles of recitation were gradually being supplanted by new styles. In Yantaq village, multiple styles of recitation competed and various Middle Eastern styles were inserted into contexts where one might normally expect a very different habitus of listening. In 2009, as part of the khätmä described in chapter 2, Märyäm delivered a passage of solo recitation. (See fig. 4.7.)

Where Märyäm begins in the middle of a line, the missing words are given in brackets. The lyrics under the transcription are rendered as she pronounces them. A standard Arabic transliteration of the Qur'anic text is given with the translation:

> Q25: 65–6 [Not recited: *Wa al-ladhīna yaqūlūna*] *rabbanā aṣrif 'annā 'adhāba jahannama. 'Inna 'adhābahā kāna gharāmāan. 'Innahā sā'at mustaqarrāan wa muqāmāan*
> [Those who say] Oh Lord! Avert from us the wrath of hell, for its wrath is indeed an affliction grievous. Evil indeed is it as an abode, and as a place to rest in.
> Q14: 41 *Rabbanā aghfir lī wa liwālidayya wa lilmu'uminīna yawma yaqūmu al-ḥisābu* (x3)
> Oh Lord! Cover (us) with thy forgiveness: ourselves, our parents, and (all) believers, on the day that reckoning will be established.
> Q7: 23 [Not recited: *Qālā*] *Rabbanā dhalamnā 'anfusanā wa 'in lam taghfir lanā wa tarḥamnā lanakūnanna mina al-khāsirīna*
> [They said]: Oh Lord! We have wronged our own souls: if thou forgive us not and bestow not on us thy mercy we shall certainly be lost.

Fig. 4.7. Märyäm recites the Qurʾan. Transcription from a recording made by the author in Yantaq village, 2009. Audio available here: http://www.soundislamchina.org/?p=1671.

Q7: 126 [Not recited: *Wa mā tanqimu minnā 'illā 'an 'āmannā bi'āyāti rabbinā lammā jā'atnā*] *Rabbanā 'afrigh 'alaynā ṣabrāan wa tawaffanā muslimīna*
[But thou dost wreak thy vengeance on us simply because we believed in the signs of our Lord when they reached us!] Oh Lord! Pour out on us patience and constancy, and take our souls unto thee as Muslims.

Märyäm recited in a distinctively local style. Her pronunciation of the Qur'anic Arabic was localized; she replaced "f" with "p," as is common in loan words from the Arabic into Uyghur, she did not distinguish between "dh" and "z," and she did not adhere to the rules of tajwid. Structurally, this passage of recitation was highly idiosyncratic. It was not a recitation of a full surah, or section of a surah, but a series of supplications (*du'a*) drawn from several parts of the Qur'an. Often—to the consternation of my research partner Hurriyät—she began in the middle of a line of the Qur'anic text. In terms of the khätmä, however, there is a clear logic to this choice of words: the repeated, insistent "Rabbana" is an appeal to God, and the emerging themes of sin and repentance prefigured the core meaning of the ritual. This was the point of the ritual at which the women's emotional responses began to build, even before they entered the zikr stage.

Märyäm's delivery was brisk, with a strong pulse, and largely syllabic except for three longer sections of melisma in the middle of phrases.[5] She traced a distinctive melodic arc, with each successive phrase reaching slightly higher than the previous, and toward a sustained, melismatic note, before falling again. This type of melodic arc and gradual movement toward a climax (*awaj*) in pitch and intensity, then a falling away, is familiar in regional music traditions, notably in the Central Asian *maqām* repertoires. Clearly we are in a Central Asian sound world here, and not in the realm of Arab maqām.[6] But this sound world was being challenged even within the same ritual. Toward the end of the ritual, Aynisa recited surah al Rahman in a very different style. (See fig. 4.8.)

Aynisa's rendition recognizably followed the classical twentieth-century Egyptian style. Aynisa had a sure grasp of tajwid, and her pronunciation of the Qur'anic Arabic was excellent. What was noticeably different from the local style was her use of the Arab mode *bayati* with its distinctive quarter tones, which are not a feature of Uyghur music. Bayati is a popular and important mode in Qur'anic recitation, more saturated with tarab than any other maqām. It has close connections with dhikr in the Egyptian context (Racy 2003), and it is the fundamental maqām for recitation in Indonesia (Rasmussen 2010a).

Fig. 4.8. Aynisa recites Surah al Rahman. Transcription from a recording made by the author in Yantaq village, 2009. Audio recording here: http://www.soundislamchina.org/?p=291.

What are we to make of the appearance of two different styles of recitation within one ritual? Clearly this suggests a situation of transition and change. Can we apply Frishkopf's (2009) semiotic system to the styles of Qur'anic recitation now circulating in Uyghur society? We might think it appropriate that the classical Egyptian style with its links to mystical Islam should be brought into the context of this strongly Sufi-influenced ritual in Xinjiang. But the situation was not so straightforward, as my subsequent conversations with Aynisa showed.

For Aynisa, the crucial thing was to recite according to the rules of tajwid. She spoke to me at length about the importance of proper recitation style and how it communicates the true meaning of the Qur'an. She told me, "I took a teacher, a woman from my own village. I followed her blindly for two years learning to recite the Qur'an. . . . Then I learned tajwid for six months from a *molla* from Kashgar, and I learned how to pronounce the 'dh' and the 'h,' and then I understood for what reason we say *bismillahi r-rahman ir-rahim*. . . . If you use the letters properly, then the meaning of the Qur'an is not spoiled" (Aynisa, Yantaq village, August 2009).

Correct pronunciation was important to her, but so was musical style. She also took great pleasure in listening to and imitating recordings of top reciters from the Middle East: "I learned the melody (*ahang*) from recordings (*dai*, from the Chinese). I bought them in the bazaar in Ürümchi. I just listened to them a couple of times. I like imitating people, so I pick it up easily. I am illiterate, I never went to school, but I studied the Qur'an for twelve years, so I can copy a voice when I hear it. . . . I learned this one from a recording of Sadiq Ali. He was a top student of Abdul Basit" (Aynisa, Yantaq village, August 2012).

Many such recordings were imported into Xinjiang by Pakistani traders during the 1990s and openly sold in town bazaars. Aynisa had learned her recitation of surah Al-Rahman from a recording of the Pakistani reciter Sadaqat Ali, who is admired for being one of the few Asian reciters able to perfectly reproduce the classical Egyptian style. In this remote Uyghur village, as Gade found in Indonesia some years earlier, we find a situation in which new styles of recitation, digitally transmitted from the Middle East, were entering local practice. Aynisa was faithfully reproducing the melody of a recording rather than improvising within a known modal framework, and yet her mimetic performance of the Egyptian style fitted comfortably into the ritual and elicited a strong emotional response from the gathered women.

Salafi Sounds in a Sufi Ritual?

In 2012, when I met with Aynisa again, we talked about Saudi reciters. "Ah yes," she said. "You mean Abdurahman Sudais. I've learned him too. I'll recite some for you at our next ritual." This ritual, led by Aynisa in August 2012, was performed to help a village woman who was recovering from an operation and is described in chapter 3. At its conclusion, Aynisa cleared her throat and recited surah Al-Fatiha in a slow, portentous manner, clearly imitating the Saudi style of recitation. The model for this performance, Abdul Rahman al-Sudais, was born 1960 in Riyadh, Saudi Arabia. He was the imam of the Grand Mosque in Mecca until his death in 2016 and a well-known reciter. He was also known as an ultra-conservative preacher who promoted the orthodox doctrine of Salafism in the global arena and caused widespread controversy over his public statements on women, Jews, and Shia Muslims.

Aynisa inserts into her ritual practice the sounds of both Abdul Basit and al-Sudais. If we follow Frishkopf's (2009) semiotic model, we might think it highly appropriate that the Egyptian style—with its links to mystic, Sufi-influenced modes of Islam—should be brought into the context of this ritual, which also draws on Sufi practices of zikr and sama' dance. The inclusion of al-Sudais, on the other hand, may strike us as bizarre. Here is a style linked to strongly, even violently, anti-Sufi ideology. It is a form of Islam that preaches, above all, a direct relationship with God and, as a result, is strongly opposed to the kind of ritual intercession in which these büwis were engaged.

The ritual practices of the büwis, along with other traditional practices, were frequently criticized by Uyghur revivalists. They argued that there was no Qur'anic basis for rituals such as these; they were un-Islamic innovations (*bidät*), local forms of "superstitious" (*khurapatliq*) practice, from which Islam should be purified. Why would Aynisa—a self-declared follower of the tärikät yol (the Sufi path)—draw on the Saudi style if it retained its semiotic associations with a school of Islam that directly preached against her practice? Surely this is a case of radical semantic and affective drift, a disjuncture of sounds and meanings.

Such forms of disjuncture are central to Veit Erlmann's (1999) discussion of the global imagination and its role in the production of global modernity. Erlmann argues that aesthetic regimes and systems of meaning produced in a globalized age emerge from encounters between different systems of knowledge, morality, and aesthetics. The global culture produced through these encounters is constituted by a series of shifts in the relationship between the subject, knowledge, and the real, as people shift the contexts of their knowledge and endow phenomena with significance beyond the immediate realm of their personal experience. Erlmann is primarily concerned with musical encounters between Africa and the West, but I argue that similar processes are apparent in the sounded encounters between the Islamic heartlands and those who perceive themselves to be on its periphery. As the disembodied sounds of Qur'anic recitation circulate around the globe with increasing ease and rapidity, their semiotic meanings are similarly detached and their sounds are resignified.

Modernity and Power

The arrival of these Middle Eastern recitation styles in rural Xinjiang demonstrates how wider trends in Islam were audibly penetrating remote villages on the fringes of the Islamic world and how the ways in which they were interpreted were strongly localized. Aynisa was mimetic in her practice. She absorbed and re-sounded these foreign styles in order to strengthen her religious practice, internalizing and bodying forth the power of this Other Islam.[7] Aynisa's appropriation of new styles of Qur'anic recitation was in fact very similar to the Uyghur ritual performers' adoption of printed versions of hikmät lyrics discussed in chapter 3. For her, Egyptian and Saudi styles—far from indexing opposing ideologies as Frishkopf demonstrates in Egypt—were interchangeable, and what they both indexed was a form of religious practice that was powerfully modern and linked directly to a technologized self. She told us, "Now our rituals are even stronger than before.... [T]he government doesn't like big gatherings of women, and so there are restrictions, but now we understand better than before. Our heads are like computers, more developed"[8] (Aynisa, Yantaq village, August 2009).

This discourse is strongly localized. It is in part a reaction to state policies, as religious practitioners sought to strengthen themselves morally and spiritually in the face of the increasing marginalization and criminalization that they faced at the hands of the state. But their statements also drew directly on prevalent state discourses of development and modernity, even as they deployed the sounds of religious practice that the state certainly heard as backward and detrimental to progress.

Many observers of the Islamic world have pitted supposedly tolerant and hybrid forms of local Islam against the purifying practices of reformist individuals and groups (Soares and Osella 2009). But, as we have seen, it is difficult to make a clear-cut distinction between orthodox Islam and Sufi-influenced Islam in Xinjiang. Senior religious leaders in mosques and madrassas throughout Xinjiang have been known to undertake leading roles within Sufi orders, and the Sufi orders have historically been closely tied to political power. Local ritual traditions derived from these Sufi orders provided just one strand within a broad spectrum of religious modalities that individuals could draw on, and they moved between, and even combined, these different strands of thought and practice with pragmatic flexibility.

The ritual practices of rural Uyghur women in the first decade of the twenty-first century were highly adaptable and responsive to social change, as their practitioners—even within their remote and impoverished villages—confronted and engaged with the complexities of a globalized society, but they engaged with global Islam on their own terms. For them, mimicking the sounds of Salafism did not necessarily denote an adoption of Salafi ideology. For Aynisa, as for other reciters, rather than indexing rival ideologies, what both the Egyptian and Saudi styles indexed was modernity. "Our level is very low," said Damolla of Uyghur Qur'anic recitation, echoing the prevalent Chinese state discourse of development. This sense of a "low" level of civilization and being "backward" is something that has been strongly internalized by China's minority peoples. Such phrases form a constant and uncomfortable refrain in encounters with ethnographers. As Louisa Schein (2000) notes, "In China the desirability of the modern—trumpeted as universally accessible—has become so hegemonic that it is sought after even by those constrained by the role of signifying its opposite" (164). In China's Muslim communities, the thirst for modernity is inescapably linked to a sense of exclusion or marginalization from the modernizing agenda of the state. Muslims in China are commonly portrayed as stubbornly and unreasonably resistant to state development projects, incapable of being modernized. Globally circulating revivalist forms of Islam offer them alternative pathways to civilized status, pathways to which they alone have privileged access.

Studies of changing patterns of religious faith among Hui Muslim Chinese communities have also emphasized the links between tropes of modernization and the adoption of new forms of Islam (Boyd Gillette 2000;

Hillman 2004). Although revivalists may use the language of authenticity, asserting a desire to return to the "original" Islam, the oil-rich countries of the Middle East provide powerful models of different kinds of modernity and an alternative ideological scale on which to evaluate themselves in terms of development and "spiritual civilization" (*jingshen wenming*). Revivalist narratives of Islam offer the enticing possibility of throwing off backward minority status, and they provide a new vision of community and a new set of relationships through which to define themselves in relation to other ethnic groups, to the state, and to the wider Islamic world. Aynisa was subject to the same set of pressures and possibilities. She too felt the need to make herself strong and to make herself modern, in part in response to pressure from state religious policies, in part in response to criticism of her own practice by Uyghur reformists. Cyborglike, magpielike, she mimetically absorbed and deployed foreign styles of recitation within a very local form of ritual, using them to resist backward status and to lay claim to alternative styles of modernity.

Notes

1. The elements of traditional culture and thinking that had to be eradicated in order for China to progress toward socialism: old customs, old culture, old habits, and old ideas.

2. He uses the term *tärägä* from the Arabic *tarawih*; like *khatam*, it denotes a complete reading of the Qur'an over the course of Ramadan: one *juz* (a thirtieth of the text) per night.

3. *Kharakteristik*; i.e., her religious ideological position.

4. See also Lauren E. Osborne's detailed modal analysis of Mishari Rashid Alafasy's recitation of surah al-Furqan (Osborne 2016).

5. Melisma is applied on the syllables of "*inna*," "*qarrāan*," and "*dayya*." These correspond to the indications of tajwid in the text, which prescribe emphasis at these points through the use of *shadd*.

6. See Harris (2008, chap. 4) for a discussion of melody and mode in the Twelve Muqam repertoire.

7. Compare Michael Taussig's (1993) rich discussion of mimesis and the paradox of absorbing the Other in order to stay the same.

8. Aynisa's vision echoes traditions of feminist thought pioneered in Donna Haraway's (1991) Cyborg Manifesto. Such metaphors are commonly used by Uyghurs to describe religious experience. Cindy Huang (2009) describes her encounter with Nurdur, who explains his understanding of Islam through an extended computer analogy about the body as hardware and the soul as software, and God as the engineer who puts the two together and sets them in motion.

Interlude 2

TUTIWALIDU (THEY'LL ARREST YOU)

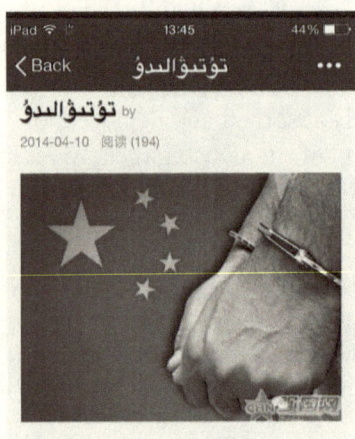

Fig. I.1. Screenshot from a WeChat feed containing the anonymous poem *"Tutiwalidu"* ("They'll arrest you").

Don't put odd things on your phone or they'll arrest you
Don't put odd things on your computer or they'll arrest you
Don't tell the truth or they'll arrest you
Don't keep books or they'll arrest you
Don't grow a beard or they'll arrest you
Don't ask people to do good deeds or they'll arrest you
Don't stop people doing wrong or they'll arrest you
Don't spend money on doing good deeds or they'll arrest you
Don't meet with the families of arrested people or they'll arrest you
Don't carry veiled women in your car or they'll arrest you
Don't pray in public or they'll arrest you
Don't listen to the recited Qur'an or they'll arrest you
There are too many things you can be arrested for

Just don't do what they don't like
Good and bad things are all in their hands

Now listen to the good news
Drink alcohol and you will *not* be arrested
Smoke and you will *not* be arrested
Visit prostitutes and you will *not* be arrested
Be corrupt and you will *not* be arrested
Cheat and you will *not* be arrested
Ignore your parents and you will *not* be arrested
Wear fashionable clothes and you will *not* be arrested
Praise them and you will *not* be arrested
Because they give you these opportunities
Report people who attend Islamic school and they will be arrested
Because they will offer you heaven
Be careful or you will spend your life in a dark cell eating steamed buns

A word from the hadith as a gift
If Allah gives you ill fortune in your destiny
All humanity cannot take that bad thing from you
If Allah gives you one good deed
All humanity cannot take that away from you
So be careful or they will arrest you.[1]

Note

1. Anonymous Uyghur-language satirical poem shared on WeChat in April 2014. Translated by Aziz Isa and Rachel Harris.

5

MOBILE ISLAM

Mediation and Circulation

The Snake-Monkey-Woman

One night in Yantaq village in summer 2012 there was a commotion in our hosts' garden. The nine-year-old daughter of the family was screaming hysterically while her mother scolded her loudly but ineffectively. The girl was refusing to go to the toilet, which lay at the end of the garden, because she was afraid that the "snake woman" might fall on her from the tree branches. Her mother complained of the girl's foolishness but asked me uneasily if such monsters might really exist. It transpired that the girl and her mother had viewed a video that morning, a meme that was circulating via the platforms Youku and WeChat right across the Uyghur community and causing a huge stir. Villagers flocked to internet cafes to watch it online and they shared it on their smartphones. It showed what appeared to be the taxidermized remains of a coiled snake, attached to the upper body and head of a monkey, and crowned with a wig of long blond hair. This object of horror was displayed on a table inside a home. The camera panned around it while hands touched it (no faces were visible) and stroked its hair. A spooky sound track of screams and pulsing synthesized beats underlined the affective impact of the video. With its digitally manipulated looped animal cries, this sound track employed familiar techniques of sound in horror films: using high frequencies to connote an unknown threat and distorting familiar sounds to create a sense of unease. The poor quality of the production only added to its aura of authenticity and its power to terrify.[1] It was particularly effective when viewed on the small screen of a smartphone. (See fig. 5.1.)

The meaning of the video was variously interpreted by people we knew in the locality, but the dominant story emerged thus: these were the

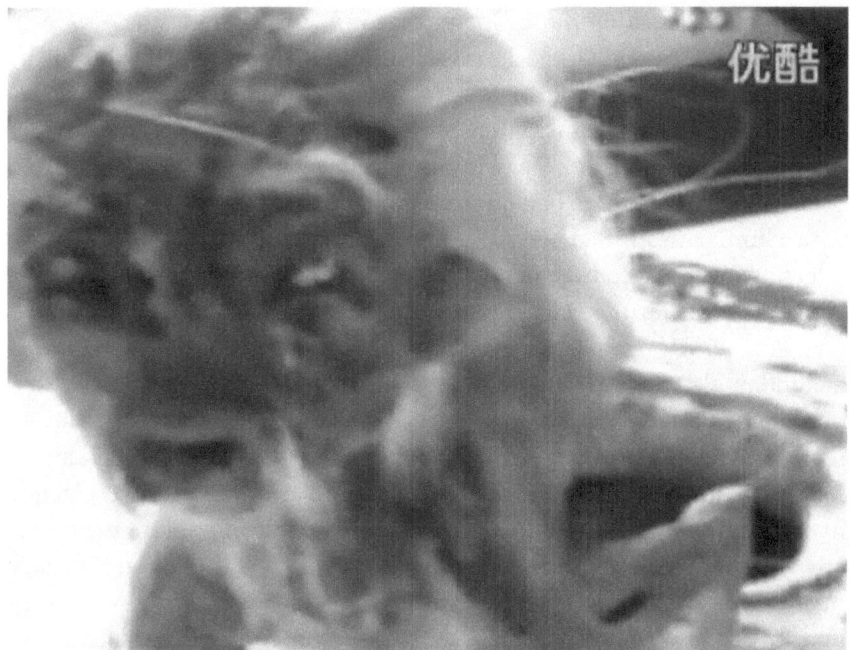

Fig. 5.1. Still from the Snake-Monkey-Woman video.

remains of a rich businesswoman from Ürümchi who was known to be fond of parties and dancing. A smartphone video of one of her parties had circulated on social media a year earlier and provoked copious disapproval from the Uyghur online community. Of particular concern to the prurient viewers was the presence of two effeminate male dancers and the fact that the women at the party had presented them with money by tucking notes into their clothing as they danced. According to rumor, the woman's husband had sent her on the hajj three times but still she wouldn't give up her bad habits. One night she came home late. Her husband asked, "What have you been doing?" She said, "I've been dancing like a snake and jumping like a monkey." The next morning he woke up to find his wife had been transformed into a snake-monkey-woman. The unfortunate man had a heart attack and died. The neighbors took the monster to the main mosque in Ürümchi, and it stayed there for several days until the government sent people to kill it by lethal injection.

My initial response to the video was to infer that it represented an attempt to police the public morality of gender identities and to discipline women by threatening those who engaged in "un-Islamic" practices such as dancing parties. But the layers of meaning that accrued around the video were quite different. Even before the video made a stir in our village, Uyghur netizens in Ürümchi were already posting online articles denouncing the snake woman as a "fake miracle." Some net-savvy individuals soon discovered that the video had originated in 2010 in Malaysia, where a "snake with a human head" had been displayed for money as a form of freak show, not in any way linked to religious ideologies. It had subsequently circulated Chinese online forums and even been the subject of a television documentary. Posts on Uyghur websites condemned the evil heart of the person who had manipulated this video, added the horror sound track, and reposted it on Uyghur sites with intent to shame Islam. They also lamented the naivety (backwardness) of the Uyghurs who believed it: "We know that Allah performed many miracles, but the ones that we find online today—the gigantic man, the girl who changed into a monkey, the pig woman—are they actually created by Allah? . . . Some people even sell these videos on the black market. These videos have such a good market that the fraudsters can't keep up with demand, but such money is haram. Our understanding of new technology is very low, so we are easily cheated."[2] By mid-August, the regional government was sufficiently alarmed to issue a news item saying that the story of the snake-monkey-woman was a fake, produced by the exile organization the World Uyghur Congress in order to incite religious extremism and separatism.[3] Uyghur netizens, on the other hand, hinted darkly that the video was actually produced by Chinese government agents who wanted to promote superstition among the Uyghurs in order to better control them.

The layers of interpretation that built up around the snake-monkey-woman provide only partial glimpses into its meanings. They attest to the complexity of the debates about Islam and Uyghur identity in this period, notions of modernity and progress, and the diversity of voices proclaiming the correct way to be a Uyghur Muslim. Gendered questions of the socially acceptable modes of behavior for Uyghur Muslim women were central to this meme. Also noteworthy is the swift response by state media, its ready attribution of this kind of online rumor to "hostile foreign forces," and the links made between separatism and religious extremism. These themes lie at the heart of the region's subsequent descent into the violence of the anti-religious-extremism campaign.

We need to listen to this item beyond the level of textual debate in order to understand more fully its potency as lived experience. The video itself was an utterance—following Davide Panagia's (2009) use of the term—entirely free from semantic meaning. We need to attend to the noisy qualities of this utterance, to think about why it was experienced so viscerally by so many Uyghur viewers and judged to be so inappropriate by elites of various political persuasions. What memories did it provoke, what connections did it make, and what trajectories did it trace through time and space? The power of the video lay in its immediate affective impact, produced through the combination of the familiar yet unnerving sound language of horror films and the possibility that the monstrous—however fake-looking—might actually be real. As with any horror film, it held a strong fascination for people we knew; it reverberated in the mind and body, and there was seductive pleasure in viewing it. A part of the video's power lay also in its openness to semantic interpretation. It was a juxtaposition of a horror film sound track and video images of a Malaysian freak show: two disparate items, free-floating on the worldwide web, with no obvious relationship either to Uyghur society or to religious belief. Only through the rumors and debates that accrued around the video did any religious meanings become attached to it.

All these issues are central to the topic of this chapter, which focuses on the circulation of religious sounds, images, and texts on social media, and in particular the rise of the social media platform WeChat. Between 2013 and 2014, WeChat flourished briefly as a space for Uyghur cultural production and mediated discourse against a backdrop of escalating violence and state intervention into religious life. In what follows, I take this WeChat discourse to be a cultural response to the growing violence and social instability of the period, which simultaneously served as a site where Uyghurs within Xinjiang and abroad negotiated what it meant to be Uyghur and what it meant to be Muslim at a time of perceived crisis. Because social media reflect and also generate popular sentiment, WeChat provides a very fruitful site to examine the interactive poetics of Uyghur identity, especially in a situation where the possibility for religious expression, and indeed expression of Uyghur identity in the public sphere, was becoming ever more tightly delimited. I pay close attention to the experience of listening to religious sounds on a smartphone, and I consider the particular sounds that conveyed experiences of collective pain and responses to the escalating violence: Qur'anic recitation, horror film sound effects, and a cappella pop.

Social Media and Religious Extremism

How did the snake-monkey-woman become a case of religious extremism? In the years after the 2009 violence in Ürümchi—the Uyghur protest against killings in Guangzhou, police intervention, riots and interethnic violence, and subsequent crackdown and mass arrests—media reports of violent local incidents became commonplace. Often these incidents culminated in the deaths of so-called Uyghur terrorists at the hands of the security forces. In the wake of the 2009 violence, a large number of young Uyghurs in Ürümchi were detained, and many Uyghur migrants from the south who had established businesses in Ürümchi returned to their hometowns. There they faced increasing surveillance and controls and ever-tightening restrictions on religious practice and belief. By 2011, such restrictions included bans on public prayer, Islamic dress, veils and beards, fasting during Ramadan, religious instruction for children, and religious gatherings like the khätmä described in chapter 2. Local police were tasked with enforcing these new rules, and many of the violent incidents reported in the Chinese press as terrorist incidents were actually sparked by heavy-handed police interventions. Particular points of conflict were the police practices of entering people's homes and forcibly removing women's veils, and breaking up religious meetings.[4]

The definition of religious extremism was deliberately broad and vague. State media frequently conflated internet memes like the snake-monkey-woman with what they termed "online jihadi propaganda." In autumn 2013, for example, a report on a new crackdown on religious media stated that "Xinjiang police were investigating 256 people for spreading 'destabilizing rumors' online.... Of those, 139 spread rumors about jihad, or Muslim holy war, or other religious ideas. More than 100 had been detained."[5] A masterly concoction of precise figures and extremely vague delineation of what "other religious ideas" might actually refer to, this report suggests that what state media referred to as extremist terrorism or jihad subsumed a far wider set of religious and political dispositions that the state regarded as threatening to stability. Also of note is the designation "spreading rumors online" as a form of religious extremism; the Xinjiang authorities seemed to fear rumors above all for the threat they posed to stability and control. In this way, the snake-monkey-woman, along with many other items of religious media circulating on Uyghur networks, became subsumed under the rubric of religious extremism and terrorism.[6]

One of the most prominent incidents designated as terrorism by Chinese media involved a car that ploughed through tourists at Tiananmen Square in 2013 before crashing into the gates of the Forbidden City, injuring thirty-eight and killing two tourists as well as the Uyghur family inside the car. Later reports suggested that the family had been in dispute with local authorities in Xinjiang over the destruction of a community-built mosque and had taken their own lives in a form of protest comparable to the earlier spate of Tibetan self-immolations (Roberts 2018; Smith Finley 2019). In her discussion of the self-immolations in Tibet that began in 2009, and the state's designation of these acts as "terrorism," Emily Yeh (2012) remarks that the linkage between terror and territory is not coincidental. Maintaining bounded spaces of territory requires the constant mobilization of threat. As Talal Asad (2007) has argued in the context of the United States' own Global War on Terror, the discourse of terror enables a redefinition of the space of violence in which the state can make bold interventions, reordering and governing everyday social relations in relation to the proclaimed state of crisis. When China declared Tibetan self-immolation to be a form of terror, it did so not because of the actual method by which the protesters chose to die or because of any possibility of harm to others, but because of the perceived threat it posed to China's territorial sovereignty over Tibet. The same logic governed the designation of terrorism in Xinjiang.

China's use of the rhetoric of terrorism in Xinjiang was directly linked to, and enabled by, the rise of this discourse in the West under the rubric of the Global War on Terror. As early as November 2001, two months after the September 11 attacks on the United States, China released a statement asserting the existence of a global network of Uyghur terrorists, supported by hostile foreign forces, which posed a major threat to China's security. The statement named Uyghur human-rights and advocacy groups as part of this terrorist network and described several earlier incidences of unrest in Xinjiang as acts of terrorism (Roberts 2018). China's discourse of religious extremism and terror has drawn on many tropes developed in the West. Arun Kundnani (2012) has noted how discussions of radicalization in the West typically exclude ascribing any causative role to the actions of Western governments or their allies. Instead, the root cause of violence is situated in individual psychological or religious journeys, largely removed from social and political circumstances, and the Islamic faith itself is viewed as the precursor for violence.[7] In Xinjiang, as I discuss in chapter 6, an equivalent process of pathologizing Uyghur faith and identity developed in state media in the post-2001 period.

In this chapter, I aim to counter these dominant narratives of terrorism and extremism by finding alternative ways of reading the circulation of sounds, images, and texts. I ask what kinds of religious sounds and ideologies were actually circulating on Uyghur social media networks in the period between 2013 and 2014, how Uyghurs consumed and interpreted the circulating media items, and what "structures of feeling" (Williams 1961; Hirschkind 2012) they conveyed. I ask why the Chinese state considered these new forms of communication and new ways of voicing religion so threatening to its control over the region and consider the impact of the state's hostility toward Islam on the development of new religious sensibilities among the Uyghurs.

Questions about the use of the internet and other forms of digital media as vehicles for religious and political mobilization have been widely addressed in the literature on Islam in the Middle East and elsewhere (Gladney 2004a; Hirschkind 2012; Ho 2010). Much of this literature has focused on the political geography of Islamic forms of knowledge and experience as it is refashioned in the context of new technologies of mediation and the weakening of the norms and institutions of traditional religious authority. Eickelman and Piscatori (2004) have argued that the spread of new media technologies has led to a fragmentation of authority in Muslim societies. With a greater diversity of people speaking about the nature of their faith on multiple media platforms, and often gaining substantial audiences, the traditional interpreters of Islam have lost their monopoly on religious authority. Whereas the Chinese state had attempted through the 1990s to maintain control of interpretations of Islamic knowledge through its strict system of training and monitoring of imams in the region's official mosques and through its periodic crackdowns on the sale of religious media, the growing use of internet and social media in the 2000s enabled the proliferation of new ideas and the development of new sensibilities, and the official imams were increasingly discredited.

As Uyghurs connected on social media, their religious experience accommodated to the architecture of the virtual environment with its specific modes of connectivity and affect. The resulting new contexts for religious experience had profound consequences for the way they learned about and experienced their faith. Together these phenomena helped to produce new structures of feeling within Uyghur society that may be best characterized as a crisis of suffering—both personally and collectively experienced—to which only Islam, in different guises, could provide a solution through its capacity to enable personal and collective transformation. For the majority, this spiritual awakening and quest for greater religious knowledge, and the projects of practice and self-discipline impelled by their new faith, were primarily personal. For some, they converged with experiences of the increasingly repressive state policies and took on a more overtly political dimension.

Religious Media in the Age of Videodiscs

The religious discourse on WeChat was rooted in the circulation of earlier forms of religious media in the region. A survey of religious videodiscs that I made in 2012 provides a snapshot of this type of consumption. A wide variety of explicitly religious videodiscs was offered for sale under the counter or in the street in bazaars in southern Xinjiang at this time. These items were enthusiastically but covertly consumed by rural women, who kept them hidden in cupboards or in chests of household linen in case of police raids on their homes, fearing that discovery would earn them a short prison sentence. The media that they contained was diverse. Some appeared to be the products of backroom commerce by opportunistic small business operators who had downloaded a seemingly random selection of Islamic music videos freely available on Chinese websites and compiled and produced them as videodiscs to sell to pious villagers. Such videodiscs could command a premium price because of the lure of the illicit.[8]

The Islamic music videos included large numbers of Arabic, Turkish, and Malaysian soft-pop-style anashid or *illahi*, predominantly with synthesized instrumental accompaniment and videos containing endless shots of waterfalls and flowers, all evidently downloaded from the mainstream Chinese equivalents of YouTube: Youku, Tudou, and 56.com. International star singers featured strongly, such as the Turkish cosmopolitan modernist Sami Yusuf; several Malaysian brother groups (a Muslim version of UK boy bands), and the veteran popular Uzbek diva Yultuz Osmanova in her religious phase, with a distinctly New Romantic take on pious performance. There were also Arab-language children's cartoons dubbed into Uyghur featuring plasticine camels explaining the meanings of the Festival of Sacrifice; an extremely poor-quality copy of the 1977 Hollywood film on the life of Mohammed, "The Message" directed by Moustapha

Fig. 5.2. Entry in a 2014 peasant art competition, part of the anti-religious-extremism campaign in Xinjiang, illustrating the dangers of listening to illegal religious media.

Akkad; and a Xinjiang government information video for pilgrims about to embark on the hajj. This was mainstream fare, publicly available and often government-sanctioned religious information and entertainment, and yet the possession of such videodiscs by Uyghurs would increasingly be figured as a criminal act and a sign of religious extremism. (See fig. 5.2.)

Other productions were equally diverse in geographical origin but seemed to be more consistent exercises in a form of religious ideology that drew on eschatological themes of suffering, death, judgment, and fear of God in order in to espouse the virtues of a pious lifestyle. The religious dispositions they promoted aligned closely with the themes of the hikmät sung poetry discussed in chapter 3. One videodisc, *Ölüm* (Death), whose cover depicted two kneeling skeletons, included a rather well produced video apparently originating in Jordan, which featured the death of a sinful young man at the hands of the angel Azra'il, portrayed by an actor in black robes holding scythe and chains. Like many other videos, it drew on classic tropes of horror film: the camera in the role of the approaching menace, and the tight close-up on the terrified victim's face. Once the young sinner is dispatched, the viewer watches with morbid fascination through the eyes of his ghost the ritual preparation and burial of his body, the grief of his relatives, and his final descent into the flames of hell. The sound track combined Qur'anic recitation with pulsing deep-pitched strings familiar from mainstream horror films. This sat alongside a video produced by the Turkish cult leader and creationist, Adnan Otkar (Harun Yahya), which juxtaposed shots of the solar system with sped-up simulations of the human aging process, set to a synthesized orchestral sound track reminiscent of 1980s disaster movies. Some videos were notable for the way they evidenced processes of transnational image remediation, remixing, and overdubbing. Several included video footage apparently of Saudi origin, showing hospital deathbeds and gruesome corpses overlaid by Qur'anic recitation and earnest sermons delivered in Uzbek and Uyghur.

Writing on the consumption of religious media in the Egyptian Islamic counterpublic, Charles Hirschkind (2006) also comments on the use of audio and visual tropes drawn directly from the language of horror films, asking whether we should feel surprise at such a juxtaposition of the affective language of Hollywood with that of the holy Qur'an. He argues that fear of the fires of hell is a religious virtue, and one of the primary tasks of the sermon is to dwell on death, rooting it in the sensory experience of the pious listener. But cassette sermons are not only religious but also commercial entities; they are rooted in popular culture, and they employ the seductive and marketable sounds and images of horror films because death sells. Uyghurs shared this popular fascination with death and judgment and actively sought out media items that provided the affective thrill of the realization of the power of the Almighty, as we can see from the widespread consumption of media items like *Ölüm* and the snake-monkey-woman.

This diverse and somewhat random collection of religious media popular with Uyghur village women in 2012 exemplifies the processes of decontextualization and abstraction often remarked on in discussions of digitally mediated productions, juxtaposing as it did a wide range of ideological and affective relationships with religious faith. It also suggests that, although some productions clearly sought to promote particular forms of Islam, Uyghurs who consumed them were not using religious media in a dogmatic way to pursue specific ideologies but were primarily seeking affective religious experiences. The affective language of horror—drawn from the sound tracks and imagery of globalized popular cinema and redirected as a way to promote the virtues of piety—was prominent among the experiences they sought. Many of these themes remained constant within the new sphere of social media, and they flourished within a context of greater connectivity, immediacy, and anonymity.

The Move to Social Media

In January 2011, the Chinese technology giant Tencent launched the smartphone app WeChat (Weixin in Chinese). Its widespread use in China was enabled by state infrastructure of third-generation networks that were established between 2010 and 2011. By 2013 it had become the media of choice for some 600 million users worldwide, 500 million of them within China. Among Uyghur users too WeChat (or Ündidar as it was called in Uyghur) became an essential communication tool. Between 2013 and 2014 almost every Uyghur we knew—both inside Xinjiang and in the diaspora—was using this app, often several times a day. They used it to chat with their friends and to participate in online groups or circles, sharing short audio messages, text, images, audio and video files, and links to other media platforms such as the US-based Facebook and YouTube and the Chinese sites Youku and Tudou. Younger people were more regular and prolific users, but older people also participated, usually as a way of keeping in touch with family members. During this period, there was a steady rise in the circulation of Islamic images, audio-video files, audio messages, and text discussion. All this communication proceeded for more than a year with little overt censorship until the Xinjiang authorities apparently caught up with the new technology and implemented a major crackdown in summer 2014. This social media platform enabled a brief window in time when we were able to sit outside Xinjiang and listen in on very open conversations about life, religion, and politics. It provided a unique snapshot of the rapidly changing and multifaceted nature of Islam in Uyghur society in this period of escalating state violence and sanctions against Islamic practice, just before the total ban on sharing religious media.

The WeChat platform provided particular affordances for the creation of new forms of association specific to its capabilities as a media platform. It offered a choice between one-to-one messaging, closed circles, and posting to all friends. People could share text messages and images including their own photos, links, and emoticons. They could record and share their own audio messages and videos and could also maintain a semipublic profile, posting regular personal status updates in order to craft an online persona. A highly flexible platform, it ranged between the intimate (especially in its capability for voice messaging) and the public. It differed from the other important platform in China, Weibo, chiefly in the fact that it was a closed-network form of communication, but the sense of privacy and intimacy that it encouraged was illusory: both platforms were monitored by the authorities (Byler 2016), and the consumption and sharing of religious media would subsequently become one of the principal signs of extremism that would condemn Uyghurs to a spell in a reeducation camp.

The term "small media" first developed in opposition to "mass media" to describe forms of media technology such as audiocassettes whose circulation is not centrally controlled or directed (Manuel 1993; Sreberny and Mohammadi 1994). Even though WeChat is now used by hundreds of millions of people, understanding it as a form of small media helps to focus on the way it can reflect, reinforce, and amplify individual and local realities and concerns. Media platforms like WeChat provide situated agency, allowing users to creatively engage with the challenges of daily life, to explore questions of faith and identity, and to find ways of dealing with political realities. They also provide particular affordances for the creation of community or social movements specific to their capabilities as media platforms (Tufekci 2017). Dorothea Schulz (2006; 2012) has noted how that this kind of small media stretch the boundaries of the audience and introduce new senses of community, so that locality is increasingly defined by circulation. Particularly relevant to this characteristic of small media was WeChat's feature of "friend circles" (*pengyouquan*); semiprivate networks that might consist of Uyghurs living within Xinjiang as well as friends, family, or new virtual acquaintances living in Los Angeles, Paris, Istanbul, or Shanghai. Within these circles, people could share links and files originating from a wide range of sources, and they could comment on them, either by text or in voice messages.

Mediated Sound and Religious Experience

Much writing in the anthropology of Islam has focused on the ways in which mediated sounds and images accessed by Muslims via social media influence the affective experience of faith. The question concerns practices of self-fashioning (Mahmood 2005), and it concerns the geographies of forms of religious knowledge and experience as they are refashioned in the context of new technologies. Accessing religious media in this way—listening to sermons and Qur'anic recitation, sharing exhortations to self-improvement—has become a part of daily practice for millions of Muslims in diverse parts of the world, part of a complex ethical and political project that promotes social responsibility, pious deportment, and devotional practice. These practices, as we saw in chapter 4, are not generally about direct forms of dissent or protest; rather, they entail and enable, in Michael Warner's (2002) influential formulation, the creation of new kinds of publics.

Many of the forms through which religious experiences and ideologies are shared are not text-based; often, the most powerful mediated religious experiences come through images and sound. The media practices that have underpinned the formation of new Muslim publics are not simply practices of exchanging ideas and opinions, they also enable shared sensory experiences: the cathartic response to a recording of Qur'anic recitation, the sense of awe provoked by listening to a sermon, or thrill at the beauty of a sung anashid. These sensory experiences are key to the transformation of the lives they mediate. Hirschkind (2006) lays emphasis on listening practices, arguing that recorded vocal performances "create the sensory conditions of an emergent ethical and political lifeworld" (8). Mediated listening practices like listening to sermons on YouTube shape new forms of religious sociality and shape religious structures of affect (Hirschkind 2012). Writing on the use of recorded sermons by charismatic sheikhs in Mali, Dorothea Schulz (2006) also focuses our attention on sound, arguing that media technologies that privilege the experience of sound address and simultaneously create communities of joint spiritual experience: "The specific capacities of particular media technologies to translate religious experience come out clearly in the ways many listeners comment on their listening experiences. For instance, they often liken the swiftness and immediacy of the sound of the spoken word to the sense of being bound tightly together and to the intimate atmosphere they experience during collective worship" (220). This facility of social media for creating powerful affective experiences of community that breach the spatial boundaries of state territory, linking Uyghurs in Xinjiang with Uyghurs in the diaspora and connecting them with other Muslims across the globe, was undoubtedly a factor in the state's designation of sharing and listening to religious media as a form of terrorism.

As Warner (2002) notes, some publics may be more public than others. Whereas the Islamic revival in Egypt was marked by the introduction of cassette sermons into shared taxis or the sounds of the recited Qur'an into cafes, audibly reshaping Cairo's public spaces, Uyghur consumption and sharing of religious media during this period became increasingly muted and furtive. The new Islamic soundscapes were contingent and fleeting.

Even in 2014, Uyghur taxi drivers might listen to recorded sermons in their taxis, but only if they were sure that their passengers shared their religious beliefs. Groups of friends continued to meet to listen to religious teachings in the relatively safe, semiprivate spaces of upstairs rooms of restaurants, but they were wary of speaking in front of strangers.[9]

Anthropologist Cindy Huang (2009) describes the consumption of religious media by one of her informants in Ürümchi in the early 2000s. When she was at home, Peride performed her daily prayers and surrounded herself with religious media. When she was working (as a shop assistant), she rarely mentioned religion, even with friends with whom it might be a natural topic of conversation. This was obviously linked to the ongoing campaigns that made people wary of appearing overly religious in public, but it also reflected a spatial division between inside and outside, a division between two different sensory worlds: inside was where Peride cultivated her faith, outside was not. Such subterranean listening practices and their particular entwining of sound and subject are increasingly common in the modern sensory landscape, especially under conditions of tight state control. Since 2009 in Xinjiang, as the anti-religious-extremism campaign tightened its hold, public expression of religious faith became too sensitive for the public sphere, but the sphere of social media gave people an illusory sense of privacy, a sense of speaking within a group of intimate friends. In this sphere, emerging forms of religiosity and new forms of affective connection flourished.

The religious media circulating during this period on Ündidar (Uyghur language WeChat) was diverse, revealing a wide range of religious sensibilities and ongoing debates on what constitutes true Islam and how to be a good Muslim. As I discussed in chapter 4, many people shared recordings of Qur'anic recitation and commented on the beauty of the sound of the recited text. The majority of postings promoted, through a range of images and text and audio files the values of daily prayer, modesty, and charity as part of an ideal Muslim lifestyle. The circulation of these posts was often transnational. One circle, for example, included people from Kashgar, Ürümchi, Ghulja, Beijing, Guangzhou, Kazakhstan, Saudi Arabia, Turkey, Dubai, the United States, and Europe. Participants were involved in raising money for the poor and sick in southern Xinjiang, and they frequently shared disturbing images of injured and sick children, along with telephone numbers and bank-account details for contributions. Such charitable practices would soon be officially designated as a sign of extremism.

Fig. 5.3. Screenshot from a WeChat feed: "Ramadan, don't end too soon."

Many women posted daily images and short texts promoting idealized notions of Muslim womanhood, piety, and self-restraint. One educated woman we followed, for example, posted regularly in four languages. On just one day, her feed included a children's poem in Uyghur Latin script, a short text in Chinese reading, "The darker the road, the brighter the light," and another in the Uyghur Arabic script: "Ramadan, don't end too soon. I wish for my sins to be taken away. Please take my sins away with you" (fig. 5.3). Another woman posted a series of hikmät in Uyghur Arabic, accompanied by large bunches of roses:[10]

> In this life, full of complications, you don't know which way to turn.
> The heart first adapts to its environment, and then it begins to love others.
> In this short, impermanent life, when you desire a stylish home, don't forget the beautiful palace waiting for you in heaven.
> One who has broken their arm knows how another person's broken arm feels.
> Choose your friends wisely and live happily. Choose the right spouse and live happily forever.

This kind of pious homily, designed to support projects of self-reform, was by far the most widespread style of expression, evident in numerous posts on Ündidar. Alongside these texts, the women exchanged links to songs and videos: an English-language Ramadan song recorded by the Swedish Muslim singer, Maher Zain, and uploaded onto Youku; an Uzbek pop music video, "Dear Heartless Father" (*Dilsiz Otajon*).

These circulating texts, images, and recordings, along with the proliferation of likes and emojis they provoked, recall Saba Mahmood's (2005) discussion of the cultivation of pious sensibilities among Egyptian women's sermon groups. In that movement, forms of bodily practice such as daily prayers, fasting, and learning to recite the Qur'an are bodily means to cultivate virtue, the outcome of their professed desire to be close to God. Such bodily practice is part of the larger project of becoming a pious Muslim in the entirety of one's life and a means of training and realizing that pious self. It is a kind of ethical self-formation, requiring constant work on the self—strengthening the desire to pray or to recite—and constant vigilance to hone the moral capacities in order to please God. As I discussed in chapter 3, this economy of bodily and moral cultivation had taken a powerful hold among Uyghur women and men in Xinjiang and in the diaspora, and they used Ündidar as a medium of solidarity and mutual support in their endeavors.

In addition to texts and images, many audio files containing religious sermons (*täbligh*) circulated on WeChat. The sermons typically focused on orthopraxy and pious living, with a particular focus on gender. Like the snake-monkey-woman, they often referred to miraculous transformations, and they often connected directly to forms of religious expression that might be termed traditional or local but that—as I have argued throughout this book—were thoroughly integrated into the global circulation of sounds and meanings. A link shared in 2013, for example, with the title "Ghost Sermon" (*jin täbligh*),[11] led to an hour-long audio file that had been accessed (at the time of viewing) by more than 280,000 users. It took the form of a smartphone recording made by a group of young men who were visiting a holy woman, a village *bakhshi* who had the reputation of being possessed by the spirit of an unnamed Muslim prophet. In the recording, the men can first be heard approaching her and asking for religious instruction. The men respond to her highly charged preaching with emotional exclamations while she scolds them in a high-pitched, increasingly excited voice:

> I will tell you one miracle. That girl over there is called Hayrinisa. She can only speak with her husband, not with anyone else. She can talk to women but not to any man. That is Allah's miracle. [Men's voices: Ya Allah! Ya Rabi!]

She is dumb. She can only talk to her husband, not to another man. You must all follow Allah! You have committed many sins. [Men cry, Allah!] ... Now so many ghosts have accepted Islam, and what are you doing? Fighting? Making money? You can't take it to the grave.... Allah didn't create you to make money. He created you to pray. Allah gave you a great opportunity when he brought you to this place to change your lives. Cry some more! Cry more! [Men sobbing, Bismillah, Ya Allah!][12]

This is a form of Islam very much in tune with the religious sensibilities expressed through the hikmät performed by rural Uyghurs in religious gatherings and discussed in chapter 3: miracle-laden, emotionally saturated, with an emphasis on the need to prepare for the Day of Judgment, the transformative potential of prayer and—as we found repeatedly in these religious media items—the importance of women's modesty. The audio recording of this ghost sermon also circulated on videodisc, and families and friends listened to it together in the privacy of their homes as an emotional affirmation of faith, taking the affective mediated sounds as proof of the existence of God, miracles, and ghosts, much in the same way that people accessed the video of the snake-monkey-woman discussed earlier.

Violence and Rumors

In 2013 and 2014, a deepening crisis took hold of the region. During this period, close to a hundred violent local incidents were reported by China's state media across southern Xinjiang (Szadziewski and Fay 2015). Most of the reported incidents involved Uyghur deaths, and they were represented as terrorist incidents by Chinese media, although, as I discussed at the beginning of this chapter, many of the confrontations were actually sparked by aggressive policing. By 2014, as the situation in Xinjiang deteriorated, a small number of these violent incidents did appear to be taking the form of premeditated, organized violence aimed at civilians. They included the Kunming train station knife attack in March 2014 that left 29 dead and 130 injured, and the Ürümchi market attack in May 2014, when two cars plowed through a busy marketplace, killing 43 and injuring more than 90.[13] The government used these incidents to justify still greater restrictions on Islam—which was now figured as the root cause of violence—and sanctioned increasingly violent methods to control the Muslim population of Xinjiang. Uyghurs on Ündidar began to comment on the intensifying anti-religious-extremism campaign and the daily experience of state violence. Soon after the Ürümchi market attack, one woman posted an audio message on her WeChat feed: "Every time I go to work it seems like everyone is looking at me like I am the enemy. You can't condemn a whole nation for the actions of a few."[14]

The satirical poem posted on WeChat "You'll Be Arrested" (*Tutiwaldiu*), translated in full in interlude 2, lists a seemingly comically bizarre set of reasons for being arrested, but in fact all were included in the official lists of signs of religious extremism.[15] Even refusing alcohol or cigarettes would soon become a valid reason for detention. Listed in this way, the poem perfectly clarifies that the real target of the campaign was not extremism but the practices of everyday Islam. The final lines of the poem refer to the sense of helplessness experienced by many Uyghurs in the face of this massive mobilization of state resources against them ("we are in their hands") and the disorientation they experienced in the face of the mushrooming and often incomprehensible regulations. Its message is clear: the campaign's true target is normal moral behavior for Uyghurs. It provides a powerful religious-based message of resistance against the campaign: do not be tempted to submit to this perversion of morality, it warns, for the only true rewards and punishments are those given by God.

The poem explicitly contrasts the norms of religious morality with the norms of civic behavior enforced by the Xinjiang security forces. If the authorities were situating Islam as the source of violence, Uyghurs were not slow to situate the authorities as the source of injustice and oppression. One user directly appealed to Uyghur police officers: "Warning! If you are a policeman and see a veiled woman, try to ignore her. They are not robbers but defenders of religion. If you are an assistant policeman in the countryside, stop torturing people who have no ID cards because their ancestors have lived here for generations; they are the owners of this land"[16] (see fig. 5.4).

One of the most serious incidents of this period encompassed a series of violent confrontations in Yarkand county in southern Xinjiang in July 2014. Chinese state media reported that ninety-six people were killed in riots that erupted after Uyghur "terrorists" attacked a police station and the authorities reacted with "a resolute crackdown to eradicate terrorists." The violence began with a police raid on an "illegal religious gathering" by a group of village women. We may assume that this was a group of büwis holding a khätmä like that described in chapter 2. Protests by the villagers after the raid led to further police violence. The World Uyghur Congress, basing its information on anonymous sources within the region, claimed

Fig. 5.4. Screenshot from a WeChat feed: "Warning! If you are a policeman and see a veiled woman, try to ignore her."

that the Chinese security forces had applied indiscriminate use of force against peaceful demonstrators and committed massive extrajudicial killings, causing possibly three thousand civilian deaths through the shooting of protesters, bombing of their villages, and further shootings in house-to-house searches.[17] The actual events are still contested. The local authorities imposed an almost total information lockdown in the wake of the violence. Internet access in Yarkand was cut off, and warnings against "spreading rumors" about the events were issued to local people. Even so, one detailed and impassioned Uyghur-language account quickly appeared on the US-based Boxun website:

> Compatriots! Our country is in an abyss of suffering. Please pass our words on to the world. We are too helpless. On July 28, in Number 14, 15, and 16 villages in Elishku Township, Yarkand County, village women gathered to recite

passages from the Qur'an on the last night of the holy month of Ramadan. There were 45 women altogether. The village men were at the mosque. Chinese government soldiers and police came to the place where the women were praying with their children and began shooting them. More than 50 people were killed. When the men came back the soldiers and police were gone. The furious men carried the corpses to the police station and were arrested for attempting to attack a police station. That night the village imam drove to three or four neighboring villages announcing, "Our women and children were slaughtered, can we continue to stand idly by? Where is our faith? This is holy war!" When the authorities heard about this, they dispatched more soldiers and there was another bloodbath.[18]

Därd (Pain, Suffering)

Baqsam bu jahangha hämmidä därd-u äläm bar,
Här adämning könglidä ming qayghu ghäm bar.
Ghämsiz kishini tapsa bolurmu, kishi izläp,
Bu päyki dilim äytadur, ghämsiz kishi kim bar?

When I look at this world, I find everyone has pain and suffering,
Every person has a thousand sorrows in his heart.
Can I find a person without grief? Seeking someone,
My sorrowful heart says, who is without grief?[19]

Uyghur religious, poetic, and musical traditions are thoroughly drenched in the perception—rooted in philosophical traditions of Sufism—of the universality of suffering and pain. Suffering is inherent in the human condition, a product of human separation (*firaq*) from the divine. Only the dissolving of self into the divine (*fanā'*) can end this mortal condition. A fundamental image within the Central Asian ghazal tradition is that of the dervish (*ashiq*) as wandering beggar, insane with love, pursuing only his quest for union with the Divine. Extensive description is lavished on the dervish/lover's suffering and anguish because of his separation from, or the cruelties of, his beloved (Light 2008), drawing on a rich vocabulary of pain: *därd, äläm, ghäm, häsrät*. Listening to this type of pain-saturated poetry performed in popular sung form and accompanied by dancing at community gatherings (*mäshräps*) is a regular and pleasurable experience for many Uyghurs.

By the mid-twentieth century, a new literary formulation of pain and suffering had emerged in Uyghur culture, one colored by modern nationalist sentiment. This gloomy nationalism, as I have characterized it elsewhere

(Harris 2012), is encapsulated in writings by the Uyghur historian and novelist Abdurehim Ötkür, who was imprisoned during the Cultural Revolution but went on to publish a series of highly influential historical novels. A sung version of one of his poems, performed at a private party and captured on smartphone, circulated widely on Uyghur social media networks in the aftermath of the 2009 Ürümchi violence:

> Qäläm sundi äläm äzdi nazuq dilimni,
> Shamal darip kekäsh qildi bulbul tilimni . . .
> Kündä teshwish kündä äläm kündä därd-u-ghäm.
> Därdimni äytäy disäm anglagha dana yoq.
>
> My pen is broken, my fragile heart is oppressed,
> A cold wind has made hoarse my nightingale voice . . .
> Daily confusion, daily suffering, daily pain and misery.
> If I say I will tell of my pain, there is no one to listen. (Harris 2012, 469)

This narrative of a Uyghur nation in pain assumed a set of power relations that fixed the Chinese state in the role of oppressor and the Uyghur nation in the role of the oppressed. The fetishization of pain as a key trope of subaltern politics resonates in the politics of minority identity in China (Bulag 2000). In Wendy Brown's (1995) formulation, subaltern subjects become invested in the wound, so that the wound comes to stand for identity itself: a transformation that fetishizes the wound and cuts it off from history, creating something that "is" rather than something that happened in time and space. (See also Ahmed 2004.) Uyghur national identity in the late twentieth century, expressed in oblique metaphors in the sphere of literature and popular song, became deeply invested in the wound (Smith 2007; Smith Finley 2013). In the Ündidar discourse of 2013–14, the narrative of national suffering took on a new religious aspect in some of the recorded sermons that circulated on these networks, as in this audio file shared in June 2013:

> On the Day of Judgment, Allah will open the doors of hell to the nation who forgets him. Allah will punish the nation who does not follow him. If he loves you, then he will tell you that he is punishing you. If he does not love you, then he will not tell you, and you will not understand you are being punished, just like us. We are under Allah's punishment now. We are like slaves under the oppressive (*zalim*) Communist regime. When will the people of this nation wake up and open their eyes, hold the holy book in their hands, and restore their decency? When will they restore their ideals (*wijdan*)? When will our girls protect their modesty (*ipät numus*)? Only then will great Allah give our nation victory.[20]

This recorded sermon links the oppression of the Uyghur nation under an atheist regime directly to a national failure to follow correct Islamic practice. The responsibility for national suffering is internalized and linked to everyday practices, including drinking alcohol and listening to music. A failure to observe the proper standards of women's modesty is also a key feature in the list of the Uyghur nation's shortcomings. If the goal here is national independence, then that can be achieved only through the reform of religious behavior. If we attend to the experience of listening to this recording, we may note that the sermon is delivered in a subdued but insistent style by a youthful, educated male voice. Also immediately obvious is the heavy use of reverb, a style that indexes recorded sermons from Saudi Arabia to Afghanistan, which has been linked to the sound acoustic of the massive Saudi mosques, whence reformist styles of Islam first emerged (Frishkopf 2009). The style is intended to underline the seriousness and weightiness of the words.

Sacrifice

The combination of this nationalist sense of pain with new religious sensibilities was manifest in other forms of sounded expression that circulated on social media. One was a smartphone video of a young woman singing a cover version of a popular song released by the well-known Kazakhstan-based Uyghur singer Saniyäm Ismayil, called My Name is Uyghur Girl (*Mening Ismim Uyghur Qizi*). Saniyäm's original song was a catchy waltz number, and it was an absolutely mainstream Uyghur folk-pop production complete with keyboards, folk instruments, and a catchy beat. It expressed the singer's emotional reunion with her family roots in southern Xinjiang, and it became a minor hit after she performed it in public concerts in Xinjiang in 2014. The cover version posted by the anonymous young woman on social media made several subtle changes that radically transformed the meaning and the emotional impact of the song. Saniyäm had worn a dress of brightly colored atlas silk, and her video featured traditional dancing and festivities; in contrast, the young woman in the new video was conservatively veiled in black and sat in front of a sky-blue background, on which were the white star and sickle moon of the banned East Turkistan flag: symbol of the Uyghur independence movement. Where Saniyäm sang of the "melodies" (*näghmä nawasi*) that flowed through Uyghur veins, the new version spoke of Uyghur blood (*Uyghurning qeni*). Where the original sang of the endless songs (*nakhsha sadasi*) of the Uyghur people, the new version praised their heroic spirit (*jengiwar rohi*). The final line of the original, "I love you, my beautiful Uyghur people," became "For your freedom I will be a flower garden," situating the performance firmly in the sphere of a Uyghur liberation struggle:

My name is Uyghur girl.	*Mening ismim Uyghur qizi.*
Uyghur blood flows through my veins.	*Tömürümdä aqudur Uyghurning qeni.*
In my soul and in my blood	*Dilimda bar, qenimda bar*
Is the endless heroic spirit of the Uyghurs.	*Uyghurumning tügümäs jengiwar rohi.*
Wherever I go, wherever I stay,	*Nägä baray, nädä turay,*
No one has the warm face of the Uyghurs.	*Hichkimdä yoq Uyghurning illiq chiray.*
For your sake I will sacrifice myself.	*Sening üchün qurban bolay.*
For your freedom I will be a flower garden.	*Ärkinliking üchün män gulkhaning bolay.*

The style of vocal production also set the new version apart. Although Saniyäm sang in the established professional Uyghur folk style, with a loud, slightly nasal delivery, melismatic and full of ethnic flavor (*puraq*), the new version was deliberately plain, quiet, and intimate, a breathy pop style designed to be delivered directly to the ear via smartphone. The young woman in the video had excised all references to music from the text, avoided instrumental accompaniment, and reformulated her performance in line with new pious styles of production that were circulating transnationally. In its production, singing style, and visual message, the video was clearly linked to a new body of musical production then beginning to circulate on Uyghur social media: anashid. Unless one knew the original, one would hardly guess that it was a direct theft from mainstream Uyghur popular music production.

Examples like this demonstrate how the mediated items circulating on social media were simultaneously imbued with new religious sensibilities and directly responsive to the current political realities; they reached out to new globalized styles of religious expression and they were deeply rooted in earlier forms of Uyghur cultural expression. Saniyäm Ismayil's emotional return to her hometown continued to have resonance with the young people producing these new kinds of song, but by discarding the old musical and performative style, they took the older nationalist cultural forms and turned them into something new. The established forms of cultural intimacy and the familiar melodies that carried them had enduring affective power. Translated into a new style of affective vocal production, they helped to create a new set of religious and political dispositions and a new Uyghur Muslim counterpublic.

Home-produced music videos like Saniyäm's provide a bridge between earlier forms of Uyghur nationalist sentiment and the emerging forms of religious and political expression. The song's emphasis on the nation is completely mainstream in Uyghur pop, rooted in Soviet and Chinese nationalities policies of the twentieth century. It is noteworthy that the line "For your sake I will sacrifice myself" is part of the original song, a formula rooted in the revolutionary discourse of twentieth-century China, endlessly reproduced and normalized in films and songs. In other audio media circulating online, the trope of sacrifice took on a new set of meanings. The media circulating on Ündidar in 2013–14 also included a number of sung anashid that sought to create empathetic bonds between listeners and an imagined community of mujahidin fighters and promoted the virtues of a liberation struggle that was increasingly being called a holy war, or jihad.

> Letter to Mother (*Anamgha yezilghan khät*)[21]
> [Spoken]: In order to fulfill my obligation to Allah to protect his religion, I have betrayed you by leaving you. I will probably be accepted and martyred. Please forgive me, and be assured that we will meet again in heaven. Dear mother of a mujahid, you are not alone. So many mothers have now sent their sons to the front line, and they are praying for us now. Never feel regret. This is not a real separation. The real separation is the choice between heaven and hell. You made us men. We have chosen this path to protect the dignity of our mothers and sisters, and to kill the unbelievers. With this letter I ask for consent from the mothers who send their sons to jihad.
>
> [Sung]: If someone says you can live for a hundred years as a rabbit,
> I reply, I wish to live for one day as a tiger.
> Please, mother, understand that your son is now a mujahid,
> I must be brave in spirit.
> The rocks and stones will be my blanket.
> As long as I live I will continue to do jihad.
> Pray to Allah for us.
> I will be happy to die on the battlefield as a mujahid.
> Maybe someday you will hear a quiet voice.
> If that voice says that your son has died,
> Mother, then your son is living joyfully in heaven.
> Never doubt that the martyrs
> Will find joy in heaven.

This powerfully affective *nashid* circulated in audio and video versions across the Uyghur diaspora and within Xinjiang, on various media platforms including Facebook and YouTube, and we found it being shared on Ündidar groups in 2013. The recording featured a young male spoken voice, heavy with sincerity and reverberation, addressing the broad constituency of Uyghur mothers, followed by a sung nashid performed by the same solo voice. The song was performed in the same quiet and intimate, breathy pop style as the young woman's smartphone video discussed earlier. Again, it was not accompanied by musical instruments, and so in orthodox interpretations could be accepted as a religiously permissible form of vocal expression. With its youthful pop voice, repeated falling melodic lines, and use of vocal counterpoint, in style it was clearly linked to the transnational sound world of Islamic anashid. The concerns expressed in the accompanying video, however, which featured footage of the 2009 Ürümchi violence and the subsequent police crackdown, were local: the bitter perception of Chinese colonization and state violence against Uyghurs. The images of the heavily armed mujahidin, and video footage of groups of armed men undergoing military training in a spacious and verdant central Asian mountain landscape, provided contrasting seductive images of freedom and power.

If the sermon discussed earlier developed the trope of suffering as the Uyghur national identity, this nashid offered a solution to the painful reality in the religious purity, brotherhood, and sacrifice of the mujahidin. These most radical examples of the new sensibilities circulating on social media were generally shared by the youngest and least well educated individuals active on WeChat: the most alienated, with the least to lose. It is important to note that, rather than any explicit engagement with the ideology they contained, the vast majority of young people accessing this material were experimenting with thrill of the illicit images and ideas and the affective impact of the musical experiences that they provided. Such media items offered fantasies of masculinity, and on WeChat feeds they were often juxtaposed with glamorous images of Lamborghinis and Porsches and comments about the unfortunate and un-Islamic assertiveness of contemporary young Uyghur women.

Traditional anashid—sung poetry praising Allah—have a long history and a wide geographical reach across the Muslim world. Today, established recording industries across the Middle East and South East Asia cater to a significant subculture of listeners who consume local popular styles of anashid. The styles are often linked to modern, reformist styles of Islam but are not overtly political or radical (Pieslak 2015; Rasmussen 2010b). In Turkey, new styles of popular religious song called anashid played a significant role in creating the new aesthetic and ethical conditions that led to the rise of the Turkish Islamist movement under Erdoğan (Stokes 2013; 2016). Examples like this Uyghur-language "Letter to Mother" belong to a subgenre of politically radical anashid that can be traced to the late 1970s and the period of violent struggle between Arab Islamist groups and governments in Syria and Egypt. Here, anashid formed an important aspect of the Islamist cultural offensive and were used to reach new youth audiences and to inspire them to join the armed struggle (Said 2012).

Uyghurs had been exposed to styles of political anashid since they were first deployed by the Afghan mujahidin who fought against the Soviets: a conflict joined by a small number of Uyghurs in the 1990s. Audio recordings of sung religious poetry, locally called *taranas*, were circulated by the Taliban (Baily 2001), first by cassette and more recently by social media; they glorified the mujahidin and promoted the necessity of jihad. The poetry and musical style of Taliban taranas was clearly rooted in local expressive traditions. They drew on Afghan cultural identifiers and historical memories to present a nationalist message of resistance and heroism. Their repetitive musical refrains, rooted in Pashtun folk song, drove home these forms of cultural intimacy with affective force (Johnson and Waheed 2011).

Anashid have been used as sound tracks for videos produced by Hamas, Fatah, and Hezbollah in the context of the Palestinian struggle (McDonald 2013) and by Da'esh to accompany videos depicting their victories in battle or the execution of hostages (Pieslak 2009; 2015). In contrast with the local sounds of the Taliban taranas, the contemporary anashid developed in Palestine and Iraq are more recognizably rooted in the globalized musical language of pop. Jonathan Pieslak (2015) notes the common use of a cappella song style, vocal harmonies, and arrangements in Al Qaeda anashid used in the Iraq war. The use of a cappella singing is in part a strategy to escape the morally dubious sphere of music. The genre's reliance on the unaccompanied voice aligns it with core sounded Islamic practices, but in these contemporary mediated anashid the style of vocalization is radically different from that of the recited Qur'an. There is no hint of tajwid here. Gone is the nasality and melisma of Qur'anic recitation. These productions draw instead on the world of pop, especially the breathy intimacy of the sentimental pop ballad, indexing the listening experience of teenagers worldwide. As Pieslak argues, Al Qaeda's anashid eschew musical instruments in order to escape problematic associations with music, but they are constructed as musical works, and their production quality and style draw directly on the technologies and the values developed within the music industry. Their carefully crafted sonic texture draws on techniques of reverb, delay, and various digitally manipulated effects familiar to listeners from the world of pop music production, with the aim of increasing the affective listening experience and thus increasing the impact of the message.

According to interviewees in Turkey, some of the Uyghur-language anashid circulating on social media networks were professionally produced by Uyghurs based in Turkey. They drew stylistically on these globally circulating models of radical anashid, using compositional styles that include multipart harmony and canon and recording effects of vocal distortion, reverb, and echo. The singer's voice in "Letter to Mother" bears the hallmarks of a trained professional pop singer. Ehsan Hajim, a Uyghur religious scholar in Istanbul, confirmed this impression: "Recently we heard that some Uyghur pop singers had come to Turkey. They regretted all the things they've done in their lives—living like unbelievers—and they repented their sins, and then they started to produce anashid" (interview, Istanbul, January 2017). In contrast to this more professional recording, another anashid circulating Uyghur networks in 2014, "They Don't Understand" (*Chüshänmäydu*), has the feeling of an amateur backroom production. A poor-quality, simply recorded young male voice sings in an undertone, almost as if he fears being overheard by the adults downstairs. The stepwise melody, with its sparing use of melisma, directly recalls the sphere of contemporary Uyghur popular song. The singing is typically pop in style—breathy and natural—and is clearly amateur, wavering in meter and pitch. The result is intimate, authentic, and affective. The lyrics are more authoritative than the musical performance, showing a strong grasp of Uyghur poetic structure and style.

> There is only one direction for the *hijrah*.[22]
> Those who haven't set out don't know its taste.
> They don't understand the rewards of jihad.
> To those who have never learned the truth,
> Night looks like day.
> Those who have never prayed
> Can never join the frontline of jihad.

Unlike "Letter to Mother," whose musical style owes much to contemporary Arab styles of radical anashid while the video conveys images of the local struggle, the song style of this production—like the cover of "My Name Is Uyghur Girl" discussed earlier—references the local sphere of Uyghur pop. But the accompanying montage of images—posing Da'esh fighters with their iconic black flags, military vehicles, hostage executions, and machine guns taken from arms company advertisements—has little directly to do with Uyghur concerns. This production moves the call to jihad beyond the sphere of nationalist struggle, calling Uyghur listeners to the global struggle. In this production, the oppressor is no longer China alone, and the images of violent resistance are those purveyed by Da'esh.

As growing numbers of Uyghurs fled the increasingly oppressive situation in Xinjiang after 2009, many arrived in Turkey, where they joined other immigrant communities who had fled war or persecution in their homelands, living in impoverished and crowded neighborhoods like Istanbul's Zeytinburnu, often without hope of permanent settlement and the right to work. In these precarious conditions, some young Uyghurs responded to calls to join the conflict in Syria.[23] There were creditable reports of small numbers of Uyghurs fighting with Da'esh in Syria in 2014 (Rosenblatt 2016). Ehsan Hajim linked anashid directly to this phenomenon: "There's no doubt that anashid played an important role in stirring up the young people and encouraging them to fight in these wars. People listen to anashid, and they cry. . . . They [the creators of anashid] try to get people emotional, excited, to inspire them. Their aim is to target young people who aren't clear in their minds, to get them to join their jihad. This is not true Islam, persuading young people to go and get themselves killed" (interview, Istanbul, January 2017). Many older-generation Uyghur migrants in Istanbul observed the circulation of anashid with dismay, alarmed by their power to attract younger listeners and fearful of the consequences of subsuming what they saw as the Uyghur nationalist struggle into narratives of global jihad. For Ehsan Hajim, the root cause of the radicalization of Uyghur fighters was not religion. Like other critics of the discourse of radicalization and terror (Asad 2007; Kundnani 2012), he situated their actions as a response to government oppression and brutality, a desperate form of resistance when all other means are blocked. For the Chinese government, however, the appearance of Uyghurs in Syria provided further evidence of the need for ever more forceful control.

Another video circulating on Uyghur networks in 2014 provided a glimpse of the grim reality faced by those who were propelled along the path of violent resistance to Chinese rule in Xinjiang. With the title "The Mujahidin of Guma" (*Guma Jihadchiliri*), it memorialized the deaths of a group of seven Uyghur men who were shot by police amid a strike-hard campaign, who were subsequently condemned as terrorists by the Chinese media.[24] The audio combined a short excerpt of Saudi-style Qur'anic recitation, followed by an Arabic-language nashid. The accompanying footage, which seems to have been taken from a Xinjiang police video, showed an unfolding police manhunt that ended with a pile of bloodied corpses lying in a cornfield.[25] One man remained alive, cowering among the corn as the armed police yelled at him to come out. We watch him shiver as he contemplates the choice whether to flee and die immediately or surrender and undergo interrogation and likely execution. Uyghur-language text imposed over the footage called for the "vengeance of the umma" (*ummätning qisasi*), but the video revealed only the desperate and pitiful condition of those men, armed with carving knives and facing the might of the Chinese military; pressed into the role of mujahidin, cornered and shot as terrorists.

* * *

What can we learn about this fatal descent into violence from listening in on the mediated circulation of sounds? Through the selection of media items this chapter has surveyed, we can see some of the responses made by Uyghurs to the escalating state violence and discrimination they experienced, and we can reflect on the effects of sharing and listening to them. Together, these diverse types of audio production circulating on social media impel us to pay attention to the affective power of the voice and the particularities of the mediated voice. Audio files shared on smartphones are particularly good at transmitting the affective properties of speech and song because the audio technologies used in smartphones highlight the frequencies used by the voice. The typically poor sound quality of these audio files—often recorded by individuals on their smartphones, uploaded and shared—means that they are also good at signifying authenticity, good at conveying the urgency and affective impact of a charged moment of experience, caught and frozen in time and shared. Dorothea Schulz (2012) has argued that the mediated voice has a special potential for mobilizing people's agentive and affective faculties. Writing on the experience of listening to recorded sermons in Mali, she notes how the human voice is considered to touch listeners in a way that is physically experienced. For this reason, she argues, it has the capacity to move individuals from passivity to action. Such views on the capacities of the voice are linked to the wider Islamic culture of orality centered on recitation of the Qur'an (Nelson 2001), and the virtues of listening (Hirschkind 2006).

For the vast majority of Uyghur listeners, the movement from passivity to action entailed no more and no less than adopting the forms of self-discipline required by a pious lifestyle: daily prayer, fasting, and especially women's adoption of codes of modesty. The strong emphasis on women's modesty was surely connected to the preponderance of young male voices active in this field of discourse. Such forms of action were now felt by many Uyghurs to be the appropriate answer to their experience of colonial rule and their sense of national pain, a sense that only through proper attention to their religious duties could they persuade God to change their fate. The appearance of radical anashid on Uyghur social media suggested the possibility of mobilizing these new religious sensibilities and refocusing them on violent resistance, yet for the majority of listeners the anashid provided no more than the thrill of the illicit, images of machine guns combined with the affective musical experience of the sentimental pop ballad. Far more commonplace than the call to jihad was the call to prayer as a means to find acceptance:

> I pressed my forehead to the prayer mat and I said, be patient.
> There is no justice or peace in this world.
> There are tears in my eyes.
> Only by praying to Allah can you find peace.
> My prayer mat is wet with my tears. (Posted on Ündidar, June 7, 2014)

By August 2014, many people began sharing messages about the new security crackdown on social media, which began with regular checks on people's smartphones as they passed through police checkpoints that were now in place at the roadside outside every town and village. People posted to their circles warning of the danger of arrest if the police discovered an illegal app on their smartphone and helpfully provided lists of apps then deemed illegal. Many people promptly deleted all the religious media from their smartphones, and posted messages like this one, shared in

August 2014: "All friends and colleagues, please read! If any of you have Islamic words or images on your profile, please forgive me if I remove you from my friends list. I am currently having a lot of problems, when I travel I am constantly being checked. I don't want to cause trouble for you."

Rumors, Anonymity, and Affect

During this period, the sounds of religious media circulating on Ündidar became increasingly detached from the soundscape experienced by a copresent community, and they became adapted to the architecture of the virtual environment. The shift in context had profound consequences for the ways that listeners experienced them and for the new forms of cultural intimacy that they promoted. Social media technologies create connections across the globe with ease and immediacy, but, as they do so, they divide the voice from the present body. The listening experience is at once personal, intimate, and secret—and also public, offering the illusory freedom of a space of communication within a private public sphere (Warner 2002). Those who engage in these practices do not necessarily think of themselves as speaking to strangers, but they are engaging with avatars and inhabiting imagined worlds predicated on anonymity. In this environment, as Hirschkind, de Abreu, and Caduff (2017) argue, rumor assumes a powerful role: "Rather than being signified in relation to an origin or a destination, anonymity has become the very expression of circulation.... Rumor's performative power derives from the absence of the author as stable point of reference. Its efficacy emerges out of its ability to maintain the indeterminacy of the source, which facilitates its errant spread. Circulation becomes the defining nature of speech without signature" (S15). The virtual environment lends itself to the circulation of extreme forms of mediated experience, with which people can engage strongly and then detach themselves with ease, creating multiple personas and compartmentalizing their lives. As new communities forged by Uyghurs on Ündidar furtively shared audio files of anonymous voices that promoted messages of pain and horror, beauty and miracles, acceptance and resistance, through the sounds of Qur'anic recitation, horror-film sound tracks, and a cappella pop, the authorities listened in on this circulation with increasing alarm.

Although they have flourished in the virtual environment, the affective power of rumors is not a new phenomenon. In his study of rioting crowds and interethnic violence in India, Stanley Tambiah (1996) identifies rumors as the currency of mass movements. Eminently oral utterances, they circulate at high velocity by word of mouth, and by their nature they cannot be traced to definite culpable sources. Crowds are highly suggestible to rumors, which can rouse them to a collective state of intensified passions in which they may commit acts normally unthinkable to them as individuals. The ease with which rumors circulate via social media, their affective power, and their capacity to provoke passionate responses may help to explain the extreme nervousness of the Xinjiang authorities about rumors, internet incidents, and more generally the circulation of religious media on Ündidar. Rumors—in the absence of credible state media reporting—played a key role in the lead-up to the July 2009 demonstrations and subsequent violence in Ürümchi. Rumors provoked another demonstration in September 2009, when a crowd of Han Chinese marched through Ürümchi to demand government action after widespread rumors that Uyghurs were stabbing Hans with hypodermic needles infected with HIV (Szadziewski 2013).

The rumors surrounding the snake-monkey-woman and other similar media were likewise alarming because of their power to circulate widely and to transform sensibilities. Of particular note are the ways in which these media items used powerfully affective sounds and imagery to communicate themes of pain and redemption. Although she did not relate to the political arena in any straightforward way, the snake-monkey-woman was threatening to the state on two levels: she defied reason and rational debate and she viscerally promoted the fundamental religious disposition of being God-fearing (*Khodadin qoqaymän*), thus diluting fear of the state's temporal power. This opposition between state power and religious sensibilities was sometimes explicitly invoked by people in Yantaq village. One büwi explained to us why she had not given up teaching children to recite the Qur'an in spite of a series of fines and beatings at the hands of the local police: "I was leading prayers one night and the police caught us. I was with one girl from Ürümchi and two from Aqsu. They put me in jail for fifteen days. After that, Allah gave me even more strength and faith, and I became even stronger. We shouldn't be afraid of them because Allah said on the Day of Judgment even a mother will forget her baby." A common theme running through much of the material we accessed on Ündidar related Islam to the question of national survival in the face of a hostile state. Repeatedly, we find the twin arguments that only by becoming true Muslims could Uyghurs withstand oppressive and assimilative rule, and only by becoming true Muslims could Uyghurs counter damaging social tendencies like drug abuse, alcoholism, fraud, and prostitution, because these immoral acts spring from living in a non-Muslim society. These perceptions suggest that the public produced and expressed through Ündidar, in the context of the marginalization and structural and physical violence experienced by Uyghurs in 2013–14, was one that rejected, implicitly or overtly, the authority of the Chinese state and embraced instead something that seemed to represent a power higher than the Chinese Communist Party.

We can also observe a dialectic of horror and modernity at play within the region in this period, a product of the clash of radically different cultures of listening. Forms of Islamic media drew on the sound world of horror films to promote a visceral fear of God, like the snake-monkey-woman, who provides a lesson for women in the monstrousness of impious behavior. Agents of the state reacted with horror at the spread of what they perceived as alien, antimodern, and hence threatening ways of being, and they invoked the globally circulating trope of Islamic terror, which enabled new violence to be unleashed against the supposed terrorists and against the Uyghur people, who were now coming to be collectively defined by this trope.

Notes

1. The video can be viewed on the Sounding Islam in China website, accessed April 3, 2019, http://www.soundislamchina.org/?p=394.

2. *Uyghurlarni aldawatqan sakhta möjuzlär* (The fake miracles confronting the Uyghurs). Message posted on the Uyghur-language blog site "bbs.alkuyi," accessed June 28, 2012. The site has since been taken down, along with many other Uyghur-language websites.

3. The Xinjiang authorities have repeatedly sought to blame incidents of violence and disorder on this predominantly secular human-rights organization; see Millward 2004; 2009.

4. Szadziewski and Fay 2015. See also World Uyghur Congress 2016b.

5. Megha Rajagopalan and Ben Blanchard, "China Police Target Online 'Jihad' Talk Amid Rumour Crackdown," *Reuters*, October 8, 2013, https://uk.reuters.com/article/uk-china-uighur/china-police-target-online-jihad-talk-amid-rumour-crackdown-idUKBRE99708J20131008.

6. Edward Wong and Xiyun Yang, "New Protests Reported in Restive Chinese Region," *New York Times*, September 3, 2009, http://www.nytimes.com/2009/09/04/world/asia/04china.html?_r=0. In 2016, Xinjiang Communist Party secretary Zhang Chunxian claimed that 90 percent of terrorism in the region was the result of radicalization by overseas propaganda videos (Qiao Long, "Man Held in China's Xinjiang for Downloading 'Terrorist' Circumvention Software," trans. Luisetta Mudie, *Radio Free Asia*, October 28, 2016, http://www.rfa.org/english/news/uyghur/software-10282016121811.html).

7. The criminalization of everyday Muslim practices in Xinjiang has its parallels in the United States, such as the New York Police Department surveillance program according to which indicators of radicalization included regularly attending a mosque, growing a beard, fasting, and wearing a hijab (Tazamal 2019).

8. I have previously noted this tendency in relation to Uyghur nationalist music productions (Harris 2002).

9. Darren Byler, personal communication, August 2017.

10. Here generically meaning "words of wisdom," not directly related to the sung poetry discussed in chapter 3.

11. The audio file can be accessed on the Sounding Islam in China website (accessed August 3, 2018): http://www.soundislamchina.org/av/Jin_tablikh.mp3.

12. Excerpt from "Jin Tabligh." Translated by Aziz Isa and Rachel Harris. Audio available at this link: http://www.soundislamchina.org/av/Jin_tablikh.mp3.

13. "China Fights Terrorism and Violent Attacks," *China Daily*, accessed July 10, 2017, http://www.chinadaily.com.cn/china/2014crackdownterrorists/.

14. Source anonymized for the safety of the individuals involved.

15. Maya Wang, "Eradicating an Ideological Virus," *Human Rights Watch*, September 9, 2018, https://www.hrw.org/report/2018/09/09/eradicating-ideological-viruses/chinas-campaign-repression-against-xinjiangs.

16. Source anonymized for the safety of individuals involved.

17. World Uyghur Congress 2016a.

18. "Xinjiang Yarkand Massacre" 2014; Uyghur Human Rights Project 2014.

19. From a poem by Huwayda, eighteenth-century Central Asian Sufi poet, sung in various renditions of the Twelve Muqam (translated in Light 2008, 124).

20. The audio file can be accessed on the Sounding Islam in China website (accessed July 17, 2017): http://www.soundislamchina.org/?p=1222.

21. The audio file can be accessed on the Sounding Islam in China website (accessed August 7, 2018): http://www.soundislamchina.org/av/Anamgha_yezilghan_xet.mp3.

22. *Hijrah* may be interpreted as the migration of the Prophet or as the road to jihad.

23. There are credible reports that Da'esh itself produced Uyghur- and Chinese-language anashid in order to recruit new Uyghur fighters, but we did not find any such on Ündidar networks.

24. Uyghur American Association, "Uyghurs Shot to Death in Guma County, amid Intense State-led Repression," press release, December 29, 2011, https://uyghuramerican.org/press-release/uyghurs-shot-death-guma-county-amid-intense-state-led-repression.html.

25. Source withheld for the safety of individuals involved.

6

SONG AND DANCE AND THE SONIC TERRITORIALIZATION OF XINJIANG

We Are as Happy as Little Apples[1]

The national hit song "Little Apple" is now in Yengisar county of Kashgar district, where peasants from every village come to the cultural center every morning and evening to dance together to "Little Apple." Today our reporter went to Mangxin village in Yengisar to watch the peasants dancing to "Little Apple." The oldest among them was over fifty and the youngest was six years old.... Dancing to "Little Apple" is intended to encourage the masses of all nationalities to develop their enthusiasm for modernity and progress, to guard against ethnic separatism and religious extremism, and to promote harmonious and civilized lifestyles.[2]

"Little Apple" (*Xiao Pingguo*), released by the Chopstick Brothers (*Kuaizi Xiongdi*) in May 2014, was a synth-heavy, retro-style, catchy love song with an insistent beat. Its bizarrely kitsch video riffed on Korean soap operas and World War II dramas alongside brightly colored Adam and Eve sequences featuring the naked, pixelated Chopstick Brothers with a group of young women in striped pajama suits and red wigs, performing a simple dance sequence. It was a national viral hit. The dance moves and the quirky humor of the video made it ripe for imitation and parody, and the tune became ubiquitous; it played in shopping malls, nightclubs, and gyms across the country, and it circulated in countless amateur videos of groups of people performing the dance, from air stewardesses to cheerleaders, and from fire fighters to students. It spilled into the public space as a ringtone on smartphones and as a sound track for many of the women who gathered in groups daily to dance in China's city squares. Some observers noted the special capacity of "Little Apple" to open out a temporary space in which participants could experience a "warm sense of human collaboration" (Stock 2016).

Even so, it was somewhat surprising—given the video's anarchic sense of humor and predilection for cross-dressing—to see "Little Apple" adopted with equal enthusiasm by China's security forces. Its unmistakable melody provided the soundtrack for a recruitment video posted on the Ministry of National Defense website, with uniformed soldiers performing the now-familiar dance moves to new lyrics that incorporated the slogan "every young person has a dream" (referring to Xi Jinping's "China Dream" slogan). Police in Anhui province recorded themselves dancing to the song, and the Shandong Police Bureau recorded a version with modified lyrics to broadcast a warning about phone-banking scams. A clip showing soldiers dancing to "Little Apple" alongside grateful child survivors of the major Yunnan earthquake of August 2014 became another viral hit. The song was also recorded by the Xinjiang SWAT Police Force (*Xinjiang tejing*) in a forceful techno-style high-quality music video production.[3] Instead of claiming "you are my little apple," the lyrics of this version promised that the Xinjiang police would serve the people and protect the (regional) capital, never faltering or flinching in their mission to maintain stability. The video underscored this message with grainy sequences of soldiers posing with high-tech military equipment, conducting mass military drills, dancing to "Little Apple," and deploying on the Ürümchi streets to protect what appeared to be an exclusively Han Chinese public.

If the Han population of Xinjiang was the target audience for this particular production, Uyghurs were certainly not excluded from the "Little Apple" phenomenon. Numerous videos of Uyghur villagers dancing in tidy lines to "Little Apple" circulated on Chinese online media and on WeChat in winter 2014 and spring 2015. They danced in schoolyards, in community centers, and in the courtyards of police stations and municipal buildings (often the largest available spaces in the village). They danced to the original release by the Chopstick Brothers, and they danced to new Uyghur-language versions. These new versions were often composed to specifically refer to the locality, as in the following played for a mass dancing session in Akto town in Kashgar district:

> In the Pamirs is a town called Akto.
> People are hardworking and live happily.
> It has fifteen villages and a town bazaar and beautiful orchards.
> All nationalities live happily together
> Under the guidance of the Communist Party.
> We will always love our home.[4]

In some parts of Xinjiang, government officials decided to mobilize the local imams to join in these organized dancing activities. *Istiqlal News*, a Turkey-based Uyghur website, ran a piece called "East Turkestan Thirty Years Ago and Today," contrasting photographs of men at prayer in front of Kashgar's Idgah Mosque taken in 1985 and images of dancing imams in the same spot in 2015. A video of imams in Uch Turpan, Aqsu, publicly dancing to "Little Apple" circulated on Uyghur exile networks and found its way into the Turkish media, where it caused a storm of outrage on behalf of their "oppressed Turkic brothers" suffering under the yoke of the "Chinese Communist infidels."[5]

Projects of Territorialization

The notion of territorialization, first developed by Deleuze and Guattari (1987), helps to explain the processes by which China's border regions (among them Tibet, Inner Mongolia, and Xinjiang) have come to be naturalized as inseparable parts of the Chinese state. Rather than viewing state territory as a preconstituted geographical unit, we can conceive it as the product of an ongoing process of territorialization through which the hegemonic spatial relationships between state and society are established, a material and embodied process that involves the transformation of both landscapes and subjectivities (Wainwright 2008, 21). Territorialization also denotes the production and imagination of political geographies and national borders. Peripheries are produced and reproduced as components of state-building projects.

Emily Yeh (2013) has argued that the ever-backward status of Tibet as a place in need of continual development is coconstitutive of Chinese state formation. In the seventeenth century, the cities of Lhasa and Kashgar served as centers of religion and culture and hubs of trade with Nepal, Kashmir, and Persia, but in the 1950s, after their incorporation into the People's Republic of China, they became peripheral backwaters with no political or economic power: places in need of development. The political order becomes imprinted onto the landscape in ways that make it seem part of the natural order, but this process of imprinting obscures the relations of power that create the landscape. When Tibetans use terms like "image engineering" to describe the transformation of their environment through state development and heritage projects like the Comfortable Housing Project of the New Socialist Countryside, they recognize the tendency of the landscape to obscure and erase the social conditions of its production. Only by investigating the struggles that go into making landscapes, Yeh argues, can the relations of power that obfuscate landscapes be understood.

This view of processes of territorialization in Tibet is useful for understanding the contemporary situation in Xinjiang, another peripheral "minority region" of China undergoing massive immigration and development and beset by violence. Of particular relevance to the situation in Xinjiang is Yeh's perception that state territorialization projects are "projects of self-fashioning" that work not only to shape the landscape but also to shape the bodies, desires, habits, and emotions of their subjects, as well as the actions that stem from those desires. The deployment of "Little Apple" and the many other examples of coerced singing and dancing that we observed during 2015 and 2016 fit well with this concept of self-fashioning.

There are many continuities between the campaigns rolled out in Tibet in 2008–9 and those rolled out in Xinjiang in 2015–16, but the fact that the indigenous peoples of Xinjiang are predominantly Muslim has allowed the Chinese government to hitch its campaigns in Xinjiang to the Global War on Terror (Roberts 2018), masking the underlying similarities between the two regions and enabling a far more wide-reaching and violent set of measures against the Uyghurs and other Muslims minorities in this region (Smith Finley 2019). In this chapter I argue that the way that Chinese media frames violence in Xinjiang, as a struggle against religious extremism and terrorism, serves to obfuscate what is better understood as an ongoing struggle over the landscape, in which state projects of development—which do not equally benefit the Uyghurs—attempt to remodel the landscape and to shape the desires and actions of its subjects; that is, to shape the ways in which they inhabit that landscape.

There are radical differences between the embodied spatial practices of Uyghur tradition and the production of state space in Xinjiang. The Taklamakan desert, for example, spreads across the heart of southern Xinjiang, and ranged around it are the "Six Cities" (*Altishahr*) that constitute the historical cultural and economic nodes of the region (Bellér-Hann et al. 2007; Thum 2014). The desert is imagined in Uyghur song as a site of desolation and fear, a place where the wandering dervish of Sufi tradition (*musapir*) weeps tears of blood remembering his beloved (Harris 2012). It was a place that one passed through, into exile, before a joyful return, or on a pilgrimage. In the 1950s, the desert was transformed in Chinese media discourse into a place of revolutionary struggle and sacrifice where the Chinese people (*zhongguo renmin*)—in the shape of the paramilitary Production and Construction Corps (*bingtuan*)—would settle and tame, transforming sand and rock into fertile agricultural land (Cliff 2016).

Work by Rahile Dawut (Dawuti 2001) and Rian Thum (2014) has eloquently described the region's sites of shrine pilgrimage and the routes through the desert traversed by Uyghur pilgrims carrying handwritten copies of *tazkira*: stories of the saints, kings, and martyrs to whom the shrines were dedicated. The repeated retreading of these routes and retelling of these stories formed a collective and sacred history etched into the landscape (Thum 2014). Dawut has described the recent transformation of these shrines into tourist destinations, often in tandem with the effective exclusion of local people from the sites where they formerly worshipped through enclosure and high ticket prices (Dawut 2007). Gardner Bovingdon (2001) also describes the construction of new tourist sites in the Xinjiang landscape, sites that tell histories of ancient Chinese domination of a historically Buddhist region and gloss over the subsequent thousand years of Islamic hegemony.[6]

This work of remodeling is also apparent in the built environment of Xinjiang. Urban development programs of the past few decades have transformed the labyrinthine street layout and Medina-type architecture of the region's oasis towns into styles of urban development that conform to the Chinese ideal of a gridlike structure of wide avenues dividing regular islets of housing (Loubes 2015; Kobi 2016). Such mathematically structured housing developments are easier to service and easier to police, but their introduction has radically transformed the structures of Uyghur community life. The radical changes are often obscured by ornamental references to local architectural traditions. Jean-Paul Loubes (2015) describes the way that forms of "neo-Uyghur" architecture have been used to overlay the new modernist structures of urban building: placing Central Asian architectural clichés such as cupolas and arches onto functionalist buildings to introduce a touch of exoticism into the urban landscape. One of the most striking examples of the neo-Uyghur architectural style is the Big Bazaar in Ürümchi, described in the introduction, which houses fast-food outlets within the architectural facsimile of a Central Asian madrassa complex.

Loubes also considers China's enthusiastic participation in UNESCO heritage schemes. He notes a piecemeal approach to heritage in which isolated monuments, which are significant because of their symbolic or tourist value, are not so much preserved as staged to suit Chinese tastes.

The transformation of the city of Kashgar remains the most notorious of these projects of architectural staging. A gradual process of destruction and reconstruction of Kashgar's old city began in the 1990s and was completed in 2013. The key heritage site of Idgah Mosque was preserved, but several other less well known historical sites were destroyed along with large swathes of residential areas. The majority of its inhabitants were rehoused elsewhere, and the old city was reopened in the form of a largely depopulated destination for tourism, with former mosques repurposed as tourist bars (Steenberg and Rippa 2019). In the eastern town of Qumul, the palace of the nineteenth-century rulers (the *Qumul Wangliri*) was reconstructed in 2005, not on the original site of the palace but on top of a bulldozed Uyghur cemetery; not in the style of the original palace but on a folklorized model designed to attract tourists. Bellér-Hann (2014) proposes this image of the bulldozer as the material embodiment of the state in its projects of spatial territorialization: an agent that physically invades, colonizes, and reorganizes space.

In this chapter, I argue that sound is a crucial aspect of these processes of territorialization, and that the soundscape is a site of struggle in ways that relate directly to—and indeed articulate—struggles over the landscape and the ways that people inhabit the landscape. I draw on the notion of sonic territorialization to explain the ways in which cultural development, state power, and the shaping of habitus are played out through sound. Just as Andrew Eisenberg (2013) has advocated turning an ethnographic ear to the affective, embodied spatial practices through which people negotiate place in the city, here I want to scale up the ethnography and listen in on the spatial negotiation of the territory of the Xinjiang Uyghur Autonomous Region as it played out through the 2015 campaign to tackle Islamic extremism by daily singing and dancing.

Sonic Territorialization

US journalists who traveled to Xinjiang after the 2015 period looking for stories on the massive securitization of the region were quick to comment on the new soundscape: "The new police state comes with an eerie soundtrack. Along the streets, you hear the same pair of Mandarin-language propaganda songs: a jolly children's song about obeying traffic laws, and a more somber acoustic tune that promotes core Communist values. The government forces shops and restaurants in Uighur neighborhoods to broadcast these two songs all day on a loop."[7] These stories were typically framed in terms of Chinese exceptionalism, but the techniques of sonic territorialization they described were developed in the United States, and they underpin everyday urban listening experiences across the globe. An early discussion of these processes by Jonathan Sterne (1997) focuses on the ways that recorded music is used to script the experience of the built environment in the context of the American shopping mall: "Programmed music can be said to territorialize the Mall: it builds and encloses the acoustical space, and manages the transitions from one location to another; it not only divides space, but also coordinates the relations among subdivisions" (31).

Crucial to discussions of sonic territorialization is an understanding of the ways in which the sounded environment works on its human inhabitants. British sociologist Tia DeNora (2000) draws particular attention to the ways that sound works on bodies in the mall: how musical sounds and styles impress themselves on the shopping body, shaping the flows of energy and money around the space of the mall, and how stores fine-tune their musical output to optimize the experience of shopping and the process of spending. These processes are always historically contingent and take place within particular economic and social regimes. Brandon LaBelle (2010) explores the historical relationship between sound and global capitalist structures in his history of Muzak, which began life in America as an early-twentieth-century project to create forms of music for the factory environment with the aim of extracting greater productivity from factory workers. The Muzak project, he argues, underpins much of our contemporary acoustic experience of public space: "The legacy of Muzak has instigated more contemporary approaches toward scripting space acoustically. Audio branding and sonification are currently active design strategies dramatically participating in the total aestheticization and crafting of contemporary social space. From advertising jingles and sound logos for particular brands or companies to ringtones and sounds for gaming devices, as well as sonified weather reports, the play of sonic memory and auditory sensing are rapidly mobilizing much of Muzak's core ideas" (186). Much of the core literature on sonic territorialization, then, attends to the experience of listening to mediated sound within the urban environments of late capitalism, and it attends to the ways that this sonic feed is manipulated in order to influence listeners. This form of sonic territorialization also plays an important role in state territorial moves in China, historically and today. It is deeply engrained in the Chinese revolutionary experience, materialized in the form of the loudspeakers that sounded in the factories and schools and on the streets of cities, towns, and villages across China, providing a nationwide soundtrack for the revolution (Mittler 2012).

The Chinese revolutionary period is also famous, however, for its techniques of mass mobilization, in particular its emphasis on mass participation in revolutionary styles of cultural performance. It is the revival of this form of sonic territorialization in contemporary Xinjiang that I consider in this chapter: the consequences of large-scale coercive musical participation and, their impact on human bodies, and their relationship with the landscape. Beginning in 2014, the anti-religious-extremism campaign in Xinjiang harnessed sound, and especially the mass performance of popular and revolutionary songs, as a tool for the reterritorialization of the region. The campaign aimed to expel Muslim noise from the soundscape and fill it instead with sounds congruent with state narratives of patriotism, unity, and a civilization with Chinese characteristics. As Uyghur villagers and urban dwellers across the region were mobilized to sing and dance to "Little Apple" and other songs, Chinese media reports explicitly linked these activities to civilizing projects: countering religious extremism and fostering modernity. I argue that these activities were intended to break down the embodied norms of religious piety inculcated by the Islamic revival by demanding forms of public behavior that violated religious norms.

By framing this campaign as a struggle over territory that was played out in sound, I am suggesting the relevance of studies of the role of sound in war contexts. This body of literature is also helpful in understanding the ongoing violence—that is, the violence inflicted by agents of the state on its citizens as well as the violent responses by a small number of citizens—that formed the backdrop to this outbreak of mass singing and dancing in Xinjiang.

In his study of the role of sound in the Iraq war, Martin Daughtry (2015) uses the notion of acoustic territories to underline the idea that hearing and listening are both embodied and emplaced. Daughtry is concerned both with the ways in which sound acts on bodies within relations of power and also with the ways that sound can bring places into being. Listening in the context of war brings together this complex of ideas with particular force: they are the sounds produced in the context of violent, technologized, and physical struggles over landscape. The direct relationship between sound and bodies is brought into focus through Daughtry's account of the physical damage and psychological trauma that the sounds of war can inflict in conflict—burst eardrums, flashbacks—or through the use of music, as in Abu Ghraib prison, as a form of torture designed to break the resistance of detainees to interrogation (Cusick 2008). The violence inherent in political territories is often implicit: unless a border is actively contested, the threat of violence remains unactivated. By contrast, sounds are transient, bounded in time as well as space, and so acoustic territories must be maintained by a constant stream of sound and are thus in a constant state of active contestation (Daughtry 2015; see also Wood 2015).

Ways of listening may imply processes of territorialization even when the sounds are not directly intended to have an effect on the listeners. Ethnomusicologist Jennifer Post recounted an experience of hearing a distant booming while she was in western Mongolia, just across the border from Xinjiang. When she asked her local companions what the noise was, they said, "The Chinese are shooting the clouds again."[8] The sonic boom of this highly interventionist irrigation strategy, developed in revolutionary-era China to shake the rain out of the clouds, was heard by the Kazakh herders across the border as a desecration of nature according to the animist beliefs they preserved and a form of theft: impelling the rain to fall on Chinese territory while drought in Mongolia decimated their herds and threatened their way of life. Post's brief account brings together the relationships between ways of listening and ways of inhabiting the environment, struggles over territory and ecological disasters (personal communication, University of Kent, April 2016; see also Post 2017).

The Anti-Religious-Extremism Campaign in Xinjiang

Rather than targeting the small number of people who might reasonably be judged vulnerable to radicalization and violent action, the anti-religious-extremism campaign in Xinjiang sought to eliminate all visible and audible expressions of Islamic faith—veiling, beards, public prayer, fasting, religious gatherings, instruction, and media—from the landscape and soundscape (see fig. 6.1).[9] Between 2011 and 2017, coercive forms of disciplinary and state power came to condition the experience of everyday life for Uyghurs, who faced controls on their appearance, their mobility, their listening, and their everyday bodily practices. The mechanisms of control extended right across the landscape and right into the family home, and they were enforced by the threat of violence. The delineation of this People's War on Terror was marked by huge demonstrations of state power, culminating in 2017 with military parades in the region's major cities of Ürümchi, Aqsu, Kashgar,

Fig. 6.1. Bilingual sign in an Aqsu park, 2012: "Praying in public spaces is prohibited." Photograph by Aziz Isa.

and Khotan involving thousands of troops and violent rhetoric. At a rally in Ürümchi in February 2017, Zhu Hailun, deputy Communist party chief, proclaimed, "We shall load our guns, draw our swords from their sheaths, throw hard punches and relentlessly beat, and strike hard without flinching at terrorists."[10] The security measures targeted people's bodily practices and their relationship with the landscape and with the soundscape in ways that were specifically aimed at the indigenous Muslim peoples of the region, predominantly Uyghurs but also Kazakhs and other Turkic Muslims.

Controlling Space

In May 2014, Xi Jinping called for the construction of "walls made of copper and steel" and "nets spread from the earth to the sky" to defend Xinjiang against terrorism.[11] The heightened rhetoric signaled the territorial nature of the campaign and the degree to which the region and its people would be isolated and immobilized. Spatial techniques of control implemented gradually over the following few years included the freezing of mobility and the circulation of information. Passports were confiscated and special passes called—in an Orwellian touch—"convenience cards" (*bianminka*) were required for any Uyghurs who wanted to travel outside their hometown.[12] In the cities, concrete road barriers and steel fences were erected on the sides of major streets. A tight network of police checkpoints was established on roads leading into cities, small towns, and even some villages. Police patrols were introduced in every village and town, alongside regular shows of force in urban areas with armed troops in military personnel carriers and even tanks patrolling city streets.[13] Authorities drew a tight net of surveillance that ranged from the high tech—security cameras, compulsory tracking devices on cars, and retina recognition software for some checkpoints—to the humanly enforced. Xinhua News Agency reported in January 2012 that eight thousand police officers had been recruited in order to apply a policy of "one officer, one village," enabling the police to "manage migrants and crack down on illegal religious activities."[14] By 2016, under the security measures introduced by the new party secretary, Chen Quanguo, this number had ballooned to more than thirty thousand new police recruits in one year, mainly young Uyghur men.[15] At checkpoints on the roads and at the entry to town bazaars, police required people to hand over their phones, plugged them into a computer, and downloaded a government application that would scan the phone for illegal material.[16] Local residents were mobilized to conduct regular antiterrorist drills, which entailed the distribution of thick wooden or metal poles and lessons in how to wield them against the enemy.[17]

Policing Bodies

Visible signs of religiosity were an early target of the anti-religious-extremism campaign. The *South China Morning Post* reported from Khotan in 2011 on a new ban on what Uyghurs called the "Arab-style" women's full covering (*jilbab*), which had become fashionable in the region during the previous decade. Women wearing this kind of veil were described as "blindly affected by extreme religious thought" and their clothing choices were directly linked to terrorist activities: "The black and loose robes enable potential attackers to hide their weapons and, hence, pose a security threat to the safety of the public," a government spokesman said. The Khotan government had launched a campaign to encourage women to avoid such clothing, he said, using slogans telling them to "show off their pretty looks and let their beautiful long hair fly."[18] An acquaintance from Khotan observed drily that life for women in that oasis town had become very difficult: if they wore a headscarf to go to work or the bazaar, they were fired, and if they did not wear a headscarf to go to work or the bazaar, they had stones thrown at them. In rural Aqsu as early as 2012, we observed signs in town centers and parks stating that it was illegal to pray or wear facial veils (*niqab*) in public; transgression would incur substantial fines. People found praying in the town bazaar were sentenced to fifteen days detention and political education. A büwi we knew complained that she had inadvertently gone out wearing an ordinary black dress and been detained for more than an hour by police for wearing "illegal Islamic dress." Not only police were actively enforcing the campaign. Professional work-unit employees were obliged to spend several hours of their work time every week patrolling the town streets dressed in army fatigues and hard hats and supplied with large sticks, charged with removing religious clothing (prayer caps and women's headscarves) from passersby.

The campaign began in rural towns and eventually spread to the major cities. "Beauty campaigns" introduced in 2014 involved communal village meetings during which women ceremonially removed their headscarves and men shaved off their beards. The Ramadan fast was disrupted by a policy requiring students and workers to drink a glass of water as they entered the classroom or the workplace. There were even media reports of public beer-drinking competitions organized for Uyghur men and women.[19] By 2016, veils and beards had disappeared from the landscape. A friend visited the religiously conservative town of Kucha and was astonished to see Uyghur women out on the streets, their heads uncovered, uniformly clad in the atlas silk dresses that were promoted in the campaign as symbols of traditional Uyghur femininity.[20]

Eradicating Noise

In May 2017, a mass rally was held at Xinjiang University. Thousands of students listened to party leaders call for the mobilization of the masses in the ongoing People's War on Terror. The goal of this People's War, according to Zhou Xuyong, the university's party secretary, was to create an atmosphere in which the public would treat those who damaged the "unity of the nationalities" like rats: screaming after them and beating them as they scurried across the street (see fig. 6.2). In the course of the campaign, he declared, all forms of "noise" (*zayin*) and "interference" (*zaoyin*) must be eliminated.[21]

Fig. 6.2. The Uyghur masses attack those who damage the unity of the nationalities like rats. Peasant art campaign, 2014. Tianshan Net (accessed May 20, 2015).

In the introduction, I discussed the rich history of noise as a metaphor, its contingency on the listening ear, and how it is often used to denote the sounds of the Other. These processes of listening and othering often have a spatial dimension. In her seminal work on black noise, Tricia Rose (1994) argues that the way rap and rap-related violence are discussed in the media is inseparable from wider discourses on the spatial control of black Americans. Highlighting the notion that spatial hierarchies are produced and upheld by ways of listening, she notes how in the early days of rap in America break-dancers transformed city sidewalks into stages because they could not access public gyms or dance studios, while disc jockeys and rappers performed in parks and on street corners because they were unable to book public theaters and concert venues. Underpinning the containment of rap culture, she argues, is the belief that black people, particularly black urban teenagers, are a threat to the American social order and need to be contained.

In the context of this rally at Xinjiang University, it was apparent that the noise Zhou Xuyong referred to was Muslim noise, and the actions of the campaign made it abundantly clear that one of its primary goals was to silence Muslim noise as part of a wider project to contain the perceived Muslim threat to social order in Xinjiang. There was little to do in terms of the public soundscape; already the call to prayer resonated only within the confines of the region's mosques or on individuals' smartphones. Instead, the campaign targeted the substrata of public-private spaces in which religious sounds resonated: inside unofficial mosques, in restaurants and family homes. It also targeted the mediated subterranean listening practices described in chapter 5. During 2015 and 2016, the Xinjiang authorities destroyed thousands of the unofficial mosques that had been constructed by local communities since the 1980s. Under the Mosque Rectification campaign launched by the Religious Affairs Department and overseen by the local police, the mosques were condemned on the grounds that they were unsafe structures that posed a safety threat for worshippers. Radio Free Asia interviewed a police officer from Khotan in 2017: "Convincing the people that one of the purposes for demolishing the mosques was for the safety of the worshipers was a bit difficult," said Eysajan Yaqup, a police officer in Toqquzaq Township. "Some of them laughed at us when we explained the purpose, and some of them stared at us to show their disagreement." Eysajan Yaqup said he and other officials ignored the laughter and the stares and "most of the prayers were silenced."[22]

Throughout the many local initiatives that made up the anti-religious-extremism campaign, there was consistent emphasis on the dangers of listening, especially listening either to unofficial sermons or to Islamic media. According to another Radio Free Asia interview in 2017, people in Kashgar were being sentenced to two to ten years in prison for listening to "illegal religious sermons." The interviewee, a police official, noted that the sermons did not contain any antigovernment rhetoric; the listeners were sentenced simply because they had listened to sermons by an unofficial imam at an unauthorized venue.[23] The Revealing Errors campaign held in Aqsu in 2017 required villagers to report to the village police office every day to confess their own "mistakes" or to report on the mistakes they had seen others make. At village meetings, residents were called to a podium one by one to confess their errors. According to a police officer in Aqsu, "The central question asked at these meetings is, 'Have you ever watched, saved, or forwarded harmful religious or separatist postings or [media] clips, or have you ever seen anyone else do this?"[24]

Also in Aqsu, Uyghur villagers were required to attend evening classes, ostensibly to learn about poverty eradication and China's "benevolent policies" in the region, but actually instructing them in what the authorities meant by "religious extremism." Villagers who had attended the classes reported:

> "We study how to watch our children carefully, so that they don't get involved in extremism...," the woman said.... "We now understand what extremism means and what is right and wrong," another Aksu [Aqsu] farmer said. "All of this has been poured into our brains.... We know now that it is wrong to send our children to religious schools," he said. "They also told us that we can no longer pray outside in the fields. We can only pray in government-designated mosques."[25]

In addition, new legislation explicitly criminalized "forcing or coercing children to participate in religious activities." Children found taking part in religious activities could be sent to special schools for correction. According to an Aqsu education official, "If anybody under eighteen prays, fasts, learns religion, or follows someone to pray or go underground religious places to learn, these are all deemed illegal."[26] The measures to cleanse Uyghur society of Muslim noise went so far as a ban on "extremist" names, which included, according to one directive from rural Khotan, not only names like Bin Laden that might possibly be taken as an expression of enthusiasm for Al Qaeda, but also common Muslim names like Mohammad and Fatima.[27] As Jacques Attali (1985) famously remarked, "noise is inscribed from the start within the panoply of power. Equivalent to the articulation of a space, it indicates the limits of a territory and the way to make oneself heard within it, how to survive by drawing one's sustenance from it. And since noise is the source of power, power has always listened to it with fascination" (6). In contemporary Xinjiang, the resurgence of Islamic sounds was heard by the state as Muslim noise: backward and oppositional, a challenge to state projects of modernization and development and marked by violence. Alongside the project of eradicating Muslim noise from the Xinjiang soundscape, the campaign mobilized other traditions of listening in order to reconfigure the soundscape.

Song and Dance

At China's National People's Congress in March 2014, delegates stood in silence to honor the victims of the Kunming train station attack which took place earlier that month. The Xinjiang representative and deputy chair of the China Dancer's Association, Dilnar Abdulla, delivered a speech complaining that religious extremists in Xinjiang were campaigning for common people not to sing and dance and were even preventing them from singing and dancing at weddings. These injunctions against dancing constituted, she claimed, "a major assault on our traditional culture."[28] Certainly, during the preceding decade, weddings had become an important site for the negotiation of customary norms and correct religious practice within the shifting terrain of religious and identity politics in Uyghur communities.

In his study of changing wedding customs in Kashgar in the period 2010–12, Rune Steenberg (2013) notes the rise in popularity of what he terms "piously oriented weddings" (*islamche toy, sünniy toy*). These *islamche toy* were simple, sober gatherings in which the religious ceremonies were central, and guesting and gift giving were kept to a minimum. Steenberg notes the onset of tensions in Kashgar society about singing and dancing at weddings. He recounts the story of a young man whose marriage plans had nearly been ruined when the bride's family walked out of the wedding venue because he and his friends started to dance. For the bride's family, dancing had no place in a proper Muslim wedding. For the groom, dancing and music were essential components in a "real Uyghur" (*milliy*, ethnic) wedding. Steenberg notes that this was "a hotly debated topic in Kashgar among almost all social groups" (249).

Dilnar Abdulla's speech reduced these debates—which echoed centuries of debates on the permissibility of music within a religious lifestyle—into a simplified and misleading opposition: "foreign" religious extremism versus "traditional" song and dance. The speech signaled the start of a new phase in the anti-religious-extremism campaign and the early stages of what would develop into extreme forms of state intrusion and interference into the everyday life of Uyghurs. The speech encapsulated the opposition drawn by state media between religious and ethnic identity: an artificial division that permitted the state to position itself as protecting Uyghur culture and upholding Uyghur tradition while effectively criminalizing all who promoted pious forms of everyday religious practice. Abdulla's speech also highlighted the central role that music, song, and dance would play in the anti-religious-extremism campaign. After the speech, local governments introduced new regulations. Families in Kashgar who wished to organize a wedding were required to pay a "playing music deposit" to the local authorities, which they could reclaim only if they could demonstrate that they had paid musicians to perform at the wedding. In Khotan, weddings could be held only at authorized municipal venues where the appropriate amount of music and dancing could be monitored.[29] But compulsory music-making was not confined to weddings; over the following year organized song-and-dance events became a cornerstone of the anti-extremism campaign.

In January 2015, the Xinjiang government Tianshan website reported that the Aqsu song-and-dance troupe had embarked on a concert tour of the province, putting on performances in rural areas for peasants and nomads in order to promote modern lifestyles and tackle religious extremism. This marked the revival of a deep-rooted Communist Party practice that went back to its early days in the revolutionary base of Yan'an during the anti-Japan war of the 1930s and 1940s: the practice of sending cultural work groups "down to the countryside" to garner support from villagers by performing songs and theatrical skits that promoted the party's messages of anti-Japanese resistance and social reforms (McDougall 1984). This practice had been an important part of the work of Xinjiang's song-and-dance troupes in the 1950s (Harris 2004; 2008), but since the 1980s the city song-and-dance troupes had gradually become more urban and sedentary, more focused on television appearances and tourist shows and the possibility of lucrative national or international tours, with little appetite for the discomforts and uncertain rewards of carrying political messages to captive audiences in the countryside. Suddenly they found themselves playing a leading role in the anti-religious-extremism campaign.

"Song and dance" (*gewu; nakhsha-usul*) has a particular history in this region. Commentators have often noted the prominence of song and dance in Communist Party policy, the huge investment in the development of minority musical traditions, and the established rhetoric of China's singing and dancing minority peoples (Harrell 2015; Harris 2004, 2008; Rees 2000). Authors such as Gladney (1994) and Schein (2000) have argued that the promotion of ethnic minority arts by the Chinese Communist Party serves as a payoff for lack of real autonomy in the political sphere. The sixtieth anniversary gala celebration of the founding of the People's Republic of China, which took place in 2009 on Beijing's Tiananmen Square at the heart of the Chinese polity, provided a spectacular evidence of the ongoing relevance of these themes. Its lavish program placed heavy emphasis on ethnic minority song and dance, deploying thousands of brightly dressed, smiling young women dancing in disciplined rows to, among others, the Uyghur revolutionary song "Salaam Chairman Mao" and the Tibetan song

"The Emancipated Serfs Have a Song to Sing" (famously performed by Peng Liyuan, professional singer and wife of President Xi Jinping).[30] The 2009 spectacle celebrated the continuities between the early revolutionary period and the first decade of the twenty-first century, and it deployed ethnic minority song and dance to symbolize the big family of nations that composed the People's Republic of China and to uphold the rule of the Chinese Communist Party over the territories that these minority groups inhabited. The core theme of these song-and-dance spectaculars was the expression of love and gratitude toward the Communist Party by minority performers. Above all, these performances are notable for the performers' smiles.

Külüsh (Smile)

> One cannot be exposed to China without being confronted by its "colorful" minorities. They sing, they dance; they twirl, they whirl. Most of all, they smile, showing their happiness to be part of the motherland. (Gladney 1994, 95)

Dru Gladney (1994) neatly characterizes the political symbolism of these smiles, but I want to probe deeper into the emotional labor performed by these smiling ethnic minority artists. As a mode of emotional expression, the smile seems to sit uneasily on the border between tropes of feeling and tropes of representation, a precariousness that is central to the discussion in this chapter. In the Introduction and in chapter 2, I discussed the classic anthropological critiques of the division between authentic emotion and outward representation and introduced Sarah Ahmed's (2004) ideas on the circulation of emotions and the ways in which emotions take shape through the repetition of actions over time. In this chapter, I shift away from the sphere of religious ritual and the embodiment of *ishq* (love or passion), and consider the embodied effects and the relationships forged by the smile in performances of Uyghur song and dance.

Arlie Hochschild (2003) has explored what occurs when everyday emotional work and the cultural rules governing the exchange of feeling are introduced into the commercial environment. She examines the work practices of flight attendants and the way they are trained to smile, deploying techniques of emotion management to serve the airline's commercial agenda. There are obvious echoes here of the Muzak project, and of course piped music is another core aspect of the in-flight experience, deployed to do work similar to that done by the attendant's smile. The difference is that the music can be delivered electronically while a living human being is needed to deliver the smile. Hochschild suggests that one effect of flight attendants' training is to estrange flight attendants from their own authentic expressions of emotion: in effect, their smiles are no longer their own.

As with Hochschild's American flight attendants, the smiles of China's professional minority performers have a strongly gendered aspect. In her ethnography of the Miao people of southwest China, Louisa Schein (2000) examines how representations of Miao identity on the national stage produce them as both feminized keepers of Chinese tradition and as the exotic Other against which the dominant Han Chinese can assert their own modernity. She notes how these relationships are replicated and upheld through numerous representations and encounters, from glamorous television shows and media reports to small-scale and often seedy tourist performances. These relationships are found across the minority regions of China, especially in areas where tourism has flourished in recent years. In Xinjiang, I have observed many such encounters between Chinese tourists and young Uyghur women in performances from Ürümchi's Big Bazaar to small restaurants in Turpan. Images of smiling young women in dance costumes serve in Chinese media depictions as instantly recognizable symbols for Han audiences of everything that is good, friendly, and welcoming about the region.

If China's professional minority performers had long been accustomed to smiling to service the requirements of nation building, the unfolding of the anti-religious-extremism campaign in Xinjiang made it clear that it was no longer sufficient for paid professionals to smile; now ordinary Uyghurs from schoolchildren to büwis were required to silence their weeping and publicly demonstrate their happiness. From 2015 on, local cultural bureaus across Xinjiang organized villagers to participate in song-and-dance performances, mass dancing displays, weekly sessions for singing revolutionary songs, and weekly mäshräp gatherings in order to counter extremism (see fig. 6.3).

A Weekly Mäshräp to Counter Extremism

In April 2015, the Xinjiang Radio website reported on a campaign in Aqsu to establish a weekly mäshräp to counter extremism, using peasant performance groups to promote love of the Communist Party, unity, and patriotism and to attack extremism and separatism. Some of these organized mäshräp gatherings were accompanied by ethnic fashion shows featuring local young women in outfits that, as far as I could see from the images

Fig. 6.3. Uyghur women participate in a mass song-and-dance event to counter extremism. Tianshan Net, 2015.

posted online, fell well short of conservative Islamic dress codes. This was no singular activity for the cameras. We learned that villagers in Yantaq were still being compelled to attend weekly, officially organized mäshräps in spring 2017.

Mäshräp denotes a loose complex of ritual and social practices among Uyghurs, which range from small informal parties to whole village events held at particular times of the year. They typically involve food, religious sermons or readings, joking, live musical performance, and dancing. Different localities have different traditions of mäshräp. In the northwestern town of Ghulja, regular mäshräps were the focus of lifelong community ties established between groups of men. They also functioned as a type of community court, with men who had committed small misdemeanors tried by the judge (*qazi*) of the mäshräp and punished by ritual humiliations such as being drenched with water. In the mid-1990s, some of these Ghulja mäshräps took on a reformist religious aspect. Mäshräp organizers attempted to enforce a more strongly Islamic lifestyle among group members and campaigned against alcohol and drug abuse among young people. The local authorities viewed these forms of community mobilization as a threat to state rule and banned the mäshräp, leading to demonstrations, police violence, and mass arrests (Dautcher 2009).

In response, the region's song-and-dance troupes began to develop an alternative form of mäshräp—a "neo-mäshräp" to echo Jean-Paul Loubes's (2015) characterization of the neo-Uyghur architecture—one centered on song and dance, smiling performers, and folkloric depictions of Uyghur culture. Alongside these moves, the Chinese government submitted the Uyghur mäshräp to the UNESCO list of Intangible Cultural Heritages in Need of Urgent Safeguarding. UNESCO duly accepted the application and inscribed the mäshräp. Mäshräp fever swept across Xinjiang in the form of videodisc sets, lavish song-and-dance troupe stage and television productions, mäshräp restaurants, mäshräp exercise classes, mäshräp household appliances, and even mäshräp paper napkins. At the same time, Uyghur villagers were finding it increasingly difficult to hold their own mäshräps, as the anti-religious-extremism campaign introduced ever-tighter restrictions on mobility and association.[31]

During spring 2015, Xinjiang media reported on organized anti-religious-extremism mäshräp gatherings in towns and villages right across the region. Some of them took the form of mass displays of staged song and dance with theatrical skits on themes of ethnic harmony and modernity, and others were small-scale local affairs that drew villagers into municipal buildings for weekly sessions of dancing to recorded music. Tianshan Net reported in March 2015 from Kashgar's Poskam County on the implementation of another "weekly mäshräp to enrich people's lives." This local campaign involved 140 party cadres stationed in sixteen towns and villages across the county, working with community elders and religious leaders in order to ensure social stability and ethnic unity and counter Islamic extremism and separatism. The cadres visited individual households to discuss every family's "problems," in other words, to discover whether they were practicing Muslims: an invasion of the private sphere that would be implemented on a massive scale as the campaign progressed.[32] They also organized peasant music groups, recruited peasants who could sing and dance, and organized a weekly mäshräp in order to enrich people's lives and achieve the campaign's goals.[33]

Singing Red Songs

Alongside the folkloric performances of Uyghur cultural heritage, another key theme of the campaign was the performance of "Red Songs": the canon of revolutionary songs created in the midtwentieth century that formed the sonic backdrop to the social chaos of the Cultural Revolution.

In launching the Cultural Revolution, Mao Zedong aimed to purge the newly established political elite in China and to transform the cultural superstructure and effect a profound transformation of Chinese society by attacking the "four olds" (old ways of thought, old culture, old habits, and old customs). Chinese society was split into supporters of Mao Zedong thought ("true revolutionaries") and reactionary forces ("demons and serpents") against whom the harshest measures were justified. It descended into an orgy of violence and unprecedented destruction of material culture, underpinned by a cult of personality around Mao. A 1981 resolution passed by the Chinese Communist Party acknowledged the Cultural Revolution as a catastrophe, and Mao's legacy was subsequently classified as 70 percent correct and 30 percent wrong. The very formulation "the Cultural Revolution," however, is itself misleading; as many have argued, by delimiting a period of ten years of chaos between 1966 and 1976, the Chinese Communist Party was able to normalize and legitimize its rule outside this time period. In fact, the techniques of revolutionary struggle normally associated with the Cultural Revolution were developed and applied much earlier, and they have had lasting legacies.

The songs of this era continued to be familiar staples of China's national soundscape into the twenty-first century: broadcast on national media at anniversary celebrations and other events, sung in China's parks by amateur choirs (Absaroka 2016). They also provided the soundtrack for the nostalgic and often commercial reinvention of Cultural Revolution culture that began in the 1990s (Mittler 2012). The overtly political mass singing of Red Songs in the twenty-first century was not unique to Xinjiang; they were also deployed in China's southwestern city of Chongqing in 2011, symbolizing a return to the "pure values" of the Cultural Revolution, as part of Bo Xilai's brief and ill-fated bid for power on the national stage (Steen 2013).

During 2015, many videos of Uyghur villagers singing Red Songs circulated on WeChat, shared by urban-educated Uyghur party members assisting the anti-religious-extremism campaign in rural areas. One video from Aqsu city, shared in June 2015, showed a local residents' committee organizing a women's choir to sing "In the Time of Liberation" (*Azad Zaman*), a revolutionary song made famous by the Uyghur singer Pasha Ishan in the 1950s. Official media also highlighted the Red Songs. Tianshan Net reported in October 2015 that "In Jiashi [Päyzawat] county, 2600 people

Fig. 6.4. "Sing Red Songs, praise the country, celebrate our home," Päyzawat County. Tianshan Net 2015.

gathered to sing Red Songs celebrating the sixtieth anniversary of the Xinjiang Uyghur Autonomous Region. They sang The East is Red in two languages, and a choral version of Long Live Chairman Mao. 61-year-old Sidiq Hasim sang in Chinese, Chairman Mao May You Live Forever, and Mixia village performed a dramatic skit on the theme of combating extremism." The Tianshan Net website published a spectacular series of photographs of local people at the rally, with young women dancing in short skirts in front of a large red banner, and older women dressed in red atlas silk dresses with Chinese flag stickers affixed to their cheeks (figs. 6.3 and 6.4). According to the report, they sang about ethnic unity and China's one family of nationalities, they praised the motherland, and they celebrated their home.[34]

Uyghurs in Turkey reposted this story as another example of "oppression in East Turkistan," citing a new Xinjiang government slogan: "Don't run to prayers, run to the dance!" (*namaz oqushqa ämäs, usul oynashqa yugur*).[35] And indeed, this part of the campaign continued to lay emphasis on involving religious personnel in the singing and dancing. Ömärjan Hakim, the governor of Awat County in Aqsu posted this on his personal blog in February 2015: "This week, Aqyar village of Tamtoghraq town organized a public gathering for religious personnel to practice singing revolutionary songs. This activity was implemented across all the county's villages and towns to promote patriotism and teach imams how to dress properly. They sang their love for their country and the Communist party and showed their happiness" (Ömärjan Hakim, blog, February 2015). Just as the Turkish Uyghur blog suggested, the campaign seemed to be actively replacing religious practice with song and dance; criminalizing the former and linking the latter inescapably to love of the Communist Party.

Responses from the Diaspora: Song and Dance as *Haram*

In November 2015, the World Uyghur Congress, a campaigning exile organization based in Munich, posted on its Facebook page images of dancing children and a traditional Uyghur music ensemble from Kazakhstan performing at the twenty-fifth anniversary celebration of the Uyghur community in Germany. The images provoked the following exchange in a Facebook thread:

USER NAME: Unsheathed Sword (*soghorulghan qilich*): Is our community still singing and dancing (*yänä nakhsha-usul bilänmu bu ummät*)?

USER NAME: Vengeance Boy (*qisasqar yigit*): Right now the Chinese government is trying to make our Uyghur people into atheists by organizing all sorts of arts events and forcing them to sing and dance. Our reporters in exile have condemned China's actions. But among our Uyghurs in the free world some people are voluntarily organizing song-and-dance activities. Do they actually think the Chinese government is doing the right thing? . . . It's like a man whose parents have died and he should be mourning, but he wraps the body in a reed mat and goes to a mäshräp. Uyghurs should be in mourning because of the daily tragedies we face, but you guys are organizing song and dance and publicizing it online. What a stupid thing! . . .

UNSHEATHED SWORD: . . . We complain we are forced to sing and dance in the homeland. I can't imagine why Uyghurs are doing this in exile, because in Islam song and dance is forbidden.

SON OF TURKESTAN: The Chinese taught this culture to them. China promotes Uyghurs as a singing and dancing nationality, and look what these people are doing here.

UNSHEATHED SWORD: How can we be, as the unbelievers say, a singing and dancing nationality? We are a nation who can shoot our arrows behind us on horseback. We can fight against oppression. We must remember this.

This Facebook thread revealed among certain parts of the Uyghur diaspora a perception of Chinese policies on minority song and dance that was remarkably in line with academic critiques, but it combined this perception with broader Islamist proscriptions on music. In this view, song and dance was both religiously inadmissible and a tool of China's oppression of the Uyghurs.

Historically in this region, musical culture has flourished as an integral part of religious expression, especially within the ritual practices transmitted by Sufi orders. In contemporary practice, musical traditions of *muqam* and *mäshräp* songs are performed at shrine festivals by dervishes (*ashiq*), and Sufi mystic poetry is sung in samaʿ rituals to the accompaniment of percussion and stringed musical instruments (Harris 2017; Light 2008; Mijit 2015). This musical-religious culture has for centuries coexisted in creative tension with more orthodox interpretations of the permissibility of music and dance in Islamic custom. These tensions and debates, which are replicated across the Islamic world, are rehearsed in some of the earliest extant religious texts from the region, including the sixteenth-century *Treatise on Audition* written by the Naqshbandi sheikh Makhdūm-i Aʿzam (also discussed in chap. 2).[36]

The treatise explains that human beings are composed of spirituality (*ruhaniyat*) and sensuality (*nafsaniyat*). If spirituality is predominant, someone who listens to fine voices will be brought to God and will progress in proximity with God since the ear of his heart is opened (*samʿ-i dilash kushada ast*). On the contrary, the careless ones (*ghafilan*) are oriented toward negligence, their hearts are black and hard, and fine sounds make no impression on them. They are inferior to animals because, when animals hear a beautiful voice, they are impressed and make spontaneous movements. If sensuality is dominant, then listening to fine voices will incline this kind of people toward fornication (*zina*) and obscenity (*fisq*). In other words, the practice of audition (*samaʿ*) itself is neither the cause nor the problem; the real foundation is the nature of the individuals (Papas 2015).

Such debates on the permissibility of music in religious life are reproduced in the folk stories that circulate across Uyghur society in multiple versions. A nineteenth-century tale collected by Gunnar Jarring recounts that on the Day of Judgment Satan will appear riding on a donkey whose tail hairs are made of the strings of musical instruments, and the sounds they produce will entice people to follow him to hell (Bellér-Hann 2000). In Yantaq village, playing music was regarded by most people as inappropriate for respectable or high-status members of the village community. Performing music was especially inappropriate for women in the village context, although dancing at mäshräp gatherings was generally considered acceptable. Mäshräps were highly valued, but the musicians who performed at them came from the lower end of village society. For leading religious figures such as haji or imam, even attending musical gatherings might provoke comment (Harris 2013a). These views, however, were by no means uniform across the region, and there was a sharp division between rural and urban attitudes to music.

Song and dance, as opposed to music, has its own particular history and set of meanings and values, dating back to the early twentieth century. Educated Uyghur urbanites still maintain considerable investment in song and dance, which they regard as a central part of modern national Uyghur culture and identity. Rather than following Unsheathed Sword and his friends in reading song and dance as a tool of control developed by the Chinese Communist Party and imposed on a passive and resentful Uyghur population, we may understand song and dance as a cocreation whose roots stretch back well beyond the founding of the People's Republic of China. Uyghur ethnomusicologist Mukaddas Mijit (2015) argues that it was the early-to-mid-twentieth-century Central Asian Muslim reformist Jadids who first developed the notion of Uyghur national culture and used musical performance to convey social reformist messages, long before the Chinese People's Liberation Army marched into Xinjiang. In part under the influence of Soviet models of cultural reform, Uyghur "Sanai Nepis" theater troupes of the 1930s produced the foundations of a new national repertoire based on local traditions of muqam, *dastan* epic stories, and the mäshräp songs of the ashiq. This national repertoire, which includes staged versions of the Twelve Muqam, operatic versions of classic love stories (Leila-Majnun, Farhad-Shirin, Ghärip-Sänäm) and many more items of staged Uyghur national culture, still resonates strongly with Uyghur listeners today (Mijit 2015; see also Harris 2008). A rejection of this culture implied, in the view of many urban intellectuals, a rejection of the development of the modern Uyghur nation.

But as the campaign hardened, Uyghur intellectuals like Yalqun Rozi began to argue that the modern emphasis on song and dance had helped to objectify, commodify, and fatally weaken the Uyghur nation.[37] Others struggled to reconcile their established sense of national identity with their love of their national music, with the growing sense that the same music was inappropriate as part of a pious religious lifestyle and that it was being used as a tool to attack Uyghur faith and religious identity. In 2014, the US-based Uyghur scientist Erkin Sidiq, a prominent member of the exile community, started an anxious discussion on music on a Uyghur language web forum:

> One of our younger brothers... asked me about the middle path of Islam, and how we should regard song and dance; is it halal or haram? Some fatwas say if its content is unhealthy then we should not listen to it. I know that in history when Muslims went to jihad or on the hajj they would sing. In olden times armies marched into battle playing music. [But then I heard] Yasir Qadhi [a conservative US Islamic scholar] explain that stringed instruments belong to Satan and it is a sin to listen to them. When I learned this, I couldn't sleep for days because music plays an important role for Uyghurs and our identity. We cannot maintain our culture without music. How to solve this problem? When Uyghurs accepted Islam we already had a very rich heritage. We cannot abandon everything for Islam, can we? We have a thousand-year-long history of song, dance and music. Have we been committing sin all this time? It is said if you have a good heart and do good deeds, Allah will accept you, and good deeds will wash away your sins. Uyghurs are a moral nation; even if we have sinned, Allah will accept us.[38]

Several discussions of these issues were conducted on various Uyghur-language message boards: what particular kinds of music might be haram and what kinds permissible, and why thinking about music distracted the Uyghur nation from its necessary task of self-discipline and improvement. Detailed fatwas on music and dance in Islam appeared on several Uyghur-language websites hosted in Turkey, with lengthy quotes from hadith explaining the particular types of music and the particular contexts where listening to music is haram.[39] Taken together, these anxious debates evidenced a growing division within the Uyghur community between the educated urban elite nationalists, who had for decades worn their religion with a light touch, and the new religiosity, which was concentrated among rural dwellers and businesspeople.

The heavy emphasis on singing and dancing in the anti-religious-extremism campaign exacerbated this division, bringing together traditional religious anxieties about music with modern antistate sentiment. It became harder for the nationalists to defend their interests in what they regarded as their national music (*milliy-muzika*) but which critics denigrated as song and dance (nakhsha-usul), precisely because it had become impossible to dissociate Uyghur music from support for—or at least acquiescence in—the Communist Party's project to cleanse the Xinjiang soundscape of Islamic sound. It was in this context, with music and Islam in Uyghur culture fixed into positions of opposition, and musical performance deployed as a tool of control by the state, that Uyghur pop singers like those mentioned in chapter 5 fled the country, arrived in Turkey "repenting of their sins"—sins that might well have included performing patriotic or revolutionary songs praising the Chinese Communist Party—and atoned for these sins recording radical anashid supporting the mujahidin.

Disciplining Bodies

In what way could these compulsory weekly song-and-dance sessions for Uyghur villagers be said to "counter extremism"? As the accounts presented in this chapter make clear, the anti-religious-extremism campaign was not aimed at the small minority of people who might be capable of carrying out acts of violence in the name of jihad. The campaign was aimed squarely at the broad-based Islamic revival among the Uyghurs, at the large numbers of people who had adopted a pious Muslim lifestyle, including embodied practices such as daily prayers, reciting the Qur'an, habits of Islamic modesty, and avoidance of tobacco and alcohol. The singing and dancing were part of wider campaign to discipline bodies, and particularly to discipline Muslim bodies—part of a raft of measures designed to disrupt and displace everyday embodied practices, including bans on public prayer, beer-drinking competitions, and bans on Islamic clothing and beards. The campaign was not simply about banning a set of religious practices; it actively sought to replace them with a different set of embodied behaviors. Daily prayer was to be replaced by daily song and dance.

In many ways, not only in that it revived the old revolutionary songs, this campaign was reminiscent of the mobilization techniques developed in China during the Cultural Revolution. The Chinese historian Ban Wang (1997) has provided a searing personal account of individual experience in the Cultural Revolution, noting the importance of embodiment, repetition, and theatricalization in the project of transforming Chinese people into revolutionary subjects: "The revolutionary rituals appealed to our senses and inner psyches, to our desires, and they worked on the surface of our bodies. They functioned on a cynical premise about individual human beings—on the supposition that the individual's mind and body are malleable, amenable to modeling and shaping by the sensuous medium of a ritual" (Wang 1997). The ubiquitous Model Operas (*yangbanxi*) of the Cultural Revolution provided people of that period with aesthetic and emotional models for becoming revolutionary heroes, but it was their embodied reproduction through the widespread practice of amateur performances that had the most significant impact on the transformation of Chinese citizens into revolutionary subjects. These amateur performances served as a way to mold people's bodies to imitate and ultimately to become revolutionary heroes.[40] As Wang recounts, "Through the constant reproductions of the plays and widespread immersion in them, the people no longer just performed the dramas and acted out the roles on the stage: they came to live these roles and act out the scenarios in daily life. They came to identify with the heroes, taking on the tone, pitch, and manner of their speech and assuming their bodily postures. They even gesticulated and moved in the same heroic and theatrical way" (Wang 1997). Fifty years later, the anti-religious-extremism campaign in Xinjiang revived these techniques of revolutionary mass mobilization. It was a battle fought not on the ideological front but over bodily habitus, directly focused on undermining the new religious forms of embodiment through the use of revolutionary traditions of embodiment and performance.

The focus on embodied practice is central to readings of the Islamic revival movement in the Middle East. As we have seen, forms of bodily practice such as veiling, daily prayers, or reciting the Qur'an do not simply express the self but also shape the self that they are supposed to signify (Mahmood 2005). Ethical self-formation, such as strengthening the desire to perform the daily prayers, can be achieved through constant vigilance, honing one's moral capacities in order to please God. In the course of this book, I have introduced several Uyghur men and women who were engaged in these kinds of ethical practice: Gulnisa Hajim in Bishkek, who ruined her eyesight crying over the sound of the recited Qur'an and dedicated herself to mastering and teaching the art of recitation; Bäkhtiyar in Karakol, who felt deep happiness when he obeyed the mysterious voice in his head telling him to pray; Aynisa in Yantaq village, who listened to black-market recordings until she could perfectly imitate the style of Abdul Basit. These new forms of habitus had become widespread and deeply sedimented in Uyghur society by 2012, and they were perceived as a challenge to state power.

Bourdieu (1984) describes habitus broadly as a system of dispositions, something nonnatural, a set of acquired characteristics that are the product of specific social conditions. As a theory of social power, Bourdieu's notion of habitus emphasizes change and process; it is formed through the changing dynamics between agents—individuals, groups, and institutions—and also between agents and their environment. Habitus transforms, but it is also transformed by the environment within which it is set into play. When Bourdieu highlighted the dynamism of habitus and emphasized that it does not apply only to stable societies, he raised the possibility of utilizing the concept to explain situations of radical social change (Hillier and Rooksby 2002, 58). Habitus is key to understanding the role of song and dance in the anti-religious-extremism campaign in Xinjiang. Chinese state responses to the Islamic revival in Xinjiang suggest a deep understanding of the role of habitus in the revival. The anti-religious-extremism campaign made a powerful intervention into these processes of Islamic subject formation, and it acted to replace them with forms of habitus developed in China's Cultural Revolution, styles of bodily behavior that were antithetical to the Islamic cultivation of a pious disposition.

Landscape

What is the significance of these interventions in habitus for the contested landscape, and how does all this singing and dancing relate to the idea of sonic territorialization? We have seen how the campaign emptied the virtual soundscape of Islamic media and filled the public soundscape with the sounds of Chinese pop songs and the old revolutionary songs, resignifying the lived spaces of Uyghur communities as a part of the territory of the People's Republic of China; a territory that was secular, modern, and absolutely dominated by the state. We may note the campaign's clear interest in the control of public space, visually marked by the ever-present array of public signage proclaiming the bans on prayer and Islamic dress in the streets, town squares, and parks. We may also note the insistent references to the local landscape in the songs of the campaign—paeans to "beautiful Xinjiang" or the beautiful orchards of Akto—and the repeated admonishments to "sing Red Songs, praise the motherland, and celebrate our home" (*jiaxiang*). But we must also return to a consideration of the ways in which embodied practices produce place.

Embodied practices and soundscapes are intimately linked. As Andrew Eisenberg (2013) explains, the Islamic soundscape recruits a set of bodily practices through which Muslims transform the public spaces of their neighborhoods into private community space. Eisenberg is concerned with the call to prayer that resonates out from Mombasa mosques five times a day, but the call to prayer has for decades been hardly audible in Xinjiang. If

Fig. 6.5. Image shared on WeChat in 2014: "When you feel the salt tears falling from your eyes, then you will understand that life is flavored by salt."

one could speak of an Islamic soundscape in this region, even at the height of the revival movement, it was one that was barely audible in public spaces. But the revival produced a resurgence of religious sounds in the private spaces of the home, and especially in the digitally mediated, public-private spaces of online forums and smartphone apps, creating a resonant virtual Islamic soundscape that served to promote and strengthen the changing bodily habitus and changing the ways in which Uyghurs inhabited the landscape (see fig. 6.5).[41]

Henri Lefebvre (2004) claims that "everywhere where there is interaction between a place, a time, and an expenditure of energy, there is rhythm" (15). Lefebvre argues that rhythms emerge from emplaced human practices and that we can identify the distinctive characteristics of place according to the ways in which changing rhythmic processes interweave with their environment. These rhythms shape our regular—daily, weekly, annual—experience of place, and they influence its ongoing material formation. This emphasis on rhythm posits the production of place as a dynamic process. Looking out his Paris window, Lefebvre considers the stop-start rhythms of pedestrians and traffic, the way they vary from day to day, and the regulatory systems that frame them: traffic lights, speed limits, and so forth. As with other habitual, everyday actions, such rhythmic systems are rarely noticeable except when they break down or are violated, but the ongoing mapping of space through repetitive, collective choreographies of congregation and interaction, rest and relaxation produce situated rhythms through which time and space are stitched together.⁴²

Drawing on these ideas, we can read the Islamic revival in Xinjiang as a set of embodied practices that reframed the landscape in ways that were deeply antithetical to state projects of modernization and development, and hence a contesting of state power. This, ultimately, is what the anti-religious-extremism campaign sought to counter. Viewed in this way, the campaign seems to be impelled by a more powerful logic than might be immediately apparent: it aimed to excise Islamic forms of habitus and replace them with revolutionary traditions of embodiment and performance, redefining the bodily practices of the Uyghur population as secular, modern, and appropriate for citizens of the People's Republic of China, and redefining the spaces where they lived as no longer Muslim space but state territory. The campaign harnessed song and dance with the aim of bringing about a thoroughgoing change in the ways that Uyghurs inhabited and moved through space, altering the rhythms of their time and place encounters. In order for this project to work at a bodily and also at a territorial level, the emphasis on participation and public performance was especially significant. As the practice of daily prayer was criminalized, and mosques and shrines were bulldozed or rendered inaccessible through regimes of surveillance, millions of Uyghurs were habituated to regular public communal dancing sessions.

We should avoid reading the song-and-dance aspect of the campaign as a project imposed by the state on a passive but largely alienated population. The sounds of the campaign formed another part of Uyghurs' sedimented sonic experience of place, formed through years of listening and embodied experience, from regular childhood participation in playground exercises and school performances to constant exposure via state media. Although some Uyghur voices that responded to the campaign identified song and dance as alien and irreligious tools of oppression, others could not so easily cast off the shared experience of song and dance as a fundamental trope of Uyghur national identity. Rather than reading this mobilization of song and dance to counter extremism as the imposition of an alien sonic regime on Muslim subjects, we may also read it as a form of cultural engagement that sought to harness these aspects of shared musical experience in pursuit of the goal of reframing Uyghurs as modern, secular Chinese citizens.

Hence the odd juxtaposition of the kitsch hit pop song "Little Apple" with classic revolutionary songs. If we are listening for the ideological messages they carry, then this juxtaposition makes little sense, but if we consider them in terms of the habitus that they evoke, then the logic is clear. Their importance lay not in their textual content, but simply in that they were part of a wider experience of being part of, and belonging to, the People's Republic of China. The fact that these experiences of singing and dancing were coercive and underpinned by state violence was completely consistent with past precedent, and this juxtaposition of song and dance and state violence would come still more sharply into focus in the new context of the mass internment camps that were already under construction across the region.

Notes

1. Caption on a video of dancing villagers posted on WeChat in March 2015 by a Uyghur party member transferred from Ürümchi to rural southern Xinjiang to assist the anti-religious-extremism campaign.

2. "Xinjiang Yingjisha County Farmers Jump for 'Little Apple' Active Rural Cultural Atmosphere," *China News*, January 24, 2015, http://www.chinanews.com/shipin/2015/01-24/news542897.shtml.

3. Sounding Islam in China [SIC], "Imams Dancing to 'Little Apple' in Uch Turpan, Xinjiang," *Sounding Islam in China*, March 25, 2015, http://www.soundislamchina.org/?p=1053.

4. Lyrics translated from a video posted on Youku, link shared on WeChat (accessed April 15, 2015).

5. David Brophy, "China's Little Apples," *The China Story*, February 16, 2015, https://www.thechinastory.org/2015/02/little-apples-in-xinjiang/.

6. See the introduction in Bellér-Hann et al. 2007 for further discussion of contending histories of the region.

7. Rob Schmitz, "Wary of Unrest among Uighur Minority, China Locks Down Xinjiang Region," NPR's *Morning Edition*, September 26, 2017, http://www.npr.org/sections/parallels/2017/09/26/553463964/wary-of-unrest-among-uighur-minority-china-locks-down-xinjiang-province.

8. Personal communication, BFE conference April 2016, University of Kent.

9. The form of prayer prohibited in figure 6.1 is explicitly Muslim: the *namaz* daily prayers (in Chinese, *zuo naimaze*).

10. Tom Philips, "Chinese Troops Stage Show of Force in Xinjiang and Vow to 'Relentlessly Beat' Separatists," *The Guardian*, February 20, 2017, https://www.theguardian.com/world/2017/feb/20/chinese-troops-stage-show-of-force-in-xinjiang-and-vow-to-relentlessly-beat-separatists.

11. "Xi Pledges Better Governance in Xinjiang," Xinhua, May 30, 2014, http://www.china.org.cn/china/2014-05/30/content_32530805.htm.

12. Andrew Jacobs, "Xinjiang Seethes under Chinese Crackdown: Uighur Identity under Siege in China," *New York Times*, January 2, 2016, https://www.nytimes.com/2016/01/03/world/asia/xinjiang-seethes-under-chinese-crackdown.html.

13. Eset Sulaiman, "New Xinjiang Party Boss Boosts Surveillance, Police Patrols," *Radio Free Asia*, December 16, 2016, http://www.rfa.org/english/news/uyghur/boosts-12162016145709.html.

14. "China Boosts Police Presence in Restless Xinjiang," *Metro News*, January 30, 2012, https://www.metro.us/news/china-boosts-police-presence-in-restless-xinjiang/tmWlaD---e2cqlpiTKZQpw.

15. Adrian Zenz and James Leibold, "Xinjiang's Rapidly Evolving Security State," *China Brief* 17, no. 4 (March 14, 2017), https://jamestown.org/program/xinjiangs-rapidly-evolving-security-state/.

16. Schmitz, "Wary of Unrest."

17. Tom Philips, "In China's Far West the 'Perfect Police State' Is Emerging," *The Guardian*, June 22, 2017, https://www.theguardian.com/world/2017/jun/23/in-chinas-far-west-experts-fear-a-ticking-timebomb-religious?CMP=Share_iOSApp_Other.

18. Choi Chi-yuk, "Ban on Islamic Dress Sparked Uygur Attack," *South China Morning Post*, July 22, 2011.

19. In 2017 video footage of public beer-drinking competitions for Uyghur women circulated on WeChat causing fresh outrage among the Uyghur diaspora.

20. Thanks to Aynur for this observation. See also figure 6.2, a depiction of women's veiling practices in a 2014 peasant art propaganda competition, part of the anti-religious-extremism campaign in Xinjiang.

21. Darren Byler "Uyghur Names as Signal and Noise," *Milestones: Commentary on the Islamic World*, June 2, 2017, https://www.milestonesjournal.net/articles/2017/6/2/uyghur-names-as-signal-and-noise.

22. Shohret Hoshur, "Under the Guise of Public Safety, China Demolishes Thousands of Mosques," *Radio Free Asia*, December 19, 2016, http://www.rfa.org/english/news/uyghur/udner-the-guise-of-public-safety-12192016140127.html.

23. Shohret Hoshur, "Village Crackdown on 'Illegal Religious Activities' Nets Dozens of Uyghurs," *Radio Free Asia*, April 26, 2017, http://www.rfa.org/english/news/uyghur/crackdown-04262017173652.html.

24. Shohret Hoshur, "Uyghurs Are Told to Confess Political 'Mistakes' in Mass Meetings," *Radio Free Asia*, February 14, 2017, http://www.rfa.org/english/news/uyghur/confess-02142017141212.html.

25. Jilil Kashgary, "Uyghur Farmers Sent to School in China 'Anti-Extremism' Drive," *Radio Free Asia*, December 13, 2016, http://www.rfa.org/english/news/uyghur/school-12132016172810.html.

26. Luisetta Mudie, "China's New Law Targets Muslim Children for 'Correction,'" *Radio Free Asia*, October 21, 2016, http://www.rfa.org/english/news/uyghur/chinas-new-law-targets-muslim-children-for-correction-10212016123917.html.

27. Xin Lin, "China Bans 'Extreme' Islamic Baby Names Among Xinjiang's Uyghurs," *Radio Free Asia*, April 20, 2017, https://www.rfa.org/english/news/uyghur/names-04202017093324.html.

28. Brophy, "China's Little Apples," 2015.

29. "Wedding Organizers in Kashgar Must Pay a Deposit to Ensure Singing and Dancing," *Radio Free Asia Uyghur Service*, November 3, 2015, http://www.rfa.org/uyghur/xewerler/kishilik-hoquq/qeshqer-toy-11032015233742.html.

30. Adam Kielman, "Selections from China's 60th Anniversary National Day Evening Gala" (subtitled), February 25, 2015, https://www.youtube.com/watch?v=DKQpov-oIRg&t=20s

31. See Harris 2020 for a detailed discussion of the history of mäshräp and its transformation into intangible cultural heritage.

32. Darren Byler, "China's Government Has Ordered a Million Citizens to Occupy Uighur Homes: Here's What They Think They're Doing," *China File*, October 24, 2018, http://www.chinafile.com/reporting-opinion/postcard/million-citizens-occupy-uighur-homes-xinjiang.

33. "Poskam County Organizes a Weekly *Mäshräp* to Enrich People's Lives," *Tianshan Net*, March 2015. The report has been removed from the website.

34. This approach was still in place in 2018 according to an official report on Labor Day celebrations in Kashgar, during which residents sang Red Songs, listened to lectures, and watched theatrical skits in order to deepen their understanding of extremism. The report has since been removed from the website.

35. "A New Opportunity from Occupational China: Run to Dance and Not Prayer," *Uyghur Net*, October 23, 2015, http://www.uyghurnet.org/namaza-degil-dans-etmeye/.

36. Ahmad Kāsānī Dahbīdī (honorific title Makhdūm-i Aʻzam), *Treatise on Audition* (*Risāla-yi samāʻiyya*). Manuscript preserved in Istanbul University, translated with commentary by Alexandre Papas 2015.

37. Yalqun Rozi, "Biz qandaqlarche nakhsha-usul milliti atilip qalduq," 2015. Uyghur National Cultural Organization. Archived at http://www.uyghurculture.org/uy/?p=1658. Yalqun Rozi was sentenced to life imprisonment for crimes relating to "separatism" in 2018. Shohret Hoshur, "Three Uyghur Intellectuals Jailed for Separatism," *Radio Free Asia*, October 10, 2018. https://www.rfa.org/english/news/uyghur/intellectuals-jailed-10102018172605.html.

38. Erkin Sidiq, *Din, Muzika we Uyghurlar*, April 2014, Bozkir website (now removed).

39. Hosted on a multilingual website supervised by Shaykh Muhammad Saalih al-Munajjid; also copied on the Turkish Uyghur site Islam House: http://islamqa.info/ug/5000 (accessed July 23, 2017).

40. See also Laurence Coderre 2016 on embodiment in amateur performances of the model operas during the Cultural Revolution period.

41. It is significant that this image was shared on the anniversary of the 2009 violence in Ürümchi.

42. See also Edensor 2010 and Madlen Kobi's 2016 discussion of urban transformation in southern Xinjiang, which draws on Lefebvre's tripartite model of social space.

7

ERASURE AND TRAUMA

Erasure

"Xi Jinping is great! The Communist Party is great! I deserve punishment for not understanding that only President Xi Jinping and the Communist Party can help me," ... a Uyghur woman who was in a center last fall, was forced to regularly repeat ... [in] self-criticism sessions. ... "My soul is infected with serious diseases," ... "There is no God. I don't believe in God. I believe in the Communist Party." ... Day after day she would say out loud that she was a traitor, a separatist and a terrorist. ... "I am so blind not to see the greatness of our strong country's laws. I am so stupid that I was not thankful for our President Xi Jinping," she would be told to recite.[1]

As I write the concluding part of this book, a climate of terror prevails in Xinjiang: surveillance on an unprecedented scale and the mass detention of more than a million of the region's citizens (Smith Finley 2019). During 2017, news gradually began to leak out of Xinjiang of the construction of a huge, secretive network of internment camps, which were dubbed "transformation through education centers" or "counter-extremism training centers" in official Chinese sources. Overseas journalists and scholars began to piece together the evidence, and by mid-2018 international organizations and national governments were raising concerns that more than a million Muslims—primarily Uyghurs but also Kazakhs and other Muslim groups, more than 10 percent of the adult Muslim population of the region—had been interned in the camps for indefinite periods of time without formal legal charge.[2] Reports by former detainees, teachers, and guards described a network of more than one hundred newly built or greatly expanded detention facilities, heavily secured with barbed wire and surveillance systems and guarded by armed police, some of them large enough to hold up to one hundred thousand inmates.[3] These reports were corroborated by careful investigation of government construction bids and satellite imagery of the new facilities (Zenz 2019).

Although international attention rightly focused on the unprecedented extent of these mass detentions, the camps were only the sharp end of a set of policies that had effectively transformed the whole region into a militarized high-security zone. These new securitization policies were introduced by Chen Quanguo, who had been appointed to the role of party secretary in Xinjiang in August 2016. Chen arrived in Xinjiang by transfer from Tibet, where he had developed a sophisticated network of surveillance and control in response to the protests of 2008.[4] In Xinjiang, the same policies were applied with great speed, on a much larger scale, taking advantage of newly available surveillance technologies, including GPS trackers, radio-frequency identification fitted on cars, and checkpoints at transport hubs and at entries into markets and shopping centers, complete with metal detectors and facial recognition or iris-recognition machines. Understanding of the extent and sophistication of these surveillance systems emerged gradually into the public domain thanks to the work of investigative journalists and Human Rights organizations.

One of the main mass surveillance systems used by the Xinjiang authorities was dubbed the Integrated Joint Operations Platform. This software collected massive amounts of personal information about the people of Xinjiang and flagged those deemed appropriate subjects for detention and reeducation. The kinds of suspicious behavior targeted built on the designated signs of extremism discussed in previous chapters and included further categories such as "not socializing with neighbors" and "often avoiding using the front door." The system also flagged the use of VPNs and social media platforms including WhatsApp and Viber.[5] When Uyghurs and other Muslims passed through a security check (Han Chinese residents were permitted to bypass these checks)—getting off a train or on the way to the bazaar—their faces and phones were scanned. If anything "suspicious" was logged against them, an alarm would be triggered, summoning extra police from a nearby "convenience police station" to interrogate and possibly detain them.

By spring 2018, the Uyghur social-media network, Ündidar, was awash with statements of passionate patriotism. Uyghur intellectuals and artists posted images of themselves gazing heroically into a bright future against the background of the Chinese flag, alongside quotations from the *Thought of President Xi Jinping*, freshly enshrined in the Chinese constitution. They added to their profiles the phrase "Love my China" (*aiwo zhonghua*) and posted a Chinese-language declaration that began "I am a citizen of the People's Republic of China. I resolutely support the leadership of the Chinese Communist Party." Uyghurs in Xinjiang replaced their former statements of piety with expressions of love for President Xi. Only very occasionally did other kinds of message creep through the "walls of steel" surrounding Xinjiang, suggesting that other sentiments lay beneath. In February 2018, one woman shared and then swiftly deleted this post:

> We don't know what fate this world will bring us. I am getting really afraid that I will fail your test. Please give me your help. Please give me peace. Right now I'm worrying about many things. The first is I don't want to go sleep at night because I'm afraid I may not be able to wake up anymore; the second is I don't know when the black hands will take me and throw me into a dark prison. These days many, many people I know are being taken away, every second, every minute, hour, or day, accused of all sorts of things.

Such fears were well founded, and more and more people were detained, often directly in connection with their digital footprints. A foreign phone number in their contacts list, an audio recording of Qur'anic recitation such as those discussed in chapter 4, or a religious image such as those discussed in chapter 5 were now all counted as sufficient evidence of religious extremism to condemn individuals, without formal charge, to a bout of reeducation of unspecified length in the camps.

Surveillance techniques also drew on the low-tech but extremely intrusive method of home stays. Under the Becoming Family policy, more than a million Han Chinese government employees were mobilized to make regular home stays with Uyghur families and to observe their enthusiasm for speaking in Chinese and singing patriotic songs. They also probed for suspicious activities, such as using the traditional greeting "*Assalam aleykum*," hiding a Qur'an in the home, or having friends or relatives in "sensitive" regions such as Turkey or Egypt. Other suspicious signs might include failure to accept a proffered cigarette or glass of beer, or hesitating to accept food that might not be halal.[6]

By 2017, the so-called anti-religious-extremism campaign had spread beyond the religious sphere; no longer simply branding everyday religious activity as terrorism, its scope had expanded to target all signs of (Uyghur) nationalist sentiment, foreign connections, or simply insufficient loyalty to the state. Official statements suggested that the whole Uyghur nation was now regarded as a problem in need of an aggressive solution. As one

Xinjiang government official said in a public speech in late 2017, "You can't uproot all the weeds hidden among the crops in the field one by one—you need to spray chemicals to kill them all; re-educating these people is like spraying chemicals on the crops... that is why it is a general re-education, not limited to a few people."[7] Any kind of links with Uyghurs in the diaspora was now regarded as evidence of anti-Chinese intent. Families who had relatives working or studying abroad were warned against receiving their phone calls, at the risk of a period of detention in one of the camps. The campaign was further broadened to include "two-faced" people such as government officials, teachers, and businesspeople who "appeared to be fighting terrorism while actually sympathizing with it."[8] Also sucked into the internment camps were hundreds of prominent Uyghur intellectuals, writers, and artists whose crimes—although they were not formally stated—seemed to be that their work in some way promoted Uyghur language, culture, or history.[9] Many of my own colleagues, long-term associates, and friends were among those detained: the iconic and much-loved musicians Sanubar Tursun and Abdurehim Heyit,[10] the popular author and scholar of Chagatay poetry, Abduqadir Jaladin, and my long-standing research partner Rahile Dawut, professor of folklore at Xinjiang University, an internationally respected scholar who had dedicated years of her life to documenting the rich culture of Uyghur shrine pilgrimage.[11] Increasingly the term "religious extremism" seemed to serve as a gloss for Uyghur culture and identity, which was now regarded as a "virus" in need of eradication. Uyghurs in exile and other commentators abroad began to describe the campaign as a form of cultural cleansing or cultural erasure.

Human Reengineering

The mass projects of representation and bodily discipline described in chapter 6 continued and deepened alongside this system of surveillance and detention. In February 2018, Chinese media carried images of crowds of Uyghur peasants brandishing flags to celebrate the Chinese New Year and standing in front of the doorways of their homes on which they had pasted the traditional Chinese New Year greetings.[12] A year later, we observed videos shared on social media of whole Uyghur communities in Khotan mobilized to celebrate the Chinese New Year by performing traditional Chinese *yang'ge* dances in the streets. Uyghurs across Xinjiang were expected to attend regular Chinese-language lessons, and officials made speeches suggesting that speaking Uyghur in public was a sign of disloyalty to the state. These new initiatives suggested that it was now no longer sufficient to reject Islam; what was required of Uyghurs was a wholesale adoption of Chinese cultural identity. As several commentators have suggested, this was a project to "reengineer" Uyghur society.[13]

The children of detainees were taken to orphanages where they were educated to regard the religion and identity of their parents as backward and dangerous.[14] Men were detained in larger numbers than women, and the Xinjiang authorities began to encourage ethnic intermarriage, offering cash incentives to Han men who were willing to marry Uyghur women. By 2019, the reengineering project had extended to the innermost bodily aspects of Uyghur identity by targeting halal eating practices. Radio Free Asia reported that detainees in the camps were being served pork and threatened with physical punishment and food deprivation if they refused to eat. Outside the camps too, Chinese media reported that pork had been distributed to poor Uyghur families as part of a Chinese New Year poverty relief effort.[15] Such radical efforts to break down these core aspects of faith and identity across the broad population were only possible because of the regime of terror enforced by the system of detention camps.

Several testimonies from former detainees provided detailed accounts of life inside the camps. Omir Bekali, a citizen of Kazakhstan, was imprisoned in 2016 during a visit to his parents in Xinjiang and released after seven months of detention when Kazakhstan diplomatically intervened.[16] After a period in jail, during which he was subjected to physical torture, Bekali was taken to a reeducation center that housed more than one thousand detainees. According to his account, detainees would wake before dawn to sing the Chinese national anthem and raise the Chinese flag. They gathered in large classrooms for history lessons in which they learned that the indigenous peoples of Xinjiang were backward and yoked by slavery before they were liberated by the Chinese Communist Party in the 1950s. They studied the dangers of Islam and took regular quizzes to test the knowledge they had acquired. Failing a test was punished by being made to stand facing a wall for several hours at a time. Refusal to follow orders was punished by solitary confinement or deprivation of food. Gulbahar Jelil, another Kazakhstan citizen who was incarcerated for more than a year, gave harrowing testimony on her experience in a camp, where she lived on a starvation diet in overcrowded cells. She observed several suicides in the camps and the widespread use of psychiatric drugs to subdue inmates.[17] Mihrigul Tursun, a resident of Egypt, was detained while trying to visit her parents in Xinjiang. She also provided testimony of suffering torture and a starvation diet, of observing the deaths of several fellow inmates, and of being separated from her young children, one of whom died under mysterious circumstances.[18]

Regimes of forced repetition and self-criticism feature strongly in these testimonies. Detainees were made to recite repeatedly, "We will oppose extremism, we will oppose separatism, we will oppose terrorism." Before meals, they were required to demonstrate their gratitude to the Communist Party by chanting "Thank the Party! Thank the Motherland! Thank President Xi!" In classes, detainees presented self-criticisms of their own religious histories. They also criticized their fellow inmates and submitted to the criticism of their peers. They admitted to learning to recite the Qur'an, to traveling outside China where they risked being exposed to extremist thought, to wearing Muslim clothing, and to praying. Those who confessed to such behaviors were made to recite repeatedly, "We have done illegal things, but we now know better." Detainees who most vigorously criticized the people and things they loved were rewarded, and those who refused were punished with solitary confinement, beatings, and food deprivation. Journalist Gerry Shih observed that "the internment program aims to rewire the political thinking of detainees, erase their Islamic beliefs and reshape their very identities."[19]

As with the techniques used outside the camps, musical performance played a key role in the reeducation program. A leaked video clip circulated on Uyghur exile networks in 2017, which appeared to show two rows of Uyghur detainees kneeling in an empty room, holding plastic bowls, and singing the revolutionary song "Without the Communist Party There Is No New China." The Uyghur intellectual Abduwali Ayup, who was assaulted, abused, and detained in 2013 in connection with his efforts to establish a Uyghur-language school, explained in a Facebook post: "This is what a Chinese (detention) center looks like. They are Uyghur detainees, they are singing 'There is no new Life without Chinese Communist Party.' They are singing for (their) meal."[20] In this context of mass incarceration and documented abuse, such coercive use of musical performance may be understood as an instance of the weaponization of music.

The weaponization of sound and music in the context of the Iraq war has been extensively critiqued. Suzanne Cusick (2008) focuses on the use of music as an interrogation technique by US forces, part of a package of measures designed to break down an individual's will and sense of self. In Abu Ghraib prison, music videos were used against Muslim detainees as part of a set of attacks on their ethical sense of self and their ability to perform the embodied practices required by their faith. In Xinjiang's reeducation centers, we find detainees subject to very similar processes, in which the coerced singing of revolutionary songs is used to break down the embodied habits of pious practice, as part of a set of attacks on detainees' will and sense of self. As Cusick argues, coerced listening takes advantage of music's unique ability to serve simultaneously as sensory experience, site of cultural belief, and medium of cultural practice.

Musical performance was also to the fore in the carefully choreographed visits to the camps organized in 2019 by the Chinese authorities for selected international media organizations.[21] Organized in response to concerns raised at the UN about mass human rights abuses in Xinjiang, these visits sought to reassure the international community that the camps were in fact voluntary "vocational training centers" designed to prepare inmates who had been led astray by "extremist thoughts" for gainful employment. Assembled inmates sang the English language song "If You're Happy and You Know It" for the press crews. The irony of this coerced display of happiness was highlighted by international observers, but this was no more than the latest manifestation of the long-standing practices, which I discussed in chapter 6, of the staged representation of China's minority peoples through singing, dancing, and smiling.

As I sit in my study on a breezy London afternoon, I contemplate what will become of my Uyghur friends, relatives, colleagues, and many interlocutors who may currently be detained in an internment camp (or who may not be detained: since calling them from abroad might result in detention, I do not call them to find out whether they are safe). Are they singing for their food "Without the Communist Party There Is No New China?" Are they repeatedly chanting that they are traitors and terrorists? How long will they be subjected to this regime? What will the experience do to them? Will it be a brief lesson to teach them the acceptable boundaries of behavior in contemporary China, a "short, sharp shock" as sections of the British media sometimes like to label prison sentences? Will it wreak some form of permanent change in them, spiritually, mentally, physically? Can I imagine a future for my friends in which these experiences will be overlaid, if not entirely forgotten, by new impressions and new memories?

Trauma

The psychological pressure is enormous, when you have to criticize yourself, denounce your thinking—your own ethnic group," said Bekali, who broke down in tears as he described the camp. "I still think about it every night, until the sun rises. I can't sleep. The thoughts are with me all the time."[22]

Many of the testimonies and interviews with Uyghurs in the diaspora have framed the experience of the campaign in terms of trauma. Like Omir Bekali, Mihrigul Tursun was reported as suffering from debilitating posttraumatic stress, including nightmares and sudden bouts of anxiety. Accounts of conversations with Uyghurs within China hint at the extreme psychological pressure, pervasive fear, and widespread depression that many people were experiencing.[23] Uyghurs in exile have also reported anxiety and trauma due to the difficulty of maintaining contact with loved ones and uncertainty about their fate, feelings of guilt and personal responsibility for the detention of family members, and direct harassment by Chinese security forces if they chose to speak out about their experience.[24]

The field of trauma studies has produced psychological models for the catastrophic long-term effects of war, persecution, and violent social upheaval. Psychologists have argued that however disparate the events that give rise to them, the psychological consequences of such events have much in common. This is now reflected in the international acceptance of the diagnosis of posttraumatic stress disorder. Part of the model is the observation that individual experiences of trauma may be transmitted within families to future generations and become part of the collective memories of whole social groups: forms of cultural trauma that arise in response to a dramatic loss of identity and meaning, or a tear in the social fabric (Argenti and Schramm 2009). Writing on the experience of trauma among Iraq war veterans in the United States, Martin Daughtry (2015) notes how sound is often singled out in veterans' testimony as a primary stimulus of traumatic stress; not a cause of trauma in itself but frequently a prominent element in the intersensorial onslaught of war.

What role might sound, and especially musical sound, play in relation to the trauma suffered by Uyghurs through their experiences of political violence, incarceration, and coercive techniques of reeducation, and how might this play out in terms of a collective remembering of these events? Many commentators have noted the revival of the political and social techniques of China's revolutionary period under Xi Jinping.²⁵ The antireligious-extremism campaign in Xinjiang, as we have seen, evokes many tropes of the Cultural Revolution, including spectacles of revolutionary fervor involving song and dance, coercive reeducation, and self-criticism. Since there are so many continuities with the Cultural Revolution era in the methods now being applied in Xinjiang, it is worth contemplating what we have learned about the impacts on people who lived through that period and were subject to similar techniques of political reeducation and self-criticism.

The psychic damage of the Cultural Revolution was expressed in some measure in the "scar" literary movement of the 1980s, but the continuity of Communist Party rule in China—in contrast to Germany, for example, where the Holocaust legacy has been thoroughly studied and memorialized—has meant that the suffering and lasting psychological impact of China's revolutionary period on those who lived through it, and on subsequent generations, has been largely sidelined. A rare collaborative project carried out by Chinese researchers working with German psychotherapists applied the methods developed in the field of trauma studies to a study of Cultural Revolution survivors and their children (Plänkers 2014). A particular source of trauma noted by Plänkers' interviewees was the habit of constant scrutiny of one's own thinking and actions for signs of political deviance that became a necessity for survival. Plänkers also argues that the traumatic psychic structures of the first Cultural Revolution generation had affected the next; interviewees displayed unconsciously powerful identifications that had led to the repetition of traumatizing behavior, accompanied by defensive stances that blocked the emotional or intellectual appreciation of these consequences (Plänkers 2014).

Some of Plänkers's interviewees cite the impact of memories of sounds in their testimonies. One interviewee recalled that "I was afraid of the sound of people being beaten.... Since then I can't listen anymore, when people are beaten ... Every time I tremble inside. I can't stand hearing beatings, or crying or screaming" (Plänkers 2014). We find other discussions of memories of music and violence in studies of the Cultural Revolution. Sinologist Geremie Barmé (1999) attends to the importance of positionality in memories of the violence of this period:

> For many older people today, the music of the operas is little less than "the threnody of the [Chinese] holocaust,"²⁶ for it was these sounds that were the

Muzak wallpaper of the violent purges and campaigns of that tumultuous time. For the children of the Cultural Revolution, however . . . the operas and the bizarre culture they represented were imbibed along with their mother's milk. What for their parents and grandparents were the shrill sounds of terror are for Feng and many of his fellows the surroundsound of nostalgia and childhood innocence. (Barmé 1999, 231)

In chapter 6, I discussed some of the responses among the Uyghur diaspora to the use of music in the anti-religious-extremism campaign, noting how some voices advocated the wholesale rejection of Uyghur national music as a cultural form, arguing that it served only to express Uyghur subjugation under Chinese rule. For others, however, sustaining this musical culture in the diaspora has become a central way to resist cultural erasure. As Daughtry (2015) notes, to imagine human experience taking place at the intersection of auditory regimes and acoustic territories is to confront the complex web of histories, actors, and influences that hides beneath the simple act of listening. This latest round of violence, coercive reeducation, and reterritorialization is not something new for the Uyghurs, and as we reflect on the possible consequences of this latest bout of terror, we need to think about the agency and the resilience of those subjected to its regime. Discourses of trauma may point to more than a clinical diagnosis. Nicolas Argenti and Katherina Schramm (2009) argue that the act of remembering violence, especially when it emerges at a collective level, is not simply a pathology but may also serve as a political act. It represents not a mere repetition over which the sufferer has no control and to which they can attribute no meaning, but more often a constructive engagement with a fractured past and a moral judgment of its political significance.

The Cultural Revolution also played out in Xinjiang, and Uyghurs were also subject to the extreme violence, social chaos, reeducation, and self-criticism of that period. As we saw in Rabiya Acha's story, recounted in interlude 1 in this book, the terror of that period was also unevenly distributed, and for people in rural areas, memories of criticism sessions and violence may well be less prominent than memories of food shortages and illness. We should also remember that the Uyghur Islamic revival was in many ways a response to the restrictions and the trauma of the revolutionary period, a remembering of former practices, and a renewal of faith that served as a form of healing and transformation. As Hurriyät Hajim suggests,

> Since I came back from the hajj I don't have pain, I feel well. All I'm thinking about is kneeling on my prayer mat and doing my daily prayers. We will all

die, and as Muslims we must pray five times a day. In Mecca every day a mulla took the lead with a microphone and taught the whole group how to pray, how to be a proper Muslim. Before I went on the hajj I didn't follow true Islam, I was careless. Then I thought to myself, here I am at home with nothing else to do so I started doing my prayers, and now I feel I have discovered true Islam. If I miss a prayer I feel uncomfortable. I only feel happy and relaxed when I do my regular prayers, so I don't go to the bazaar much these days because I worry I'll miss my prayer. I am very happy, because Allah has blessed me and given me that spirit, so my inner world is very bright. Allah has given me the chance to be a haji. When you're on the hajj you don't feel hungry, you don't think about your family, you forget about this world, you just want to pray. (Hurriyät Hajim, Yantaq village, 2012)

This powerful sonic memory of a mulla with a microphone during her hajj sustained Hurriyät Hajim through her experience of physical pain. Such memories easily resurface at times of need. Among the accounts in chapter 4 from people who had recently returned to their faith, it was often the case that childhood memories of early religious experiences within the home, especially learning the forms of the daily prayer from an older relative, were driving factors in their adoption of a pious lifestyle. For these people, even forty years of social upheaval and secularization was not sufficient to erase these early memories and lessons in embodied religious practice.

Repetitive Rhythms

If one theme ties this book together, it is this question of repetition: the repetitive rhythms that lie at the heart of the practice of zikr and the motions of daily prayer, the repetitive performance of Chinese revolutionary songs and the repeated acknowledgment of the self as infected with ideological virus of extremism. The relationship between sound, place, and body, and the role of these repetitive rhythms in forming and re-forming the self lie at the heart of this study. In the introduction to this book, I evoked the ideas of Judith Butler, who argues that all social forms—civilization, gender, nation—are effects of repetition and that it is through the repetition of norms that worlds materialize, and that boundary, fixity, and surface are produced (Butler 1993). I showed how Butler's ideas are taken up by Sarah Ahmed (2004) in her writing on the circulation of emotions and the ways in which emotions take shape through the repetition of actions over time. The büwis in Yantaq village often emphasized the spiritual necessity of repetition—"we have to repeat the shahadah 72,000 times for a death"—and repetition lay at the heart of their regular practice of khätmä, with its repeated rhythmic recitation of Arabic prayers and phrases from the Qur'an. This embodied repetitive practice allowed the büwis in Yantaq village to do spiritual work on themselves and to bring spiritual benefits to village society. Repetition underpins this form of religious practice just as it underlies the bodily disciplines of China's revolutionary culture and the regime in Xinjiang's camps.

In chapter 6, I introduced the "rhythmology" of Henri Lefebvre (2004): the notion that repetitive, collective choreographies of congregation and interaction, rest and relaxation produce situated rhythms through which time and space are stitched together. I suggested this theory as a way of understanding how the anti-religious-extremism campaign and mass displays of song and dance sought to discipline Muslim bodies and transform the Xinjiang soundscape. I drew parallels with Ban Wang's (1997) account of amateur performances of the Cultural Revolution model operas and the way that through constant reproductions of the plays and widespread immersion in them people came to live these roles and act out the scenarios in daily life. Lefebvre's focus frequently turns to this kind of social disciplining of the body. He refers to the regulation of embodied rhythms as "dressage": a means to train the body to perform and condition it to accede to particular rhythms: "Humans break themselves in (*se dressent*) like animals. They learn to hold themselves. Dressage can go a long way: as far as breathing, movements, sex. It bases itself on repetition. One breaks in another human living being by making them repeat a certain act, a certain gesture or movement" (Lefebvre 2004: 39). From everyday systems of traffic control to the extremes of the reeducation regime in Xinjiang's camps, systems of power often seek to impose rhythmic conformity on their subjects. Such attempts at "dressage" are most clearly observable and often at their most brutal under systems of colonial rule in which the ruling powers have attempted to "break in" a whole subject group by habituating them to new rhythmic and spatial norms.

Coloniality and Palimpsests

Both in terms of the measures being employed and the ideological justification of its actions, the Chinese state project to securitize Xinjiang and reengineer its Muslim peoples may be read as a colonial project. As Dibyesh Anand (2019) has argued, coloniality is about proprietorial control, dispossession, and difference in power. Built into it is the assumption that the

Other is inferior to the progressive Self, which has the duty and the right to mold the violent and backward Other into its own image. The campaign's relentless focus on embodied practices in Xinjiang is far from unique; we can find many similarities in its approach to reengineering Uyghurs in other, historical colonial projects around the world.

In many cases, the imposition of colonial rule entailed an almost obsessive interest in the embodied, performative practices of the subjugated—rituals, songs, or dances—suggesting an understanding of the importance of such practices as sites for the expression and transmission of identity and memory, and a focus on the body as the prime locus for imposing new regimes of knowledge and being. Diana Taylor (2003) argues that an important aspect of the colonizing project throughout the Americas consisted of discrediting autochthonous ways of preserving and communicating historical understanding. Just as Uyghur religious and cultural practices are dubbed religious extremism and terrorism in China, so indigenous performance practices were dubbed devil worship under colonial rule in the Americas. The numerous prohibitions imposed under colonial rule in the Americas sought to limit the indigenous peoples' capacity for movement, economic independence, self-expression, and community building, and they attempted to interrupt social memory and embodied memory. The many edicts against performance practices suggests that the colonial rulers recognized that such practices functioned as ways of organizing knowledge as well as remembering knowledge (Taylor 2003).

But Taylor's account also makes clear that the persistent attempts by the colonizers to erase these performance practices were matched only by their obstinate resurgence: both in their own ways were performances of power and resistance: "the performance of the prohibitions seems as ubiquitous and continuous as the outlawed practices themselves. Neither disappeared" (Taylor 2003, 43). Lefebvre (2004) also urges us to avoid assuming that the managed normative rhythms imposed by systems of power possess an overarching force that compels individuals to march to their beat. Thus, we should not assume for one moment that the effects of the anti-religious-extremism campaign in Xinjiang will be a permanent erasure of the religious sensibilities and the cultural identity of its subjects and to rewire them as patriotic automatons. In the crowded cell of the internment camp where Gulbahar Jelil was detained, the detainees were under constant surveillance, and strict punishments were enforced against anyone seen to be performing the movements of prayer. Gulbahar recounts how the women in her cell whispered to each other to "pray on the inside."[27] Even when inaudible, the Islamic soundscape may be reactivated—internally, repetitively—through simple acts of remembering engrained bodily practices. Such small acts of resistance hint at the possibility of sustaining embodied memory even under the most extreme conditions of coercion and control, and they suggest the inevitable failure of state projects of social reengineering.

The trope of the palimpsest—a manuscript on which earlier writing has been effaced and later writing has been superimposed—is helpful for thinking through these issues. The palimpsest, as Martin Daughtry (2013) notes, is defined by a paradox: it is formed of multiple layers inscribed by multiple authors and composed of repeated but unsuccessful attempts to erase that which came before. We can see these processes of erasure and overwriting at work in multiple spheres in Xinjiang: across the landscape and the soundscape, and inscribed on and within the bodies of its citizens. In the visual sphere we may note the overnight bulldozing of unofficial mosques,[28] acts of painting over religious inscriptions on gravestones (see fig. 7.1), and removing the word *halal* from restaurant signs (Smith Finley 2019).

In the digital sphere too, palimpsests abound. Although Uyghurs strove to demonstrate their loyalty and patriotism on their social media feeds, it was impossible to fully delete their digital footprint. Many people were detained after they were stopped at a checkpoint and a simple form of retrieval software was used on their phones, easily revealing deleted images of prayer or audio files of Qur'anic recitation.

In the same way, we can think of the sonic aspects of the campaign—the mass singing and dancing, the forced singing of revolutionary songs and repeated denial of faith in detention centers—as acoustic palimpsests based on political acts of erasure and attempts to inscribe new ideological orientations on a populace through sound. As Daughtry (2013) argues, the palimpsest often entails violence: "The twin acts of erasure and reinscription that are the palimpsest's minimal condition can easily be construed as an aggressive move with respect to the past. The desire to erase the past and start afresh is one of the hallmarks of modernism, and the palimpsest metaphor retains some of the violent energy of this movement. While the persistence of the *scriptio inferior* points toward the impossibility of fully erasing history, the palimpsest is nonetheless infused with the desire to do so" (28). If we can read the Xinjiang soundscape as an acoustic palimpsest, composed of layers of sonic memories that can be reanimated and activated

Fig. 7.1. Images of the sickle moon and phrases from the Qur'an are painted over in a Kazakh graveyard in northern Xinjiang. Image shared on Facebook July 2018.

at any time, then arguably the task of the scholar is to listen through the layers, to perceive not only the dominant and immediately audible present of the soundscape but also the things that have been submerged and overwritten but never fully erased. Ildikó Bellér-Hann (2014) has described the bulldozing of a Uyghur graveyard in the eastern town of Qumul and the construction of the new Muqam Heritage Centre on the site. She observed the way that the Uyghur cultural officials entered the new building for the first time in 2009, offering a prayer to the displaced dead before they passed through the doors. The new building could not erase their memories of the former landscape, and their whispered prayer served to reanimate that landscape and perhaps to mitigate the violent memories of its erasure. Stories such as this attest that soundscapes are entwined with bodies and with places, dynamic, contested, and layered.

Again, scholarship on the Americas provides helpful insights for reflecting on the current situation in Xinjiang. Ruth Hellier-Tinocco (2019) introduces the notion of "palimpsest bodies," figuring the human body as both container and transmitter of histories. Pasts, she argues, are deposited within bodies as forms of corporeal memory. Embodied memories are built up in sedimented layers, and they may be reactivated in performance. Thus, the idea of the palimpsest is inherently concerned with transtemporality, and the understanding of past and present not as successive but as simultaneously produced. Hellier-Tinocco reflects on contemporary postcolonial strategies of performing palimpsest bodies. Such performances draw on embodied and sedimented collective memories of colonial violence, and they rework them in ways that permit the imagination of other potential political realities and other futures. Performance practices like this offer the possibility of a counternarrative to the fears of erasure that now haunt Uyghur communities. We can see performative moves already afoot among the Uyghur diaspora, as in the dancing body of Mukaddas Mijit, who provocatively positioned herself amid the passersby on Brooklyn Bridge in 2018, performing Uyghur dance moves for the camera of artist Lisa Ross.[29]

In 2017, as the police checks and intrusions into daily life became more intense and the penalties for possessing religious material became more severe, people started to dispose of their personal collections. Stories circulated of streams clogged with religious books hastily disposed of by throwing them into the water. People deleted apps and files containing religious material from their phones. But the new regulations, and even the new high-tech surveillance measures, could not completely erase the Islamic soundscape. Apart from the sonic memories people retained, they also carefully hid away many of their prized religious artifacts. Just as their parents or grandparents had during the Cultural Revolution, they buried books in their gardens, and they hid their prayer mats and prayer beads in food stores and animal shelters. In a contemporary refraction of this practice, some people downloaded their digital libraries onto spare SIM cards, inserted them into dumplings and preserved them in the freezer.[30]

Far from internalizing understandings of their culture and faith as an infectious disease that led inexorably to terrorist violence, I suggest that Uyghurs are well accustomed to the periodic and transient nature of political campaigns (see fig. 7.2), and they know how to attune themselves to the requirements of the present. "Five or six years ago they even dared to play Qur'anic recitation on the village loudspeakers. Now they say it is religious extremism," Rabiya Acha told us in 2009.

Fig. 7.2. A faded and cracking propaganda mural in July 2018, with dirt from some new construction project already piled in front of it, suggesting the impermanence of the current security measures. Photograph courtesy of Lisa Ross.

Others responded to political persecution in ways that strengthened their religious faith. In Yantaq village, büwi Nisakhan recounted an incident when local government officials raided their family home looking for illegal religious books in an early phase of the anti-religious-extremism campaign in 2011. They discovered her mother's carefully preserved handwritten collection of hikmät:

> The government people looked at the book, and they said, "This is worse than reading the Qur'an. It is not acceptable because it says, if you don't do your prayers, if you don't follow the rules of Islam, you will die a bad death." That's why the administration banned it. It also says this kind of thing in the Qur'an, but it's in Arabic so people can't understand it. But these hikmät say very directly that if you are not a good Muslim you will die a bad death. The religious affairs people said, "We can't give you permission to recite this. If we allow it then many people will follow these kinds of practices, so we have to ban it." (Nisakhan, Yantaq village, August 2012)

Nisakhan took the officials' assessment of her hikmät as a validation and an affirmation of the power of her religious practice. If they wanted to ban it, she reasoned, it must be worth doing. Her mother's book was taken, but she hid away her own copy, and she preserved the memory of how to reanimate the hikmät in ritual performance. Coercive political campaigns may temporarily silence her practice and overwrite the Islamic soundscape with new layers of sound, but they cannot fully erase it.

Notes

1. Nathan Vanderklippe, "'It Is about Xi as the Leader of the World': Former Detainees Recount Abuse in Chinese Re-education Centres," *Globe and Mail*, July 3, 2018, https://www.theglobeandmail.com/world/article-former-detainees-recount-abuse-in-chinese-re-education-centres/.

2. UN Committee on the Elimination of Racial Discrimination, "Concluding Observations on the Combined Fourteenth to Seventeenth Periodic Reports of China (including Hong Kong, China, and Macao, China)," advance release, August 30, 2018, https://tbinternet.ohchr.org/Treaties/CERD/Shared%20Documents/CHN/CERD_C_CHN_CO_14-17_32237_E.pdf. The US government's annual report on human rights in China estimated between 800,000 and 2 million people detained (US Department of State, "2018 Country Reports on Human Rights Practices: China [includes Tibet, Hong Kong, and Macau]—China," March 13, 2019, https://www.state.gov/reports/2018-country-reports-on-human-rights-practices/china-includes-tibet-hong-kong-and-macau-china/).

3. John Sudworth, "China's Hidden Camps," *BBC* online, October 24, 2018, https://www.bbc.co.uk/news/resources/idt-sh/China_hidden_camps.

4. Zenz and Leibold 2017.

5. Human Rights Watch 2019.

6. Darren Byler, "China's Government Has Ordered a Million Citizens to Occupy Uighur Homes: Here's What They Think They're Doing," *China File*, October 24, 2018, http://www.chinafile.com/reporting-opinion/postcard/million-citizens-occupy-uighur-homes-xinjiang.

7. Shohret Hoshur, "Chinese Authorities Jail Four Wealthiest Uyghurs in Xinjiang's Kashgar in New Purge," *Radio Free Asia*, January 5, 2018, https://www.rfa.org/english/news/uyghur/wealthiest-01052018144327.html.

8. Shohret Hoshur, "Xinjiang Jails Uyghur Civil Servants over Lack of Enthusiasm for Anti-Extremist Campaigns," *Radio Free Asia*, May 30, 2018, https://www.rfa.org/english/news/uyghur/servants-05302018154833.html.

9. Uyghur Human Rights Project, "Update: Detained and Disappeared," press release, May 21, 2019, https://uhrp.org/press-release/update-%E2%80%93-detained-and-disappeared-intellectuals-under-assault-uyghur-homeland.html.

10. Rachel Harris, "'Uyghur Dutar King' Detained in China," *Freemuse Report*, November 1, 2017, https://freemuse.org/news/uyghur-dutar-king-detained-in-china/; "Sanubar Tursun, Voice of the Uyghurs, Missing Presumed Detained in Xinjiang's Internment Camps," *Freemuse Report*, November 28, 2019, https://freemuse.org/news/china-sanubar-tursun-voice-of-the-uyghurs-missing-presumed-detained-in-xinjiangs-internment-camps/.

11. Chris Buckley and Austin Ramzy, "Star Scholar Disappears as Crackdown Engulfs Western China," *New York Times*, August 10, 2018, https://www.nytimes.com/2018/08/10/world/asia/china-xinjiang-rahile-dawut.html.

12. Darren Byler, "Images in Red: Han Culture, Uyghur Performers, Chinese New Year," *Art of Life in Chinese Central Asia*, February 23, 2018, https://livingotherwise.com/2018/02/23/images-red-han-culture-uyghur-performers-chinese-new-year/.

13. Interview with Adrian Zenz cited in Darren Byler, "Imagining Re-engineered Muslims," *Art of Life in Chinese Central Asia*, April 26, 2017, https://livingotherwise.com/2017/04/26/imagining-re-engineered-muslims-northwest-china/.

14. Emily Feng, "Uighur Children Fall Victim to China Anti-Terror Drive," *Financial Times*, July 9, 2018, https://www.ft.com/content/f0d3223a-7f4d-11e8-bc55-50daf11b720d.

15. Shohret Hoshur, "Kazakh and Uyghur Detainees of Xinjiang 'Re-education Camps' Must 'Eat Pork or Face Punishment,'" *Radio Free Asia*, May 23, 2019, https://www.rfa.org/english/news/uyghur/pork-05232019154338.html.

16. Gerry Shih, "China's Mass Indoctrination Camps Evoke Cultural Revolution," *AP News*, May 17, 2018, https://apnews.com/6e151296fb194f85ba69a8babd972e4b.

17. Pidailar Biz, "Olum Lagirgha alaqidar dehshetler," https://www.youtube.com/watch?time_continue=3&v=VlLgyCn-gS0; see also English translation and commentary by Darren Byler, "'As If You've Spent Your Whole Life in Prison': Starving and Subdued in Xinjiang Detention Centers," *SupChina*, December 5, 2018, https://supchina.com/2018/12/05/starving-and-subdued-in-xinjiang-detention-centers/.

18. Mihrigul Tursun, "I Did Not Believe I Would Leave Prison in China Alive," interview by Gulchehra Hoja, trans. Mamatjan Juma and Alim Seytoff, *Radio Free Asia*, November 1, 2018, https://www.rfa.org/english/news/uyghur/detentions-11012018100304.html.

19. Shih, "China's Mass Indoctrination."

20. Translated with further discussion in Byler, "Images in Red."

21. Ben Blanchard, "China Defends Xinjiang Camps As It Takes Reporters on Tour," *Irish Times*, January 7, 2019, https://www.irishtimes.com/news/world/asia-pacific/china-defends-xinjiang-camps-as-it-takes-reporters-on-tour-1.3750070.

22. Shih, "China's Mass Indoctrination."

23. Gene Bunin, "The Happiest Muslims in the World," *Art of Life in Chinese Central Asia*, July 31, 2018, https://livingotherwise.com/2018/07/31/happiest-muslims-world-coping-happiness/.

24. "Uighurs Live with Fear, Trauma," *ABC News*, updated October 5, 2018, https://www.abc.net.au/news/2018-06-24/uighur-community-in-australia-fear-reports-of-crackdown-in-china/9824554.

25. See, for example, Gao Wenqian, "Mao's Cultural Revolution Legacy and Xi Jinping's Governance Model," *Human Rights in China*, https://www.hrichina.org/cht/node/17318.

26. Noah Rosenbloom, "The Threnodist and the Threnody of the Holocaust," as cited in Barmé 1999 (231); see also *Threnody for the Victims of Hiroshima* (Polish: *Tren Ofiarom Hiroszimy*), composed in 1960 by Krzysztof Penderecki.

27. Biz, "Olum Lagirgha."

28. See the Bitter Winter blog: https://bitterwinter.org/disappearing-mosques-of-xinjiang/ (accessed August 2, 2018).

29. "I Can't Sleep," http://www.chinafile.com/reporting-opinion/culture/i-cant-sleep-homage-uyghur-homeland (last updated January 6, 2020).

30. Darren Byler "Ghost World," *Logic* 7 (May 1, 2019), https://logicmag.io/07-ghost-world/.

REFERENCES

Abrahamov, Binyamin. 2003. *Divine Love in Islamic Mysticism: The Teachings of al-Ghazālī and al-Dabbāgh*. London: Routledge Curzon.
Absaroka, Ruard. 2016. *Hidden Musicians and Public Musicking in Shanghai*. PhD diss., SOAS, University of London.
Abu-Lughod, Lila. 1993. "Islam and the Gendered Discourses of Death." *International Journal of Middle East Studies* 25, no. (2): 187–205
———. 2015. *Do Muslim Women Need Saving?* Cambridge, MA: Harvard University Press.
Ahmed, Sara. 2004. *The Cultural Politics of Emotion*. Edinburgh: Edinburgh University Press.
———. 2010. "Killing Joy: Feminism and the History of Happiness." *Signs* 35, no. 3: 571–94.
Anand, Dibyesh. 2019. "Colonization with Chinese Characteristics: Politics of (In)security in Xinjiang and Tibet." *Central Asian Survey* 38, no. 1: 129–47.
Anwar, Aynur [Ainiwa'er, Ayinu'er]. 2013. *Shache xian dangdai weiwu'erzu sufei zhuyi jiaotuan nvxintu (buwei) dike'er yishide renleixue diaocha yanjiu* [The zikir activities of female sufis in Yarkand county: an anthropological enquiry]. MA thesis, Xinjiang Normal University.
Argenti, Nicolas, and Katharina Schramm. 2009. Introduction to *Remembering Violence: Anthropological Perspectives on Intergenerational Transmission*, edited by Nicolas Argenti and Katharina Schramm, 1–29. New York: Berghahn.
Asad, Talal. 1986. *The Idea of an Anthropology of Islam*. Center for Contemporary Arab Studies Occasional Papers. Washington, DC: Georgetown University.
———. 2007. *On Suicide Bombing*. New York: Columbia University Press.
Attali, Jacques. 2011. *Noise: The Political Economy of Music*. Minneapolis: University of Minnesota Press.
Azmun, Yusuf. 1994. *Hoca Ahmed Yesevi: Divan-i Hikmet*. Istanbul: Tek-Esin.
Baily, John. 2001. *Can You Stop the Birds Singing? The Censorship of Music in Afghanistan*. Copenhagen: Freemuse.
Barmé, Geremie R. 1999. *In the Red: On Contemporary Chinese Culture*. New York: Columbia University Press.
Becker, Judith. 2001. "Anthropological Perspectives." In *Music and Emotion: Theory and Research*, edited by Patrik N. Juslin and John A. Sloboda, 135–60. New York: Oxford University Press.
Becquelin, Nicolas. 2004. "Criminalizing Ethnicity: Political Repression in Xinjiang." *China Rights Forum* 1: 39–46.
Bellér-Hann, Ildikó. 2000. *The Written and the Spoken: Literacy and Oral Transmission among the Uyghur*. Berlin: ANOR.
———. 2001. "Making the Oil Fragrant: Dealings with the Supernatural among the Uyghurs in Xinjiang." *Asian Ethnicity* 2, no. 1: 9–23.
———. 2008. *Community Matters in Xinjiang 1880–1949: Towards a Historical Anthropology of the Uyghur*. Leiden, Neth.: Brill.

———. 2014. "The Bulldozer State: Chinese Socialist Development in Xinjiang." In *Ethnographies of the State in Central Asia: Performing Politics*, edited by Madeleine Reeves, Johan Rasanayagam, and Judith Beyer, 173–97. Bloomington: Indiana University Press.

Bellér-Hann, Ildikó, Cristina Cesáro, Rachel Harris, and Joanne Smith Finley. 2007. *Situating the Uyghurs: Between China and Central Asia*. Farnham, UK: Ashgate.

Blacking, John. 1983. "The Concept of Identity and Folk Concepts of Self: A Venda Case Study." In *Identity: Personal and Socio-cultural*, edited by A. Jacobson-Widding, 47–65. Stockholm: Almqvist and Wiksell.

Born, Georgina. 2005. "On Musical Mediation: Ontology, Technology and Creativity." *Twentieth Century Music* 2, no. 1: 7–36.

Bourdieu, Pierre. 1984. *Distinction: A Social Critique of the Judgement of Taste*. London: Routledge.

Bovingdon, Gardner. 2001. "The History of the History of Xinjiang." *Twentieth Century China* 26, no. 1: 95–139.

Boyd Gillette, Maris. 2000. *Between Mecca and Beijing: Modernization and Consumption among Urban Chinese Muslims*. Stanford, CA: Stanford University Press.

Brophy, David. 2015. "Little Apples in Xinjiang." *China Story*, February 16, https://www.thechinastory.org/2015/02/little-apples-in-xinjiang/.

———. 2016. *Uyghur Nation: Reform and Revolution on the Russia-China Frontier*. Cambridge MA: Harvard University Press.

———. 2018. "Confusing Black and White: Naqshbandi Sufi Affiliations and the Transition to Qing Rule in the Tarim Basin." *Late Imperial China* 39, no. 1: 29–65.

Brown, Wendy. 1995. *States of Injury: Power and Freedom in Late Modernity*. Princeton, NJ: Princeton University Press.

Bulag, Uradyn E. 2000. "From Inequality to Difference: Colonial Contradictions of Class and Ethnicity in 'Socialist' China." *Cultural Studies* 14, no. 34: 530–61.

Butler, Judith. 1993. *Bodies that Matter: On the Discursive Limits of 'Sex.'* London: Routledge.

Byler, Darren. 2016. "Internet and Social Media, Uyghur." In *Pop Culture in Asia and Oceania*, edited by Jeremy A. Murray and Kathleen M. Nadeau, 248–51. Santa Barbara, CA: ABC-CLIO.

Christian, William A. Jr. 2004. "Provoked Religious Weeping in Early Modern Spain." In *Religion and Emotion: Approaches and Interpretations*, edited by John Corrigan, 33–50. Oxford: Oxford University Press.

Clark, William, and Ablet Kamalov. 2004. "Uighur Migration across Central Asian Frontiers." *Central Asian Survey* 23, no. 2: 167–82.

Clayton, Martin, Byron Dueck, and Laura Leante. 2013. *Experience and Meaning in Music Performance*. New York: Oxford University Press.

Cliff, Thomas. 2016. *Oil and Water: Being Han in Xinjiang*. Chicago: University of Chicago Press.

Coderre, Laurence. 2016. "Breaking Bad: Sabotaging the Production of the Hero in the Amateur Performance of Yangbanxi." In *Listening to China's Cultural Revolution: Music, Politics, and Cultural Continuities*, edited by Pang Laikwan, Paul Clark, and Tsai Tsan-Huang, 65–83. London: Palgrave Macmillan.

Corbin, Alain. 1998. *Village Bells: Sound and Meaning in the 19th-Century French Countryside*. Translated by Martin Thom. New York: Columbia University Press.

Corrigan, John. 2004. "Introduction: Emotions Research and the Academic Study of Religion." In *Religion and Emotion: Approaches and interpretations*, edited by John Corrigan, 3–32. Oxford: Oxford University Press.
Cusick, Suzanne G. 2008. "'You Are in a Place That Is Out of the World...': Music in the Detention Camps of the 'Global War on Terror.'" *Journal of the Society for American Music* 2, no. 1: 1–26.
Dähnhardt, Thomas. 2012. "Breath and Breathing." In *Encyclopaedia of Islam, THREE*, edited by Gudrun Krämer, Denis Matringe, John Nawas, and Everett Rowson. Brill Online. http://dx.doi.org/10.1163/1573-3912_ei3_COM_24357.
Dammen McAuliffe, Jane. 2006. Introduction to *The Cambridge Companion to the Qur'an*, edited by Jane Dammen McAuliffe, 1–20. Cambridge: Cambridge University Press.
Danielson, Virginia. 1997. *"The Voice of Egypt": Umm Kulthum, Arabic Song, and Egyptian Society in the Twentieth Century*. Chicago: University of Chicago Press.
Daughtry, J. Martin. 2013. "Acoustic Palimpsests and the Politics of Listening." *Music and Politics* 7, no. 1. DOI: http://dx.doi.org/10.3998/mp.9460447.0007.101.
———. 2015. *Listening to War: Sound, Music, Trauma, and Survival in Wartime Iraq*. New York: Oxford University Press.
Dautcher, Jay. 2009. *Down a Narrow Road: Identity and Masculinity in a Uyghur Community in Xinjiang China*. Cambridge, MA: Harvard University Press.
Dawut, Rahile. 2007. "Shrine Pilgrimage and Sustainable Tourism among the Uyghurs: Central Asian Ritual Traditions in the Context of China's development policies." In *Situating the Uyghurs between China and Central Asia*, edited by Ildikó Bellér-Hann, Cristina Cesaro, Rachel Harris, and Joanne Smith Finley, 149–63. Farnham, UK: Ashgate.
Dawut, Rahile, and Elise Anderson. 2015. "Dastan Performance among the Uyghurs." In *The Music of Central Asia*, edited by Theodore Levin, Saida Daukeyeva, and Elmira Köchümkulova, 406–20. Bloomington: Indiana University Press.
Dawuti, Reyila. 2001. *Weiwuerzu Mazha Wenhua Yanjiu*. Ürümchi: Xinjiang daxue chubanshe.
De Certeau, Michel. 1998. *The Capture of Speech and Other Political Writings*. Translated by Tom Conley. Minneapolis: University of Minnesota Press.
Deleuze, Gilles, and Felix Guattari. 1987. *A Thousand Plateaus*. Translated by Brian Massumi. Minneapolis: University of Minnesota Press.
DeNora, Tia. 2000. *Music in Everyday Life*. New York: Cambridge University Press.
DeWeese, Devin. 1996a. "Yasavī "Šayḫs" In The Timurid Era: Notes on the Social and Political Role of Communal Sufi Affiliations in the 14th and 15th Centuries." *Oriente Moderno*. n.s. 15, no. 76, 2/I: 173–88.
———. 1996b. "The Masha'ikh-I Turk and the Khojagan: Rethinking the Links between the Yasavi and Naqshbandi Sufi Traditions." *Journal of Islamic Studies* 7, no. 2: 180–207.
———. 1999. "The Politics of Sacred Lineages in 19th-Century Central Asia: Descent Groups Linked to Khwaja Ahmad Yasavi in Shrine Documents and Genealogical Charters." *International Journal of Middle East Studies* 31, no. 4: 507–30.
———. 2006. Foreword to *Early Mystics in Turkish Literature*, edited by Mehmed Fuad Koprulu. Translated by Gary Leiser and Robert Dankoff. Abingdon-on-Thames, UK: Routledge.
———. 2011. "Ahmad Yasavi and the Divan-i Hikmat in Soviet Scholarship." In *The Heritage of Soviet Oriental Studies*, edited by Michael Kemper and Stephan Conermann, 262–90. Abingdon-on-Thames, UK: Routledge.

Doubleday, Veronica. 2009. *Three Women of Herat: A Memoir of Life, Love and Friendship in Afghanistan*. London: Tauris Parke.

Doumato, Eleanor Abdella. 2000. *Getting God's Ear: Women, Islam and Healing in Saudi Arabia and the Gulf*. New York: Columbia University Press.

Ebersole, Gary L. 2000. "The Function of Ritual Weeping Revisited: Affective Expression and Moral Discourse." *History of Religions* 39, no. 3: 211–46.

Edensor, Tim. 2010. "Introduction: Thinking about Rhythm and Space." In *Geographies of Rhythm: Nature, Place, Mobilities and Bodies*, edited by Tim Edensor, 1–20. Abingdon-on-Thames, UK: Routledge.

Edgar, Iain, and David Henig. 2010. "Istikhara: The Guidance and Practice of Islamic Dream Incubation through Ethnographic Comparison." *History and Anthropology* 21, no. 3: 251–62.

Eickelman, Dale F., and James Piscatori. 2004. *Muslim Politics*. Princeton, NJ: Princeton University Press.

Erie, Matthew. 2016. *China and Islam: The Prophet, the Party, and Law*. Cambridge: Cambridge University Press.

Eisenberg, Andrew. 2009. *The Resonance of Place: Vocalizing Swahili Ethnicity in Mombasa, Kenya*. PhD diss., Columbia University.

———. 2013. "Islam, Sound and Space: Acoustemology and Muslim Citizenship on the Kenyan Coast." In *Music, Sound, and Space: Transformations of Public and Private Experience*, edited by Georgina Born, 186–202. Cambridge: Cambridge University Press.

Eisenlohr, Patrick. 2018. *Sounding Islam: Voice, Media, and Sonic Atmospheres in an Indian Ocean World*. Oakland: University of California Press.

Erkin, Adila. 2009. "Locally Modern, Globally Uyghur: Geography, Identity and Consumer Culture in Contemporary Xinjiang." *Central Asian Survey* 28, no. 4: 417–28.

Erlmann, Veit. 1999. *Music, Modernity and the Global Imagination: South Africa and the West*. New York: Oxford University Press.

———. 2004. "But What of the Ethnographic Ear? Anthropology, Sound and the Senses." In *Hearing Cultures: Essays on Sound, Listening and Modernity*, edited by Veit Erlmann, 1–20. Oxford, UK: Berg.

Faruqi, Lois Ibsen al. 1985. "Music, Musicians and Muslim Law." *Asian Music* 17, no. 1: 3–36.

Feld, Steven. 1996. "Waterfalls of Songs: An Acoustemology of Place Resounding in Bosavi, Papua New Guinea." In *Senses of Place*, edited by Steven Feld and Keith H. Basso, 91–135. Santa Fe, NM: School of American Research Press.

———. 2015. "Acoustemology." In *Keywords in Sound*, edited by David Novak and Matthew Sakakeeny, 12–21. Durham, NC: Duke University Press.

Fernea, Elizabeth Warnock. 1965. *Guests of the Sheik: An Ethnography of an Iraq Village*. New York: Doubleday.

Fiesler, Casey, and Nicholas Proferes. 2018. "'Participant' Perceptions of Twitter Research Ethics." *Social Media and Society*, January–March 2018: 1–14.

Finnegan, Ruth. 2014. *Literacy and Orality: Studies in the Technologies of Communication*, 2nd ed. Oxford, UK: Callender.

Frishkopf, Michael. 2009. "Mediated Qur'anic Recitation and the Contestation of Islam in Contemporary Egypt." In *Music and the Play of Power in the Middle East, North Africa and Central Asia*, edited by Laudan Nooshin, 75–114. Farnham, UK: Ashgate.

Fuller, Graham E., and Jonathan N. Lipman. 2004. "Islam in Xinjiang." In *Xinjiang: China's Muslim Borderland*, edited by S. Frederick Starr, 320–52. Armonk, NY: M. E. Sharpe.
Gade, Anna. 2004. *Perfection Makes Practice: Learning, Emotion, and the Recited Qur'ān in Indonesia*. Honolulu: University of Hawai'i Press.
Gill, Denise. 2017. *Melancholic Modalities: Affect, Islam and Turkish Classical Musicians*. New York: Oxford University Press.
Gladney, Dru C. 1994. "Representing Nationality in China: Refiguring Majority/Minority Identities," *Journal of Asian Studies* 53, no. 1: 92–123.
———. 2004. *Dislocating China: Muslims, Minorities, and Other Subaltern Subjects*. Chicago: University of Chicago Press.
Graham, William, and Navid Kermani. 2006. "Recitation and Aesthetic Reception." In *The Cambridge Companion to the Qur'an*, edited by Jane Dammen McAuliffe, 115–41. Cambridge: Cambridge University Press.
Grima, Benedicte. 1992. *The Performance of Emotion among Paxtun Women: "The Misfortunes Which Have Befallen Me."* Austin: University of Texas Press.
Gupta, Akhil. 2006. "Blurred Boundaries: The Discourse of Corruption, the Culture of Politics, and the Imagined State." In *The Anthropology of the State: A Reader*, edited by Aradhana Sharma and Akhil Gupta, 211–42. Oxford, UK: Blackwell.
Habermas, Jürgen. 2003. "Fundamentalism and Terror." In *Philosophy in a Time of Terror: Dialogues with Jürgen Habermas and Jacques Derrida*, edited by Giovanna Borradori, 25–43. Chicago: University of Chicago Press.
Haraway, Donna. 1991. *Simians, Cyborgs and Women: The Reinvention of Nature*. Abingdon-on-Thames, UK: Routledge.
Harrell, Stevan. 2015. "Introduction: Civilizing projects and the reaction to them." In *Cultural Encounters on China's Ethnic Frontiers*, edited by Stevan Harrell, 3–36. Seattle: University of Washington Press.
Harris, Rachel. 2002. "Cassettes, Bazaars and Saving the Nation: The Uyghur Music Industry in Xinjiang, China." In *Global Goes Local: Popular Culture in Asia*, edited by Timothy Craig and Richard King, 265–83. Vancouver: University of British Columbia Press.
———. 2004. *Singing the Village: Music, Memory and Ritual among the Sibe of Xinjiang*. Oxford: Oxford University Press.
———. 2008. *The Making of a Musical Canon in Chinese Central Asia: The Uyghur Twelve Muqam*. Farnham, UK: Ashgate.
———. 2012. "Tracks: Temporal Shifts and Transnational Networks of Sentiment in Uyghur Song." *Ethnomusicology* 56, no. 3: 450–75.
———. 2013a. "Doing Satan's Business: Negotiating Gendered Concepts of Music and Ritual in Rural Xinjiang." In *Gender in Chinese Music*, edited by Rachel Harris, Rowan Pease, and Shzr Ee Tan, 229–46. Rochester, NY: University of Rochester Press.
———. 2013b. "Harmonizing Islam in Xinjiang: Sound and Meaning in Rural Uyghur Religious Practice." In *On the Fringes of the Harmonious Society: Tibetans and Uyghurs in Socialist China*, edited by Ildikó Bellér-Hann and Trine Brox, 293–317. Copenhagen: NIAS.
———. 2017. "Theory and Practice in Contemporary Central Asian Maqām." In *Theory and Practice in the Music of the Islamic World: Essays for Owen Wright*, edited by Rachel Harris and Martin Stokes, 215–35. New York: Routledge.
———. 2020. "'A Weekly Meshrep to Tackle Religious Extremism': Music-Making in Uyghur Communities and Intangible Cultural Heritage in China." *Ethnomusicology* 64, no. 1.

Hellier-Tinocco, Ruth. 2019. *Performing Palimpsest Bodies: Postmemory Theatre Experiments in Mexico*. Bristol, UK: Intellect.
Helmreich, Stefan. 2010. "Listening against Soundscapes." *Anthropology News* 51: 10.
Henig, David. 2012. "'This Is Our Little Hajj': Muslim Holy Sites and Re-Appropriation of the Sacred Landscape in Contemporary Bosnia." *American Ethnologist* 39, no. 4: 752–66.
Hillier, Jean, and Emma Rooksby. 2002. *Habitus: A Sense of Place*. Farnham, UK: Ashgate.
Hillman, Ben. 2004. "The Rise of the Community in Rural China: Village Politics, Cultural Identity and Religious Revival in a Hui Hamlet." *China Journal* 51: 53–73.
Hirschkind, Charles. 2006. *The Ethical Soundscape: Cassette Sermons and Islamic Counterpublics*. New York: Columbia University Press.
———. 2012. "Experiments in Devotion Online: The YouTube Khuṭba." *International Journal of Middle East Studies* 44: 5–21.
Hirschkind, Charles, Maria José A. de Abreu, and Carlo Caduff. 2017. "New Media, New Publics? An Introduction to Supplement 15." *Current Anthropology* 58: S15.
Ho Wai-Yip. 2010. "Islam, China and the Internet: Negotiating Residual Cyberspace between Hegemonic Patriotism and Connectivity to the Ummah." *Journal of Muslim Minority Affairs* 30, no. 1: 63–79.
Hochschild, Arlie. 2003. *The Managed Heart: The Commercialization of Human Feeling*. Berkeley: University of California Press.
Huang, Cindy. 2009. *Muslim Women at a Crossroads: Gender and Development in the Xinjiang Uyghur Autonomous Region*. PhD diss., University of California–Berkeley.
Human Rights Watch. 2019. *China's Algorithms of Repression*. New York: Human Rights Watch. https://www.hrw.org/report/2019/05/01/chinas-algorithms-repression/reverse-engineering-xinjiang-police-mass-surveillance.
Ingold, Tim. 2007. "Against Soundscape." *Autumn Leaves: Sound and the Environment in Artistic Practice*. Edited by A. Carlyle. Paris: Double Entendre, 10–13.
Johnson, Thomas H., and Ahmad Waheed. 2011. "Analyzing Taliban Taranas (Chants): An Effective Afghan Propaganda Artefact." *Small Wars and Insurgencies* 22, no. 1: 3–31.
Kadir, Aynur. 2010. "Ehmed Yessewiy she'irlirining Uyghur folklorida ishlitilishi." *Bulaq* 2010, no. 6: 93–102.
Kahn, Douglas. 1999. *Noise, Water, Meat: A History of Sound in the Arts*. Cambridge, MA: MIT Press.
Kandiyoti, Deniz, and Nadira Azimova. 2004. "The Communal and the Sacred: Women's Worlds of Ritual in Uzbekistan." *Journal of the Royal Anthropological Institute* 10, no. 2: 327–50.
Kapchan, Deborah. 2009. "Singing Community/Remembering Common: Sufi Liturgy and North African Identity in Southern France." *International Journal of Community Music* 2, no. 1: 9–23.
———. 2017. "The Splash of Icarus: Theorizing Sound Writing/Writing Sound Theory." In *Theorizing Sound Writing*, edited by Deborah Kapchan, 1–24. Middletown, CT: Wesleyan University Press.
Kassabian, Anahid. 2013. *Ubiquitous Listening: Affect, Attention, and Distributed Subjectivity*. Berkeley: University of California Press.
Keil, Charles. 1987. "Participatory Discrepancies and the Power of Music." *Cultural Anthropology* 2, no. 3: 275–28.
Kheshti, Roshanak. 2015. "On the Threshold of the Political: The Sonic Performativity of Rooftop Chanting in Iran." *Radical History Review* 121: 51–70.

Kirmse, Stefan. 2013. *Youth and Globalization in Central Asia: Everyday Life between Religion, Media, and International Donors*. Frankfurt: Campus.

Kleinmichel, Sigrid. 2000. *Halpa in Choresm (Hwārazm) und Ātin Āyi im Ferghanatal: zur Geschichte des Lesens in Usbekistan im 20. Jahrhundert*. Berlin: Arabische Buch.

Kobi, Madlen. 2016. *Constructing, Creating, and Contesting Cityscapes: A Socio-Anthropological Approach to Urban Transformation in Southern Xinjiang, People's Republic of China*. Wiesbaden, Ger.: Harrassowitz.

Koprulu, Mehmed Fuad. 2006. *Early Mystics in Turkish Literature*. Translated by Gary Leiser and Robert Dankoff. Abingdon-on-Thames, UK: Routledge.

Kundnani, Arun. 2012. "Radicalisation: The Journey of a Concept." *Race and Class* 54, no. 2: 3–25.

LaBelle, Brandon. 2010. *Acoustic Territories: Sound Culture and Everyday Life*. London: Continuum.

Lee, Tong Soon. 1999. "Technology and the Production of Islamic Space: The Islamic Call to Prayer in Singapore." *Ethnomusicology* 42, no. 1: 101–34.

Lefebvre, Henri. 2004. *Rhythmanalysis: Space, Time and Everyday Life*. London: Continuum.

Leibold, James, and Timothy A. Grose. 2016. "Veiling in Xinjiang: The Struggle to Define Uyghur Female Adornment." *China Journal* 76: 78–102.

Light, Nathan. 2008. *Intimate Heritage: Creating Uyghur Muqam Song in Xinjiang*. Berlin: Lit.

Lipman, Jonathan N. 2014. "Head-Wagging and the Sounds of Obscenity: Conflicts over Sound on the Qing-Muslim Frontiers." *Performing Islam* 3, no. 12: 43–58.

Liu Xiangchen (dir.). 2010. *Ashiq: The Last Troubadour*, 128 minutes. Ürümchi: Xinjiang Normal University.

Lomax, Alan. 2009. *Folk Song Style and Culture*. New Brunswick, NJ, Transaction.

Lord, Albert B. 1960. *The Singer of Tales*. Cambridge, MA: Harvard University Press.

Loubes, Jean-Paul. 2015. *La Chine et la ville au XXIe siècle: la sinisation urbaine au Xinjiang Ouïghour et en Mongolie intérieure*. Paris: Sextant.

Lutz, Catherine, and Geoffrey White. 1986. "The Anthropology of Emotions." *Annual Review of Anthropology* 15: 405–36.

Mahmood, Saba. 2003. "Ethical Formation and Politics of Individual Autonomy in Contemporary Egypt." *Social Research* 70, no. 3: 837–66.

———. 2005. *Politics of Piety: The Islamic Revival and the Feminist Subject*. Princeton, NJ: Princeton University Press.

Manuel, Peter. 1993. *Cassette Culture: Popular Music and Technology in North India*. Chicago: University of Chicago Press.

Marsden, Magnus. 2005. *Living Islam: Muslim Religious Experience in Pakistan's North-West Frontier*. Cambridge: Cambridge University Press.

———. 2007. "All-Male Sonic Gatherings, Islamic Reform, and Masculinity in Northern Pakistan." *American Ethnologist* 34, no. 3: 473–90.

Marsden, Magnus, and Konstantinos Retsikas. 2013. *Articulating Islam: Anthropological Approaches to Muslim Worlds*. Dordrecht: Springer.

McBrien, Julie. 2006. "Extreme Conversations: Secularism, Religious Pluralism, and the Rhetoric of Islamic Extremism in Southern Kyrgyzstan." In *The Postsocialist Religious Question: Faith and Power in Central Asia and East-Central Europe*, edited by Chris Hann. Berlin: Lit Verlag.

McDonald, David A. 2013. *My Voice Is My Weapon: Music, Nationalism, and the Poetics of Palestinian Resistance*. Durham, NC: Duke University Press.

McDougall, Bonnie. 1984. *Popular Chinese Literature and Performing Arts in the People's Republic of China, 1949–1979*. Berkeley: University of California Press.

Mijit, Mukaddas. 2015. "Sufism and the Ceremony of Zikr in Ghulja." In *The Music of Central Asia*, edited by Theodore Levin, Saida Daukeyeva, and Elmira Köchümkulova, 304–10. Bloomington: Indiana University Press.

Millward, James. 2004. *Violent Separatism in Xinjiang: A Critical Assessment*. Policy Studies 6. Washington, DC: East-West Center.

———. 2009. "Introduction: Does the 2009 Urumchi Violence Mark a Turning Point?" *Central Asian Survey* 28, no. 4: 347–60.

Mittler, Barbara. 2012. *A Continuous Revolution: Making Sense of Cultural Revolution Culture*. Cambridge, MA: Harvard University Press.

Montgomery, David W. 2016. *Practicing Islam: Knowledge, Experience, and Social Navigation in Kyrgyzstan*. Pittsburgh, PA: University of Pittsburgh Press.

Morey, Peter, and Amina Yaqin. 2011. *Framing Muslims: Stereotyping and Representation after 9/11*. Cambridge, MA: Harvard University Press.

Mostowlansky, Till. 2017. *Azan on the Moon: Entangling Modernity along Tajikistan's Pamir Highway*. Pittsburgh, PA: University of Pittsburgh Press.

Mukhlis, Nijat. 1985. "Diwani Hikmet: Ehmet Yessewiy." *Bulaq* 16: 1–35.

Mu Qian. 2019. *Experiencing God in Sound: Music and Meaning in Uyghur Sufism*. PhD diss., SOAS, University of London.

Nelson, Kristina. 2001. *The Art of Reciting the Qur'an*. Cairo: American University in Cairo Press.

Novak, David. 2013. *Japanoise: Music at the Edge of Circulation*. Durham, NC: Duke University Press.

Novak, David, and Matthew Sakakeeny. 2015. *Keywords in Sound*. Durham, NC: Duke University Press.

Novetzke, Christian Lee. 2015. "Note to Self: What Marathi Kirtankars' Notebooks Suggest about Literacy, Performance, and the Travelling Performer in Pre-Colonial Maharashtra." In *Tellings and Texts: Music, Literature and Performance in North India*, edited by Francesca Orsini and Katherine Butler Schofield, 169–84. Cambridge, UK: Open Book.

Oliveros, Pauline. 2005. *Deep Listening: A Composer's Sound Practice*. New York: iUniverse.

Osborne, Lauren E. 2016. "Textual and Paratextual meaning in the Recited Qur'ān: An Analysis of a Performance of Sūrat al-Furqān by Sheikh Mishari Rashid Alafasy." In *Qur'ānic Studies Today*, edited by Angelika Neuwirth and Michael A Sells, 228–46. Abingdon-on-Thames, UK: Routledge.

Panagia, Davide. 2009. *The Political Life of Sensation*. Durham, NC: Duke University Press.

Papas, Alexandre. 2015. "Creating a Sufi Soundscape: Recitation (*dhikr*) and Spiritual Audition (*samāʿ*) according to Ahmad Kāsānī Dahbidī (d. 1542)." *Performing Islam* 3, no. 12: 23–41.

Pasilov, Bahodir, and Adham Ashirov. 2007. "Revival of Sufi Traditions in Modern Central Asia: 'Jahri Zikr' and Its Ethnological Features." *Oriente Moderno* n.s. 87, no. 1: 163–75.

Pieslak, Jonathan. 2009. *Sound Targets: American Soldiers and Music in the Iraq War*. Bloomington: Indiana University Press.

———. 2015. *Radicalism and Music*. Middletown, CT: Wesleyan University Press.

Pink, Sarah. 2009. *Doing Sensory Ethnography*. London, UK: Sage Publications.

Plänkers, Tomas. 2014. *Landscapes of the Chinese Soul: The Enduring Presence of the Cultural Revolution.* Translated by John Hart. London: Karnac.
Post, Jennifer C. 2017. "Ecological Knowledge, Collaborative Management and Musical Production in Western Mongolia." In *Ethnomusicology: A Contemporary Reader*, edited by Jennifer C. Post, 2: 161–80. Abingdon-on-Thames, UK: Routledge.
Privratsky, Bruce G. 2001. *Muslim Turkistan: Kazak Religion and Collective Memory.* Richmond, UK: Curzon.
Qureshi, Regula Burckhardt. 1994. "Exploring Time Cross-Culturally: Ideology and Performance of Time in the Sufi Qawwālī." *Journal of Musicology* 12, no. 4: 491–528.
Racy, Ali Jihad. 2003. *Making Music in the Arab World: The Culture and Artistry of Tarab.* New York: Cambridge University Press.
Rasanayagam, Johan. 2006. "Post-Soviet Islam: An Anthropological Perspective—Introduction." *Central Asian Survey* 25, no. 3: 219–33.
——. 2011. *Islam in Post-Soviet Uzbekistan: The Morality of Experience.* Cambridge: Cambridge University Press.
Rasmussen, Anne. 2010a. *Women's Voices, the Recited Qur'an, and Islamic Musical Arts in Indonesia.* Berkeley: University of California Press.
——. 2010b. "Performing Religious Politics: Islamic Musical Arts in Indonesia." In *Music and Conflict*, edited by John Morgan O'Connell and Salwa El-Shawan Castelo-Branco, 155–76. Champaign: University of Illinois Press.
Raudvere, Catharina. 2002. *The Book and the Roses: Sufi Women, Visibility, and Zikir in Contemporary Istanbul.* London: I. B. Tauris.
Reichl, Karl. 2015. "Memory and Textuality in the Orality-Literacy Continuum." In *Orality and Textuality in the Iranian World: Patterns of Interaction across the Centuries*, edited by Julia Rubanovich, 19–42. Leiden, Neth.: Brill.
Rees, Helen. 2000. *Echoes of History: Naxi Music in Modern China.* New York: Oxford University Press.
Reeves, Madeleine, Johan Rasanayagam, and Judith Beyer. 2014. *Ethnographies of the State in Central Asia: Performing Politics.* Bloomington: Indiana University Press.
Roberts, Sean R. 2018. "The Biopolitics of China's 'War on Terror' and the Exclusion of the Uyghurs." *Critical Asian Studies* 50, no. 2: 232–58.
Rosaldo, Michelle Z. 1984. "Toward an Anthropology of Self and Feeling." In *Culture Theory: Essays on Mind, Self, and Emotion*, edited by Richard Shweder and Robert LeVine, 137–57. Cambridge: Cambridge University Press.
Rose, Tricia. 1994. *Black Noise: Rap Music and Black Culture in Contemporary America.* Hanover: Wesleyan University Press.
Rosenblatt, Nate. 2016. *All Jihad Is Local: What ISIS' Files Tell Us about Its Fighters.* Policy Paper. Washington, DC: New America 2016. https://www.newamerica.org/international-security/policy-papers/all-jihad-is-local/.
Said, Behnam. 2012. "Hymns (Nasheeds): A Contribution to the Study of the Jihadist Culture." *Studies in Conflict and Terrorism* 35, no. 12: 863–79.
Sakakeeny, Matthew. 2010. "'Under the Bridge': An Orientation to Soundscapes in New Orleans." *Ethnomusicology* 54, no. 1: 1–27.
——. 2015. "Music." In *Keywords in Sound*, edited by David Novak and Matthew Sakakeeny, 112–24. Durham, NC: Duke University Press.

Samuels, David W., Louise Meintjes, Ana Maria Ochoa, and Thomas Porcello. 2010. "Soundscapes: Toward a Sounded Anthropology." *Annual Review of Anthropology* 39: 329–45.

Schafer, R. Murray. 1994. *The Soundscape: Our Sonic Environment and the Tuning of the World*. Rochester, VT: Destiny.

Scharlipp, Wolfgang Ekkehard. 1998. "Two Eastern Turki texts about reading and writing." *Turkic Languages* 2, no. 1: 109–25.

Schein, Louisa. 2000. *Minority Rules: The Miao and the Feminine in China's Cultural Politics*. Durham, NC: Duke University Press.

Schimmel, Annemarie. 1975. *Mystical Dimension of Islam*. Chapel Hill: University of North Carolina Press.

Schrode, Paula. 2008. "The Dynamics of Orthodoxy and Heterodoxy in Uyghur Religious Practice." *Welt des Islams* 48, nos. 3–4: 394–433.

Schulz, Dorothea E. 2006. "Promises of (Im)mediate Salvation: Islam, Broadcast Media, and the Remaking of Religious Experience in Mali." *American Ethnologist* 33, no. 2: 210–29.

———. 2012. "Dis/Embodying Authority: Female Radio "Preachers" and the Ambivalences of Mass-Mediated Speech in Mali." *International Journal of Middle East Studies* 44, no. 1: 23–43.

Sells, Michael. 1991. "Sound, Spirit, and Gender in Sūrat al-Qadr." *Journal of the American Oriental Society* 111, no. 2: 239–59.

Shannon, Jonathan. 2004. "The Aesthetics of Spiritual Practice and the Creation of Moral and Musical Subjectivities in Aleppo, Syria." *Ethnology* 43, no. 4: 381–91.

Sharma, Aradhana, and Akhil Gupta. 2006. *The Anthropology of the State: A Reader*. Oxford, UK: Blackwell.

Shinjang Uyghur Aptonum Rayonliq az sanliq millet qedimki eserlirini toplash, retlesh, nesher qilishni pilanlish rehberlik guruppa ishanishi. 1989. *Uyghur, Ozbek, Tatar Qedemki Eserler Tizimliki*. Kashgar, China: Qeshqer Uyghur Neshriyati.

Shirazi, Faegheh. 2016. *Brand Islam: The Marketing and Commodification of Piety*. Austin: University of Texas Press.

Smith, Joanne. 2007. "The Quest for National Unity in Uyghur Popular Song: Barren Chickens, Stray Dogs, Fake Immortals and Thieves." In *Music, National Identity and the Politics of Location: Between the Global and the Local*, edited by Ian Biddle and Vanessa Knights, 115–41. Farnham, UK: Ashgate.

Smith Finley, Joanne. 2013. *The Art of Symbolic Resistance: Uyghur Identities and Uyghur-Han Relations in Contemporary Xinjiang*. Leiden, Neth.: Brill.

———. 2019. "Securitization, Insecurity and Conflict in Contemporary Xinjiang: Has PRC Counter-Terrorism Evolved into State Terror?" *Central Asian Survey* 38, no. 1: 1–26.

Soares, Benjamin, and Filippo Osella. 2009. "Islam, Politics, Anthropology." Special issue, *Journal of the Royal Anthropological Institute* 15, no. S1: S1–S23.

Sreberny, Annabelle and Ali Mohammadi. 1994. *Small Media Big Revolution: Communication, Culture and the Iranian Revolution*. Minneapolis: University of Minnesota Press.

Steen, Andreas. 2013. "Voices of the Mainstream: Red Songs and Revolutionary Identities in the People's Republic of China." In *Vocal Music and Contemporary Identities: Unlimited Voices in East Asia and the West*, edited by Christian Utz and Frederick Lau, 225–47. Abingdon-on-Thames, UK: Routledge.

Steenberg, Rune Reyhé. 2013. *Uyghur Marriage in Kashgar: Muslim Marriage in China*. PhD diss., Freien Universität Berlin.
Steenberg, Rune Reyhé, and Alessandro Rippa. 2019. "Development for All? State Schemes, Security, and Marginalization in Kashgar, Xinjiang." *Critical Asian Studies* 51, no. 2: 274–95.
Sterne, Jonathan. 1997. "Sounds like the Mall of America: Programmed Music and the Architectonics of Public Space." *Ethnomusicology* 41, no. 1: 22–50.
———. 2012. "Sonic Imaginations." In *The Sound Studies Reader*, edited by Jonathan Sterne, 1–18. Abingdon-on-Thames, UK: Routledge.
Stewart, Alexander. 2016. *Chinese Muslims and the Global Ummah: Islamic Revival and Ethnic Identity among the Hui of Qinghai Province*. Abingdon-on-Thames, UK: Routledge.
Stock, Jonathan P. J. 2016. "Sounding the Bromance: The Chopstick Brothers' 'Little Apple' Music Video, Genre, Gender and the Search for Meaning in Chinese Popular Music." *Journal of World Popular Music* 3, no. 2: 167–96.
Stokes, Martin. 1994. "Introduction: Ethnicity, Identity, and Music." In *Ethnicity, Identity and Music: The Musical Construction of Place*, edited by Martin Stokes, 1–24. Oxford/Providence: Berg.
———. 2013. "New Islamist Popular Culture in Turkey." In *Music, Culture and Identity in the Muslim World: Performance, Politics and Piety*, edited by Kamal Salhi, 15–35. Abingdon-on-Thames, UK: Routledge.
———. 2016. "Islamic Popular Music Aesthetics in Turkey." In *Islam and Popular Culture*, edited by Karin van Nieuwkerk, Mark LeVine, and Martin Stokes, 41–57. Austin: University of Texas Press.
Sultanova, Razia. 2011. *From Shamanism to Sufism: Women and Islam in Central Asian Culture*. London: I. B. Tauris.
Sykes, Jim. 2015. "Sound Studies, Religion and Urban Space: Tamil Music and the Ethical Life in Singapore." *Ethnomusicology Forum* 24, no. 3: 380–413.
Szadziewski, Henryk. 2013. *Rumors, Suspicion and Hysteria: Urumchi's Han Residents Target Uyghurs in September 2009 Pinprick Attack Scare*. Washington DC: Uyghur Human Rights Project.
Szadziewski, Henryk, and Greg Fay. 2015. *Legitimizing Repression: China's "War on Terror" under Xi Jinping and State Policy in East Turkestan*. Washington, DC: Uyghur Human Rights Project. http://docs.uyghuramerican.org/pdf/Legitimizing-Repression.pdf.
Tambiah, Stanley. 1996. *Leveling Crowds: Ethnonationalist Conflicts and Collective Violence in South Asia*. Berkeley: University of California Press.
Tapper, Nancy, and Richard Tapper. 1987. "The Birth of the Prophet: Ritual and Gender in Turkish Islam." *Man* 22, no. 1: 69–92.
Taussig, Michael. 1993. *Mimesis and Alterity: A Particular History of the Senses*. Abingdon-on-Thames, UK: Routledge.
Taylor, Diana. 2003. *The Archive and the Repertoire: Performing Cultural Memory in the Americas*. Durham, NC: Duke University Press.
Tazamal, Mobashra. 2019. "China Justifies Its Concentration Camps Using 'War on Terror' Discourse." *Bridge*, January 12. https://bridge.georgetown.edu/research/chinas-justifies-its-concentration-camps-using-war-on-terror-discourse/.
Thum, Rian. 2014. *The Sacred Routes of Uyghur History*. Cambridge, MA: Harvard University Press.

Tufekci, Zeynep. 2017. *Twitter and Tear Gas: The Power and Fragility of Networked Protest.* New Haven, CT: Yale University Press.
Uyghur Human Rights Project. 2013. *China's Iron-Fisted Repression of Uyghur Religious Freedom.* Washington, DC: Uyghur Human Rights Project.
Van Nieuwkerk, Karin. 2013. *Performing Piety: Singers and Actors in Egypt's Islamic Revival.* Austin: University of Texas Press.
Wainwright, Joel. 2008. *Decolonizing Development: Colonial Power and the Maya.* Oxford: Blackwell.
Waite, Edmund. 2006. "The Impact of the State on Islam amongst the Uyghurs: Religious Knowledge and Authority in the Kashgar Oasis." *Central Asian Survey* 25, no. 3: 251–65.
———. 2007. "The Emergence of Muslim Reformism in Contemporary Xinjiang." In *Situating the Uyghurs: Between China and Central Asia*, edited by Ildikó Bellér-Hann, Cristina Césaro, Rachel Harris, and Joanne Smith Finley, 165–81. Farnham, UK: Ashgate.
Wang Ban. 1997. *The Sublime Figure of History: Aesthetics and Politics in Twentieth-Century China.* Stanford, CA: Stanford University Press.
Warner, Michael. 2002. "Publics and Counterpublics." *Public Culture* 14, no. 1: 49–90.
Weidman, Amanda. 2014. "Anthropology and Voice." *Annual Review of Anthropology* 43: 37–51.
Widdess, Richard. 2014. "Orality, Writing and Music in South Asia." *Musicology Today* 19: 1–17.
———. 2015. "Text, Orality, and Performance in Newar Devotional Music." In *Tellings and Texts: Music, Literature and Performance in North India*, edited by Francesca Orsini and Katherine Butler Schofield, 231–45. Cambridge, UK: Open Book.
Williams, Raymond. 1961. *The Long Revolution.* London: Chatto and Windus.
Wolf, Richard. 2006. "The Poetics of "Sufi" Practice: Drumming, Dancing, and Complex Agency at Madho Lal Husain (and Beyond)." *American Ethnologist* 33, no. 2: 246–68.
Wood, Abigail. 2015. "The Cantor and the Muezzin's Duet: Contested Soundscapes at Jerusalem's Western Wall." *Contemporary Jewry* 35, no. 1: 55–72.
World Uyghur Congress. 2016a. "East Turkestan: Anniversary of Yarkand Massacre Marked by Uyghur Community amid Chinese Silence." Brussels: Unrepresented Nations and Peoples Organization. http://unpo.org/article/19342.
World Uyghur Congress. 2016b. *2016 Report on Human Rights Violations in East Turkestan (Events of 2015).* Munich: World Uyghur Congress. http://www.uyghurcongress.org/en/wp-content/uploads/WUC-2016-Report-Human-Rights-in-East-Turkestan.pdf.
"Xinjiang Yarkand Massacre: Ramadan Prayers Trigger Soldiers and Police to Kill Thousands." 2014. *Boxun News*, August 25. http://en.boxun.com/2014/08/25/xinjiang-massacre-no-distinction-between-men-women-old-and-young-and-no-one-left-alive/.
Yeh, Emily T. 2012. "On 'Terrorism' and the Politics of Naming." Hot Spots, *Fieldsights*, April 8. https://culanth.org/fieldsights/on-terrorism-and-the-politics-of-naming.
———. 2013. *Taming Tibet: Landscape Transformation and the Gift of Chinese Development.* Ithaca, NY: Cornell University Press.
Yessewi, Ehmed. 2012. *Diwan Hekmet.* Translated from Chagatay into modern Uyghur by Abdureshid Jelil Qorluq. Beijing: Milletler Neshriyati.
Zarcone, Thierry. 2000. "Ahmad Yasavï héros des nouvelles républiques centrasiatiques." *Revue des Mondes Musulmans et de la Méditerranée*, 89–90: 297–323.
———. 2001. "The Sufi Networks in Southern Xinjiang during the Republican Regime (1911–1949): An Overview." In *Islam in Politics in Russia and Central Asia: Early Eighteenth*

to Late Twentieth Centuries, edited by Stéphane A. Dudoignon and Komatsu Hisao, 119–32. London: Kegan Paul.

———. 2002. "Sufi Lineages and Saint Veneration in Twentieth Century Eastern Turkestan and Contemporary Xinjiang." In *The Turks*, edited by Hasan Celâl Guzel, C. Cem Oguz and Osman Karatay, 534–41. Istanbul: Yeni Turkiye.

———. 2016. "Writing the Religious and Social History of Some Sufi Lodges in Kashgar in the Twentieth Century." In *Kashgar Revisited: Uyghur Studies in Memory of Ambassador Gunnar Jarring*, edited by Ildikó Bellér-Hann, Birgit N. Schlyter, and Jun Sugawara, 207–31. Leiden, Neth.: Brill.

Zenz, Adrian. 2019. "'Thoroughly Reforming them Toward a Healthy Heart Attitude': China's Political Re-Education Campaign in Xinjiang." *Central Asian Survey* 38, no. 1: 102–28.

Zenz, Adrian, and James Leibold. 2017. "Chen Quanguo: The Strongman Behind Beijing's Securitization Strategy in Tibet and Xinjiang." *China Brief* 17, no. 12 (September 21). https://jamestown.org/program/chen-quanguo-the-strongman-behind-beijings-securitization-strategy-in-tibet-and-xinjiang/.

Zhou Ji. 1999. *Zhongguo Xinjiang weiwu'erzu yisilanjiao liyi yinyue*. Taibei: Xinwenfeng chuban gongsi.

INDEX

Abd al-Wahhab, Muhammad ibn, 36n2
Abdul Basit 'Abd us-Samad, 28, 104–5, 114, 117–19, 122, 127
Abdul Rahman al-Sudais, 105, 114, 128
Abdulla, Dilnar, 183
abstraction, 143
Abu Ghraib prison, 176, 209
a cappella pop, 137
acoustemology, 13
adhan (call to prayer): as banished, 19–20; space, demarcating and sacralizing of, 19; as temporal marker, 19
Adiläm, Hajim, 91–97, 114
aesthetics, 30–31, 129
Afaq Khoja, 55
affect: and emotion, 42–43
Afghanistan, 155
Africa, 129
African Americans, 24
agency, 13, 16, 27, 212; as situated, 145
Ahmad, Qul Khoj'. *See* Yasawi, Khoja Ahmad
Ahmed, Sarah, 185, 213; economies of affect, 31; experiential, messiness of, 43; inside-out dichotomy, 42, 63; text-based discourse, 43
Akkad, Moustapha, 141–42
AK Party, 103
Alafasy, Mishary Rashid, 28, 104–5, 109, 114, 118–21
al-Ghazali, 73
al Hussari, Khalil, 116
Ali, Sadiq, 127
Almaty (Kazakhstan), 73
Al Qaeda, 159, 182
Al-Rahman, 127
Altishahr, 55–56; hand-copied manuscripts, tradition of, 86–87. *See also* Xinjiang

Americas, 218; indigenous performance practices, as devil worship, 215
Anand, Dibyesh, 214
anashid, 74, 141, 156, 162, 167n23; geographical reach of, 158–59; Islamist cultural offensive, as aspect of, 159; listeners and imagined community, bonds between, 157; politically radical subgenre, 159, 161, 163, 195; pop music, influence of, 159–60; as video sound tracks, 159
Ankara (Turkey), 73, 83–84, 99
anthropology: and agency, 16; ethnography of the ear, 13; and representation, 16; and sound, 13; and subjectivity, 16
anti-religious-extremism campaign, 46, 136, 151, 173, 177, 181, 194; and music, 212; public space, control of, 197; song and dance, role of, 197, 199, 211; state power, countering of, 199; Uyghur nationalist sentiment, targeting of, 205–6; and Uyghurs, 150, 183, 188–89, 195, 205, 212, 219; in Xinjiang, 4, 34–35, 147, 175–76, 178, 184, 186, 196–97, 199, 211, 214–15
Aqsu (China), 55, 117–18, 165, 170, 176–77, 179, 181–82, 184, 186, 189–90
Aqsu Religious Affairs Committee, 54
Argenti, Nicolas, 212
Arslan Baba, 77
Arzu Style Restaurant, 101–2
Asad, Talal, 139
Ashiq: The Last Troubadours (film), 99n2
ashiqs, 99n2
Ashirov, Adham, 80
Asia, 2–5, 7–9, 11, 18, 23–24, 26, 28, 31, 33, 50, 55, 77–78, 82–83, 95, 99, 104, 106, 108, 120, 158; Muslim publics in, 103; shamanism in, 52
Attali, Jacques, 182
authenticity, 131, 162; and recordings, 31

Ayup, Abduwali, 208
Azimova, Nadira, 28, 50

Barmé, Geremie, 211–12
Basmachi rebellion, 56
Becker, Judith, 63
Becoming Family policy, 205
Beijing (China), 29, 34, 147, 184
Bekali, Omir, 207, 210
Bellér-Hann, Ildikó, 6, 68, 217
Bin Laden, Osama, 182
Bishkek (Kyrgyzstan), 27, 29, 103, 112–15; Uyghur women in, 116
black Americans: spatial control of, 180
Blacking, John: bodily resonance, 63
black noise, 180
bodily habitus, 196
bodily practice, 149; daily prayers, 34, 115; ethical self-formation, 196; habitus, as form of, 115; Qur'anic recitation, 34, 115
bodily resonance, 63
Bourdieu, Pierre, 196–97
Bovingdon, Gardner, 172
Bo Xilai, 189
Boxun, 152–53
Brazil, 29
Brown, Wendy, 154
Bulaq (magazine), 83, 98
Butler, Judith, 42, 213
büwi, 40, 46, 63, 64, 69n9, 69n12, 75, 103, 114, 121, 151, 165, 179, 219; Jahriyya traditions, links between, 57; masculine lines of transmission, 54; repetition, spiritual necessity of, 213–14; respect toward, 53; ritual practices of, 128; spiritual power of, 51; Sufi groups, 54–55; Sufi-inflected traditions, 65–66; as tärikätchi (people of the path), 54, 57; transnational Islamic culture, 105; and weeping, 67; and women, 49–53, 66–68

Caduff, Carlo, 164
Cairo (Egypt), 29, 101, 102–4; adhan (call to prayer) in, 19; Islamic revival in, 24; public spaces in, 146
Canada: First Nation peoples, 19
Chagatay literary culture, 65; poetry, 206

"Chairman Mao May You Live Forever" (song), 190
Chen Quanguo, 178, 204
China, 1–3, 9, 18, 21, 23–24, 29, 34–35, 47–48, 100n7, 117, 120, 130, 131n1, 144–45, 150, 157, 161, 169–71, 176, 182, 195, 197, 208, 211, 215; adhan (call to prayer) in, 20; Belt and Road Initiative, 91; communization drive, 91; and exceptionalism, 174; four olds campaign, 91, 189; human rights in, 220n2; internal security policies, justification of, 10; Islam in, 5; Islamic institutes, 8; Islamic sounds, 25; Middle Kingdom, 5–6; minority musical traditions, 184–85, 192, 209; Muslims in, 5–6; professional musical minority, gendered aspect of, 186; Red Songs, 189; religious practice in, between tolerance and criminalization, 5; sonic territorialization in, 174–75; terrorism, rhetoric of, 139; UNESCO heritage schemes, participation in, 172; Uyghurs in, 210. *See also* People's Republic of China (PRC), Uyghurs
China Dancer's Association, 183
Chinese Communist Party (CCP), 6–8, 86, 166, 186, 189, 191, 193–95, 203, 207–8, 211; song and dance, prominence of, 184–85
Chinese Islam, 20
Chinese Muslims, 6; ethnic categories of, 7; Hui Chinese-speaking, 7; marginalization of, 130; modernity, thirst for, 130; mosque land, as protected, 8; sharia courts, 8
Chinese People's Liberation Army, 193
Chongqing (China), 189
Chopstick Brothers, 168–69
chorzarb, 80
Christian, William, 67
circulation, 10, 30, 161; of emotions, 185, 213; of hikmät, 73–74, 80, 97–98; of information, 177–78; and locality, 145; of media items, 34; of mediated experience, 164; patterns of, 33, 73; of religious media, 28, 99, 102, 108, 137, 141, 144, 147, 165; of sounds, 122–23, 140, 149, 162; transnational networks of, 29, 31
circuits of affect, 31
circuits of connection, 29, 34

circuits of transmission, 74, 99
Clayton, Martin, 43
collectivity: entrainment, form of, 43; as shared groove, 43; through synchronized movement, 43
colonialism: performance practices, attempt to erase, 215
coloniality, 214–15
community schools, 86
communization, 3–4
Corbin, Alain, 19
cultural authenticity: as tools of governance, 5
cultural cleansing, 206
cultural erasure, 35, 206
Cultural Revolution, 1, 8, 34–35, 37, 48–49, 154, 189, 197, 212, 218; four olds campaign, 106; mass mobilization, techniques of, 175, 195–96; Model Operas of, 195–96, 214; music and violence, memories of, 211; psychic damage of, 211; scar literary movement, 211; song and dance, 211; and trauma, 211
Cusick, Suzanne, 208–9

Da'esh, 159, 161, 167n23
Damolla, 117–18, 130
Damolla, Abla, 54, 57
Damolla, Mohammad Ali, 85–86
Daughtry, Martin, 175, 210, 212, 216
dawa'chi (preachers), 106
dawah missionary movement, 9
Dawut, Rahile, 88, 172, 206
de Abreu, Maria José A., 164
"Dear Heartless Father" (video), 149
decontextualization, 143
Deleuze, Gilles, 170
DeNora, Tia, 63, 174
Deobandi movement, 9, 56
detention camps, 2, 151, 179, 207–8, 210, 216; musical performance, 209. *See also* internment camps, reeducation centers
deterritorialization: and place, 30
DeWeese, Devin, 100n5
dhikr, 125. *See also* zikr
digital media, 140
disciplining bodies, 195

discourse, 10, 15, 18, 28, 32, 51, 55, 65, 102, 137, 139, 154, 157, 161, 163, 171–72; corporeal experience, 43; as localized, 129; and perception, 17; religious, 30, 141; as text-based, 43; of trauma, 212
disjuncture, 16, 36, 128; acoustemological, 24
Diwan-i Hikmät, 73, 77, 79–81, 83–84, 87–90, 93–95, 97–98; ishq, as central concept in, 82; as term, 78
Dubai, 147
Dueck, Byron, 43
Durkheim, Émile, 42

"East Is Red, The" (song), 190
East Turkistan, 3, 155, 190. *See also* Xinjiang Uyghur Autonomous Region
Ebersole, Gary L., 69n5
Egypt, 9, 27, 103, 106, 109–10, 122, 129, 159, 205, 208; Islamic revival in, 146; Saudi style, of Qur'anic recitation, 117; women's mosque movement, 115
Egyptian Islamic counterpublic, religious media consumption, 143
Ehsan, Hajim, 160–61
Eickelman, Dale F., 140
Eisenberg, Andrew, 20, 173, 197; acoustemological disjuncture, 24
Eisenlohr, Patrick, 31
"Emancipated Serfs Have a Song to Sing, The" (song), 184–85
embodied behavior, 34–35
embodied practices, 20, 35, 195–96, 215; and landscape, 199; soundscapes, as linked, 197
embodied religious practice, 213
embodied spatial practices, 171, 173
embodiment, 28, 31, 43, 54, 66, 118, 173, 185, 195; of faith, 14; and performance, 196, 199; and representation, 34; of social values, 42
emotions, 46, 213; affect, contagious forms of, 31; authentic v. outward representation, 185; dard (suffering), 31–32; effects of circulation, 31; inside-out dichotomy, 42, 63; ishq (divine love, passion), 31–32; and rituals, 41–43; sociality of, 31; as sticky, 31
emplacement, 30; and soundscapes, 20, 198
Emre, Yunus, 83

entrainment: belonging, sense of, 44; collectivity, sense of, 43; as rhythmic, 63; ritual performance, 43; shared groove, 43–44
erasure, 215; cultural, 35, 206, 212; fears of, 218; political acts of, 216
Erdoğan, Recep Tayyip, 159
Erlmann, Veit, 128
ethical listening, 101–2
ethical self-formation, 149; bodily practice, 196
ethnomusicology, 16–17
Europe, 18–19, 67, 147

Facebook, 144
Fatah, 159
Fayruz, 123
Feld, Steven: histories of listening, 13
Festival of Sacrifice, 141
56.com, 141
Finley, Joanne Smith, 23
Finnegan, Ruth, 84
France, 19, 64
Frishkopf, Michael, 117, 120, 127; semiotic model, 127, 128

Gade, Anna, 111, 122, 127
Gansu (China), 25
gender, 25, 31, 42, 46, 53, 66, 149, 213; Chinese minority performers, 186; listening practices, 15–16; and modesty, 32, 74; performative weeping, 48; politics of, 44; public morality of, 135–36; sacred space, 6; and soundscape, 26; of space, 36; spatial binaries, 27; of territorialization, 36
geographies of form, 145
Germany, 211; Uyghur community in, 191
gham (sadness or suffering), 48
"Ghost Sermon," 149
Ghulja (China), 91, 93–96, 99, 147, 187
Giddens, Anthony, 105
Gill, Denise, 15–16
Gladney, Dru, 184–85
globalized capitalism, 23
Global War on Terror, 10, 48, 139, 171
Great Wall, 5–6
Grima, Benedicte, 48
Guangzhou (China), 138, 147

Guattari, Félix, 170
Gulnisa, Hajim, 104, 112–15, 196

habitus, 35–36, 173, 200; bodily practice, 115; of community, 19; contested landscape, 197; Islamic forms of, 199; of listening, 122; of senses, 19; as system of dispositions, 196
hajj, 7–9, 14, 46, 75, 92, 104, 106, 109, 112–15, 135, 142, 194, 212–13
halal food, 106–7
halal industry: and identity, 120
halpa, 50
hälqä-sohbät, 79. *See also* samaʿ rituals
Hamas, 159
Han Chinese, 1–2, 165, 169, 186, 204–5
Haraway, Donna: Cyborg Manifesto, 131n8
Hasim, Sidiq, 190
Hellier-Tinocco, Ruth, 218
Heyit, Abdurehim, 206
Hezbollah, 159
hijrah, 167n22
hikmät, 32–33, 40, 66, 70–71, 83, 86–90, 92–94, 100n6, 100n11, 129, 142, 150, 219–20; affective work of, 72, 79–80; circulation of, 73–74, 80, 97–98; dastan, performances of, 79; as diverse, 79; as laments, 74; as living performance, 73–74, 76–77, 79; oral circulation, 97; oral traditions of, 74; as panegyrics, 78–79; patterns of circulation, 73–74; oral circulation of, 80; performative traditions of, 84, 98; printed and oral circulation of, 97–98; reciters of, 98; rituals of mourning and healing, 73; sung performance of, 73; transnational circulation of, 74; and weeping, 79
Hirschkind, Charles, 19, 24, 30, 32, 62, 101, 143, 164; ethical listening, 16, 102; Islamic counterpublics, 102; listening practices, emphasis on, 146
Hochschild, Arlie, 185–86
Holocaust, 211
Homeric epics, 84
horror: affective language of, 143–44; and videodiscs, 142–43
horror films, 166; sound effects, 137; sound tracks, 164
Huang, Cindy, 46, 131n8, 147

Hui Chinese Muslims, 5, 10, 25, 130
Hurriyät, Hajim, 75–76, 125, 212–13
Huwayda, 167n19
huzn, 84, 121; as moral state, 72–73

Ibn Khaldun, 115
identity, 136, 215; in public sphere, 137
identity formation: and music, 105
"If You're Happy and You Know It" (song), 209
image engineering, 170
indigenous people, 215
India, 9, 55, 106, 164–65
Indonesia, 125–27; Qur'anic recitation in, 122
Integrated Joint Operations Platform, 204
interiority: inside-out model, 42
internet, 4, 29–30, 34, 109, 118, 134, 138, 140, 152, 165
internment camps, 2, 35, 200. *See also* detention camps, reeducation centers
"In the Time of Liberation" (song), 189
Iran, 26
Iranian revolution, 26
Iraq, 159
Iraq war, 39, 159, 208, 210; sound in, 175
Isa, Aziz, 3
Ishan, Pasha, 189
ishq (love), 82, 185; and weeping, 48, 65, 68
Islam, 4, 7, 9–10, 14–15, 23, 28, 31–33, 36n2, 53, 61, 108, 112, 131n8, 136, 144–45, 151, 194; cassette sermons, and popular music, 29–30; in China, 5, 8; as commercialized transnational, 120–21; counterpublic, as discursive arena, 102; counterpublics, 30; digital media, 140; ethical listening, 16, 101–2; everyday religious experience, complexity of, 12; four olds campaign, as part of, 8; global, 129; and hearing, 20; local, hybrid forms of, 130; media forms, 29; music videos, 141; mystical, 127; national survival, 165; original, 131; Other, 129; political geography, 140; pure, 106–7; reformist styles of, 34, 94, 155, 159; restrictions on, 150; revivalist narratives of, 117, 130; sacred sounds of, as noise, 18–19; semiotic associations of, 128; sounded practice, 99; Sufi-influenced modes of, 127; true, 6, 11, 104–5, 147; as virus, 1. *See also* Islamic revival, Islamic soundscapes
Islamic Association of China, 7–9, 117
Islamic Institute, 8, 53, 117
Islamic revival, 2–3, 16, 27, 103, 175, 196–97, 199; media, listening to, 30; Muslims, as passive Others, 15; religious sounds, in private spaces, 198; visual, privileging of, 15
Islamic soundscapes, 20, 30, 220; adhan (call to prayer), 19; as contingent and fleeting, 146; as form of resistance, 23; in private space, 198; in public space, 197–98; reactivated, 216
Israel, 16
Istanbul (Turkey), 15–16, 29, 73, 145, 160–61

Jadidists, 7, 50, 54–55, 83
Jadids, 193
Jakarta (Indonesia), 19, 123
Jaladin, Abduqadir, 206
Jännät, Hajim, 13, 25–27
japakesh, 46–47
Jarring, Gunnar, 81, 100n10, 192
Jelil, Gulbahar, 207, 215–16
Jerusalem (Israel), 26; Western Wall, as contested site, 16
jihad, 157, 159, 161, 163, 167n22, 195
Jordan, 142

Kadir, Aynur, 79, 97–98
Kahn, Douglas, 18
Kandiyoti, Deniz, 28, 50
Kapchan, Deborah, 15, 44, 64
Kashgar (China), 25, 55–56, 78–79, 81, 97, 106, 108, 147, 169–70, 173, 176–77, 181, 188, 202n34; wedding customs in, 183–84
Kashmir, 170
Kassabian, Anahid, 15
Kazakhstan, 3–4, 33, 74, 77, 80, 91–93, 97, 104, 107–8, 114, 118, 147, 191, 207; Uyghur diaspora in, 13, 103
Keil, Charles: participatory discrepancies theory, 64
khaniqa, 69n12
khätmä ritual, 28, 31–32, 49–50, 53–54, 57–60, 75, 77, 92–93, 99n3, 106, 121, 123–25, 151, 213–14; body-sound interactions, 63; weeping participants in, 62–63

Khazini, 80
Khesti, Roshanak, 26–27
Khotan (China), 5, 55, 176–78, 181–82, 184
kolkhoz collective farms, 91
Köprülü, Mehmet Fuad, 82–83
Kulthum, Umm, 122
Kundnani, Arun, 139
Kunming (China), 150, 182
Kyrgyzstan, 3–4, 10, 29, 33, 102, 107; Uyghur diaspora in, 13, 103

landscape, 1, 9, 20, 147, 158, 170, 172, 198; as contested, 197; embodied practices, 36, 199; and erasure, 217–18; and power, 171; and soundscape, 23, 176–77, 216; struggles over, 173, 175
Leante, Laura, 43
LaBelle, Brandon, 174
le Coq, Albert von, 80, 100n7
Lefebvre, Henri, 198, 215; embodied rhythms, as dressage, 214; rhythmology of, 214
"Letter to Mother," 157–61
Lhasa (Tibet), 170
Light, Nathan, 96–97
Linxia (China), 20, 25
Lipman, Jonathan, 5
listening, 25, 27, 35, 212; coerced, 209; dangers of, 181; deep, 15; ethical, 16; genres of, 15; new ways of, 105; permissibility of, 18; religious sounds, on smartphones, 137; and sound, 30; and space, 20; spatial dimension of, 180; tactical, 15; territorialization, processes of, 176; transnational networks of circulation, 31; ubiquitous, 15
listening experience: freedom, as illusory, 164; as personal and public, 164
listening practices, 14, 34, 36, 103, 115, 147; gendered nature of, 15–16; as mediated, 146; as social markers, 13
literacy, 86; and orality, 73–74, 84–85
"Little Apple" (song), 168–71, 175, 200
Liu Xiangchen, 99n2
lived experience, 5, 23; snake-monkey-woman video, 136
locality, 50, 105, 169; and circulation, 145
"Long Live Chairman Mao" (song), 190
Lord, Albert B., 84

Los Angeles (California), 145
Loubes, Jean-Paul, 172, 188
Lutz, Catherine, 42

madrassas, 86, 107, 130
Mahmood, Saba, 12, 34, 115, 149
Makhdum-i A'zam, 55, 64–65, 192
Malaysia, 136
male space: and mosques, 112–13
Mali, 146, 163
manuscript copying: and feedback loops, 99
Mao Zedong, 38, 189–90
maqām, 121, 125
Marsden, Magnus, 28
mäshräp, 10, 79, 153, 187–88, 193; extremism, countering of, 186
Mashrab, Baba Rahim, 96
Mauritius, 31, 62
Mecca (Saudi Arabia), 29, 104, 117
media technology, 158; audiocassettes, circulation of, 145, 157, 162, 164; deletion of, 163–64; mass media v. small media, 145; sacrifice, trope of, 157; sound, and joint spiritual experiences, 146
mediated circulation of sounds, 162
mediated experience, 164
mediated listening, 122
mediated sound: social media, 145; sonic territorialization
mediated voice: mobilizing potential for, 162–63
Medina (Saudi Arabia), 117
memory, 31, 220; collective, of colonial violence, 218; corporeal, 218; embodied, 215–6, 218; social, 215; sonic, 218
Message, The (film), 141–42
Miao people, 186
Middle East, 6, 9, 30, 33–34, 57, 102–5, 117–19, 123, 127–28, 130, 140, 158; Islamic revival movement in, 196
Mijit, Mukaddas, 193, 218
mobility, 23, 176–78; across borders, 74; contact and circulation, 74; restrictions on, 188
modernity, 21, 23–24, 32, 129–30, 186, 216; global imagination, 128; in globalized world, 105; and horror, 166;

snake-monkey-woman video, 136; social relations, disembedding of, 105
modernization, 18–19, 23, 182, 199; Islam, new forms of, 130
Mombasa (Kenya), 20
Mongolia, 170, 176
morality, 31, 129, 135–36, 151
Morocco, 29
Mosque Rectification campaign, 181
Muhammad, Prophet, 36n3, 57, 65, 67, 109
mujahidin, 157–59, 162, 195
"Mujahidin of Guma, The," 162
Mukhlis, Nijat, 83, 98
Muqam Heritage Centre, 217
muqam texts, 96
music, 210–11; anti-religious-extremism campaign, role in, 183–84; cultural belief, site of, 209; cultural practice, medium of, 209; deterritorialization and place, oscillation between, 30; identity formation, as agent of, 30; interrogation techniques, 208–9; as problem, 17; as sensory experience, 209; and trance, 63; weaponization of, 208
music making: community building, 64
musiqa: permissibility, debates around, 17
Muslims: counterpublics, 35; mass internment of, 203; new publics, 145–46; social media, 145; true Muslims, 165–66; womanhood, notions of, 148–49
Muzak, 174, 185
"My Name Is Uyghur Girl" (song), 155–57, 161

nagamat rast, 121
nagamat saba, 121
Namangoni, Mazdub, 80
nashid, 158. *See also* anashid
National People's Congress, 182
Nawa'i, Ali Shir, 96
näzir (death ritual), 11–12, 36n4, 45
Nelson, Kristina, 110, 121
Nepal, 85, 170
New Orleans (Louisiana): soundscapes of, 24
New Socialist Countryside: Comfortable Housing Project of, 170–71
New York City, 10
Night of Barat, 58–59, 66–68, 106, 121

Night of Forgiveness, 68
Nizamidin, Hurriyät, 69n15
noise: eradication of, 180; as metaphor, 18, 180; music, in opposition to, 18; Other, sounds of, 18, 180; and power, 182; and sound, 18; as subversion, 18
Novak, David, 17
Novetzke, Lee, 85

O Clone (The Clone) (telenovela), 29
Olivero, Pauline, 15
Ölüm (Death) (videodisc), 142–43
Ömärjan, Hakim, 190–91
orality, 163; and literacy, 73–74, 84–85; and text, 85, 96–97
oral poetry, 84
oral transmission: and canonization, 98–99
orthopraxy, 149
Osmanova, Yultuz, 141
Others, 15; and noise, 18, 180; normative narratives, 16–17; progressive Self, 214–15
Otkar, Adnan, 143
Ötkür, Abdurehim, 154
Ottoman Turkey, 7

Pakistan, 9, 64, 106, 109; samaʿ rituals, 60
Palestine, 159
palimpsest: mass singing and dancing, 216; palimpsest bodies, 218; revolutionary songs, forced singing of, 216; as soundscape, 216–17; transtemporality, 218; and violence, 216
Panagia, Davide, 18, 137; politics of utterance, 34
Paris (France), 145, 198
Parry, Milman, 84
participatory discrepancies theory, 64
Pasilov, Bahodir, 80
Päyzulla, Hajim, 13
Peng Liyuan, 185
People's Republic of China (PRC), 4, 6, 34–35, 170, 184–85, 193, 197, 199–200, 205; freedom of religion, 8. *See also* China
People's War on Terror, 18, 176, 179
performative behavior, 34
performative tears, 69n5
Persia, 170. *See also* Iran

Pieslak, Jonathan, 159–60
pilgrimages, 7, 10, 25, 29, 77–78, 172, 206
Piscatori, James, 140
Plänkers, Tomas, 211
political geographies, 29–30
positionality, 13, 24, 211
postcolonial movements, 35, 218
Post, Jennifer, 176
praise poetry: bada notebooks, 85
Privratsky, Bruce G., 83
public space, 2, 25, 147, 168, 198; control of, 197; freedom, as illusory, 164; insiderness and outsiderness, 24; Islamization of, 103; masculine v. feminine, 26–27; private community space, transforming into, 197; reshaping of, 146; rumor, powerful role of, 164; Uyghur identity in, 137
Punjab (India), 85
punk, 18

Qing Empire, 21, 55–56
Qinghai (China), 10
Qorluq, Abdureshid Jelil, 83
Qumal (China), 173, 217
Qur'an, 213–14; self-study of, 108–9; four olds campaign, target under, 106; texts of, 114–15. *See also* Qur'anic recitation
Qur'anic recitation, 17–18, 28, 31–33, 36n4, 40, 46, 49–50, 53, 59–60, 74–75, 90, 107, 112–15, 123, 130, 137, 143, 146, 149, 159, 164–65, 195–96, 205, 208, 219; affective impact of, 110–12, 122; affective states, of unanticipated tension, 110–11; bayati, Arab mode of, 121–22, 125; cadences, importance of, 122; cassettes, 109, 117; changing styles of, 117; correct pronunciation, 127; in digital media, 103, 127; as divine revelation, 110; Egyptian style, 117, 122, 125–27, 129; emotional engagement in, 104; enthusiasm for, upsurge in, 105; as global halal industry, 120; and huzn, 73; as localized, 129; and maqām, 121, 125; mäwlud celebrations, 106; melodic and expressive aspects of, 116; mode, use of, 121; mujawwad style, 116–17; murattal style, 116–17; musical sound of, 105, 116–17; nasality, use of, 111–12; Night of Power, 58; orality, culture of, 163; in public places, 101–3; Qur'an recitals, 73; reciter, role of, 110; recordings of, 99, 101, 103, 109, 121, 127, 147; repetition, meaningfulness of, 61–63; revival of practices around, 106, 108; Saudi style, 117, 120, 128–29, 162; semiotic meanings, 128; as sound, 61–62; styles of, 127; tajwid, rules of, 110–12, 116, 125–26; transnational media, circulation through, 120–21; Uyghur reciters, 118; vocal quality of, 110–11; and women, 117
Qureshi, Regula, 60–61

Rabiya Acha, 3, 37–39, 47–48, 69n7, 212, 218
Racy, Ali Jihad, 121–22
Radio Free Asia, 181, 207
rap culture: containment of, 180
Rasmussen, Anne, 19, 58, 122–23
reciprocal hospitality, 44; religious custom, 45
reciprocity: networks of, 53
Red Guards, 8, 106
"Red Songs," 188–90, 197, 202n34
reeducation centers, 2, 204, 209. *See also* detention camps, internment camps
reengineering, 215–16; as colonial project, 214
Reichl, Karl, 84
religious extremism, 5, 10, 20, 29, 39, 48, 75, 136, 138–39, 142, 151, 168, 171, 175, 182–83, 215, 219; as term, for Uyghur culture, 206
religious media, 140; accessing of, by Muslims, 145–46; audio files, 149–50; banning of, 144; deletion of, 163–64; extremism, as sign of, 147; as form of terrorism, 146; images and texts, 148–49; and rumors, 165; sharing of, 145
religious revivals: marginalized people, 23; state, relationship between, 4
religious sociality: mediated listening practices, 146
repetition, 214, 216; social forms, 213
representation, 16, 34–35, 44; bodily discipline, 206; smile, trope of, 185
resilience, 212
reterritorialization, 175, 212
Revealing Errors campaign, 181
Rif'at, Sheikh, 121

ritual performance: belonging, sense of, 44; bodily movement, 43; and entrainment, 43
ritual practices, 49, 99; collectivity, and synchronized movement, 43; embodied practices, 13; sounded practices, 13; and weeping, 48
Rose, Tricia, 180
Ross, Lisa, 218
Rozi, Yalqun, 193, 202n37
rumors: mass movements, as currency of, 164–65; performative power of, 164; in social media, 165

sacred space, 25; gendered divisions of, 6
Saddam Hussein, 39, 48
Sakakeeny, Matt, 17, 24
Salafism, 20, 128, 130
sama' rituals, 40, 49–50, 60, 64, 68n2, 128, 192; as defined, 65. *See also* hälqä-sohbät
Samuels, David, 20
Saniyäm Ismayil, 155–57
Saudi Arabia, 9, 36n2, 106, 109, 118, 147, 155
Schafer, Murray, 24; World Soundscapes, 19
Schein, Louisa, 130, 184, 186
Schramm, Katherina, 212
Schrode, Paula, 9
Schulz, Dorothea, 145–46, 162–63
securitization, 3–4, 35, 213–14
self-fashioning, 145; coerced singing and dancing, 171
sensory studies, 14–15
September 11 attacks, 10
shamanism, 52
Shanghai (China), 145
shared groove: belonging, sense of, 44; and entrainment, 43–44
Shih, Gerry, 208
Shir, Ali, 104
Shirazi, Faegheh, 120
Shurbäk Imam, 107–8, 118–20
Sidiq, Erkin, 194
silsila (spiritual genealogy), 77
Singapore, 19–20, 24
Six Cities, 171
smile: gendered aspect of, 186; political symbolism of, 185; symbolic potential of, 34
snake-monkey-woman video, 149–50, 166; affective impact of, 137; as fake miracle, 136; horror films, similarity to, 137; as lived experience, 136; meaning of, 134–36; online jihadi propaganda, 138; public morality, policing of, 135–36; and modernity, 136; religious extremism, 138; rumors surrounding, 165; semantic interpretation, openness to, 137; as threatening, to state, 165; as utterance, 136–37; Uyghur identity, 136; Uyghur online community, 135–36; Uyghur Muslim women, gendered questions, 136; visceral response to, 137
sociality, 25; of emotion, 31; of women, 27
social media, 26, 28–29, 120, 135, 137, 144, 147, 154–56, 162–63, 204, 206, 216; affective experiences of community, creating of, 146; affective experience of faith, 145; anashid, 160; ease and immediacy of, 164; masculinity, fantasies of, 158; mediated sounds, 145; and rumors, 165; structures of feeling, 140; and taranas, 159
social space: audio branding, 174; and Muzak, 174
song and dance, 18, 214; state violence, 200
sonic architecture, 102
sonic imagination, 13, 19; emancipatory potential of, 14; senses, democracy of, 14–15. *See also* sound
sonic memory, 174
sonic territorialization, 35, 175, 197; American shopping malls, 174; mediated sound, listening to, 174; song and dance, 197; techniques of, 174
SonoCairo, 116
sound, 13; bodies, direct relationship between, 175–76; circulation of, in commodity form, 122; as dangerous noise, 18; embodied relationships with, 20; identity, expression of, 18–19; and listening, 30; meanings attached to, 17; media technologies, and joint spiritual experience, 146; metaphors for, 17–19; power, relations of, 175; as sacred, 18; social and religious change, patterns of, 2; and space, 19; territory, conflict over, 19; torture, as form of, 175–76; traumatic stress, 210–11;

in war contexts, 175, 210; weaponization of, 208. *See also* sonic imagination
sounded practices, 14, 17, 24, 99, 101, 115; weeping rituals, 48
soundscape, 1, 5, 29, 34–36, 105, 164, 173, 176, 181, 197, 214, 216–17; as contested, 24–26; as culturally inflected, 23; as discursive tradition, 24; embodied practices, as linked, 197; emplacement, 20; experientiality, 24; and gender, 25–27; and identity, 20; landscape, equating with, 23; and music, 17; positionality, 24; of public squares, 21; sounds not heard, 2; and space, 25; and time, 25; urban, 24. *See also* listening
soundscape studies, 19
sound studies, 13–14, 17
Soviet Union, 3, 18, 120
space: contrastive understandings of, 24; demarcation of, 19; as gendered, 26–27, 36; and listening, 20; sacralizing of, 19; sonic contestation of, 26; spatial techniques of control, 177–78
Spain, 67
spatial territorialization: reorganizing of space, 173
spiritual civilization, 5
spiritual geographies, 29
spirituality, 192
Stalin, Joseph, 78, 83
Steenberg, Rune, 183
Sterne, Jonathan, 174; sonic imagination, notion of, 13–14
Stokes, Martin, 30, 103
subaltern subjects, 154
subjectivity, 16, 18
Sufism, 20, 33, 58, 68n1, 83, 86, 90, 96–97, 122, 127, 128, 130, 153, 192; Chisti order, 55; dervishes, 171; and drummers, 64; hälqä-sohbät ritual gatherings, 106; Jahriyya branch, 56–57; khaniqa (Sufi lodges), 50, 54–57; Khufiyya branch, 56; mysticism, 88–89; mystic poetry, 78; Naqshbandi order, 7, 50, 55–57, 64–65, 77; Qadiriyya order, 25, 50, 55; samaʻ (listening), 18; spiritual audition, 64; Yasawi order, 77; women's community-based practice, relationship between, 50

Sunna, 36n3
Sykes, Jim, 24
Syria, 159; Uyghurs in, 161

Tablighi Jama'at organization, 9, 106–7
tajwid, 111–12, 116, 121, 125–27, 159
Taklamakan desert: shrine pilgrimage, 172; Six Cities, 171
Taliban, 159
Tambiah, Stanley, 164–65
tarab, 121–22
taranas, 159
tärikät yol, 73, 84
Tashkent (Uzbekistan), 73, 78, 80, 83–84
Taussig, Michael, 131n7
Taylor, Diana, 215
tazkira manuscript tradition, 87, 172; and copying, 97
technological determination, 84
temporal rupture, 33
Tencent, 144
territorialization, 36, 170–71, 173; and listening, 176; as self-fashioning, 171
terrorism, 29, 138–39, 171, 177, 205–6, 208, 215; and extremism, 140; religious media, as form of, 146
"They Don't Understand" (song), 160
Thum, Rian, 7, 87, 97, 100n8, 172
Tianshan Net, 188, 190
Tibet, 139, 170–71, 204
Timur, Amir, 77
Timurid dynasty, 77
transmission, 9, 53, 73, 111, 215; chains of, 31, 50, 74; complex circuits of, 90; literate forms, 55; masculine lines of, 54; oral, 31, 33, 74, 96, 98–99; performative, 31; textual, 31; transnational circuits, 33; written, 33
transtemporality: and palimpsest, 218
trauma, 210; constant scrutiny, 21; sounds, memories of, 211
trauma studies, 210–11
Troitskaya, Valery, 80
Tudou, 141, 144
Turkey, 9, 27–28, 30–31, 33, 67, 78, 83, 90, 95, 102–3, 106–7, 112–15, 147, 160, 194–95, 205; Turkish Islamist movement, 159; Uyghurs in, 161, 190–91

Turkistan, 77–78, 83, 99
Turpan (China), 78, 97–99, 186
Tursun, Mihrigul, 208, 210
Tursun, Sanubar, 206
"Tutiwalidu," 132–33
Twelve Muqam, 79, 96–98, 167n19, 193

Ündidar networks, 167n23, 204
UNESCO, 172, 188
United Nations (UN), 209
United States, 10, 18–19, 139, 147, 167n7, 174, 210
Ürümchi (Xinjiang), 1, 8, 11–12, 47, 73, 99, 102–3, 136, 147, 169, 176–77; Big Bazaar, 172, 186; halal consumption, 121; Islamization of, 21–23; market attack, 150–51; violence in, 138, 150–51, 154, 158, 165
Uyghur Islam, 7, 29; nexus of sound, debates and conflict about, 14; sounded practices, 17; soundscapes of, 23–24
Uyghur Islamic revival, 128, 130; halal consumption, patterns of, 121; healing and transformation, as form of, 212; soundscapes approach to, 35–36
Uyghurs, 1, 12–13, 20–22, 25, 29, 35, 64, 70, 73, 79–80, 83–85, 90–93, 96, 103, 114, 131n8, 203, 216, 219; and agency, 212; anashid, 159–60, 163, 167n23; anti-religious extremist campaign, 136, 183, 195, 205–6, 212, 219; Arab-style women's covering, ban on, 178–79; assimilation, policies of, 23; "beauty campaigns," 179; bodily practices, as secular, 199; büwi tradition, 50; Central Asia, trading links with, 9; Chinese cultural identity, adoption of, 207; Chinese rule, resistance to, 162; circulation of religious media, 28; "cleansing" campaign against, 2, 206; community life, 7; control of, 176–78; convenience cards, 178; as cosmopolitan, 9; counterpublics, 34; dard, 31–32, 153; detention camps, 206–9; diaspora, 146, 149, 158, 191–92, 206, 210, 212, 218; din chay, 27; disciplining bodies, 195; discrimination against, 4; and erasure, 206, 217–18; ethnic identity, 23; exile networks, 208, 210; gloomy nationalism of, 153–54; helplessness, feeling of, 151; hikmät in, 74, 86–87, 97–98, 129, 150; and identity, 136–37; independence movement, 155; ishq, 31–32; Islamic soundscape, 5–6; Islamic soundscape, emptying of, 197; khätmä, reciting of, 68; language message boards, 194; literary and musical traditions, canonization of, 98–99; "Little Apple," 169, 175; local form of Islam in, as distinctive, 7; male rituals, 49–50; marginalization of, 5, 8, 23, 166; mäshräp among, 187–88, 193; mass internment of, 3; migrations of, 3–4, 33; Muslim noise, attempt to eradicate, 182; Muslim revivalists, 104; national identity, 154, 158, 199; nationalist sentiment, and religious expression, 156–57; nationalist sentiment, targeting of, 205–6; national music, rejection of, 212; new ways of listening, 105; online community, 135–36; oppression of, 154–55, 161, 192, 199; and orphanages, 207; pathologizing of, 139–40; permissibility of music, in religious life, 192–93; persecution of, 161; piety, rise of, 10; pilgrimage practices, 7; place, sonic experience of, 199; pop music, 155–57, 160–61; prison camps, 48; public space, control of, 197; Qur'anic recitation, 118; reading in, 86; Red Songs, performance of, 188–91; reeducation camps, 145, 212; reeducation programs, and musical performance, 208; reengineering of, 207, 214–15; religious extremism, 138–39; religious extremism, culture and identity of, 206; religious life, restrictions on, 4; religious media, deletion of, 163–64; religious media, and extremism, 145; religious media, sharing of, 144–47; religious piety, breaking down of, 175; religious practice, longing for, 104; and resilience, 212; and reterritorialization, 212; and rumors, 165; Sanai Nepis theater troupes, 193; separation, illegal religious activities, conflation with, 10; snake-monkey-woman video, 135–37; social media networks, 140–41, 154–57, 160, 165; song and dance, 18, 193; song and dance, and forced smile, 185; song-and-dance sessions, as counter extremism, 195; song-and-dance troupes, as alternative

form of mäshräp, 188; state violence against, 158, 162; and suffering, 153–55, 158; Sufi traditions in, 7, 192; surveillance of, 178, 203; and Syria, 161; tazkira manuscript tradition, 97, 172; and trauma, 210; Twelve Muqam repertoire, 65; videodiscs, 143; videodiscs, possession of, as criminal act, 142; violence against, 166, 171; violent resistance, 163; WeChat, users of, 137, 144; and weeping, 68; *zikr*, practice of, 14. *See also* Xinjiang

Uzbekistan, 10, 50, 55, 80, 83, 90

van Nieuwkerk, Matthijs, 69n11
videodiscs, 141; horror film, tropes of, 142–43
violence, 4, 11–12, 21, 34, 47–48, 137–38, 144, 152, 154, 158, 166, 171, 175–76, 182, 188–89, 210–11, 216; of anti-religious-extremism campaign, 136; and jihad, 195; and rap, 180; redefinition of, 139; remembering, act of, 212, 218; and rumors, 164–65; song and dance, 200; sounds, mediated circulation of, 162

Waḥḥabis, 12–13, 33; as religious revivalists, 11; and sharia, 11; Sunni Islam, branch of, 36n2
Waite, Edmund, 106, 108
Wang, Ban, 195–96, 214
Warda, 123
Warner, Michael: influential formulation, 146
WeChat, 134, 144, 147, 150–51, 158, 169, 201n19; audio files, 149; as closed-network form, 145; friend circles, 145; religious discourse on, 141; religious media, sharing of, 145, 149; situated agency, providing of, 145; Uyghur cultural productions, as space for, 137
weeping, 46, 62–63; as gendered performative, 48; and ishq (love), 48, 65, 68; male violence, as tool against, 47; as public act, 47
Weibo, 145
Weidman, Amanda, 16
West Turkistan, 80
White, Geoffrey, 42

Widdess, Richard, 85
"Without the Communist Party There Is No New China" (song), 208–9
Wolf, Richard, 64
women, 64, 91, 149, 201n19; assertiveness of, 158; büwi tradition, 49–53; cooking, significance of, 66, 68; frying in oil, 66; global Islam, 130; hikmät, performing of, 32–33, 86; invisibility of, 27; ishq, 32; khaniqa-based practices, 57; khätmä ritual, 28, 31–32, 58–60; modesty, emphasis on, 150, 155, 163; Qur'an, studying of, 112–15; reciprocal hospitality, 44–45; religious practice, 27; religious tea parties, 103; ritual practice, 130; ritual practice, and spiritual work, 66; rituals of, 40–41, 80; snake-monkey-woman, gendered questions of, 136; sociality of, 27; soundscape of, 29; tradition, as repositories of, 28; and trances, 40–41; victimhood, perception of, 47; as voiceless, 27; and weeping, 41, 46–48, 66–67; zikr, 32
Women of the Wall, 26
Wood, Abigail, 16, 26
World Uyghur Congress, 136, 151–52, 191

Xi Jinping, 169, 177, 185, 203, 205, 208, 210–11
Xinjiang (China), 12, 18–19, 27–28, 32–33, 44, 46–50, 54–57, 64–65, 77–79, 87, 90–91, 94–95, 104, 107, 114, 118, 123, 127, 138, 141, 144, 155, 166n3, 193; adhan (call to prayer) in, 20; anti-religious-extremism campaign, 4, 34–35, 147, 150–51, 173, 175–76, 177–78, 181, 186, 188, 194, 196–97, 199, 205–6, 211, 215; Chinese architecture, 172–73; control, spatial techniques of, 177–78; convenience cards, 4–5; cultural identity, erasure of, 215; Cultural Revolution, 212; dawah movement in, 9; embodied practices, 215; erase of, 216; expression of Islamic faith, elimination of, 176; Han Chinese population, 1, 169; hikmät in, 74, 100n6; human rights abuses, 209; illegal religious activities, 10; illegal religious activities, and religious extremism, conflation with, 10–11; Islamic revival in, 199; Islamic soundscape, cleansing of,

194–95; literacy in, 86; mäshräp fever, 10, 188; mass detention, 203–4; mass internment camps, 35; mass performances of revolutionary songs, 5; Middle Eastern recitation styles, arrival of, 129; as minority region, 171; Muslim counterpublic, 35; Muslim noise, attempt to eradicate, 179–82; Muslim practices, criminalization of, 167n7; new soundscape of, 173; new tourism, 172, 186; noise, eradication of, 179; orthodox Islam, 130; propaganda songs, 173–74; Red Songs, 189; reeducation centers, 209, 214–15; religion, domestication of, 8; religious extremism, 183; religious practice in, 7–9; religious revivalism in, 23; remodeling in, 172; and rumors, 165; securitization of, 3–4, 173, 204, 214; self-study, of Qur'an, 108–9; song-and-dance troupes, 183–84, 186, 197; sonic territorialization, 175; soundscape, as acoustic palimpsest, 216–17; soundscape, of mass song and dance, 35, 175, 214; strike hard campaigns, 10; Sufi-influenced Islam, 130; SWAT Police Force, 169; terrorism in, 139; Uyghur communities in, 2, 13–14, 20, 29, 80, 103, 137, 145, 149–50, 158, 161–62, 205–7; Uyghur reciters of Qur'an, 118; violence in, 4, 150–53, 171, 175; and Wahhabis, 11. *See also* Altishahr, Uyghurs
Xinjiang News Agency, 178
Xinjiang Production and Construction Corps, 92
Xinjiang Radio, 186
Xinjiang University, 18, 21; Folklore Unit, 88; rally at, 179, 181
Xinjiang Uyghur Autonomous Region, 1, 3, 21, 173, 190. *See also* East Turkistan, Xinjiang

Yan'an (China), 184
Yang Zengxin, 56
Yaqup, Eysajan, 181
Yarkand Khanate, 55
Yasawi, Khoja Ahmad, 32, 73, 79, 81–82, 86, 90, 93–94, 97, 100n5; hikmäts, 83; Jadidists, link to, 83–84; land pilgrimages, 78; retreat of, 88; shrine of, 77–78, 80; Sufi mystic poetry, 78; Turks, as literary forefather of, 84; veneration of, 78
Yasawi Sufism: communal solidarity and identity of, 77–78; legacy of, 77, 83
Yeh, Emily, 139, 170–71
"You'll Be Arrested" (poem), 151
Youku, 141, 144, 149
YouTube, 141, 144, 146
Yugoslavia, 84
Yunnan (China), 10, 169
Yusuf, Sami, 141

Zain, Maher, 149
Zarcone, Thierry, 56
Zhang Chunxian, 166n6
Zharkent (Kazakhstan), 90–9, 118, 119
Zhou Ji, 100n6
Zhou Xuyong, 179, 181
Zhu Hailun, 177
zikr, 16, 18, 32, 40, 46, 49–50, 53, 56–58, 64, 70, 77–78, 80, 90, 93, 98, 99n3, 128; body-sound interactions, 63; building community, 44; as nonmusic, 14; repetitive rhythms of, 213. *See also* dhikr

RACHEL HARRIS is Professor of Ethnomusicology and Director of Research for the School of Arts at SOAS, University of London. Her research focuses on religious and expressive culture among the Uyghurs and cultural policy in China. She is author of *The Making of a Musical Canon in Chinese Central Asia* and *Singing the Village,* and she has coedited several books, including *Theory and Practice in the Music of the Islamic World* and *Ethnographies of Islam in China*. Her research projects include Sounding Islam in China and An Alternative Approach to Sustainable Development: Uyghur Meshrep in Kazakhstan.

www.ingramcontent.com/pod-product-compliance
Lightning Source LLC
Chambersburg PA
CBHW030616230426
43661CB00053B/2021